The Partnership Book

How to Write Your Own Small Business Partnership Agreement

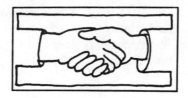

Attorneys Denis Clifford & Ralph Warner
Illustrations by Linda Allison

Nolo Press

Important

Please read this: We have done our best to give you useful and accurate information. But please be aware that laws and procedures are constantly changing and are subject to differing interpretations. You have the responsibility to check all material you read here before relying on it. Of necessity, neither Nolo Press nor the authors make any guarantees concerning the information in this book or the use to which it is put.

Nolo Press is committed to keeping its books up-to-date. Each new printing, whether or not it is called a new edition, has been completely revised to reflect the latest law changes. This book was printed and updated on the last date indicated below. Before you rely on information in it, you might wish to call Nolo Press, (415) 549-1976 to check whether a later printing or edition has been issued.

Printing History

Difference between new *editions* and *printings:*

New *printing* means there have been some minor changes, but usually not enough so that people will need to trade in or discard an earlier printing of the same edition. Obviously, this is a judgment call and any change, no matter how minor, might affect you.

New *edition* means one or more major—or a number of minor—law changes since the previous edition.

First Edition:	1981
Second Printing:	May 1982
Second Edition:	September 1984
Second Printing:	April 1985
Third Printing:	January 1986
Third Edition:	March 1987

ISBN 0-87337-041-4

ACKNOWLEDGEMENTS

Putting this book together was a surprisingly big—and humbling—job. Without the caring kibbitzing of many friends, we would have produced a less accurate work and had less fun doing it. So a tip of the hat and a hearty *muchas gracias* to the following friends: Ted Lyman, Bill Petrocelli, Jim Braghetta of P&J Braghetta and Associates, Larry Baskin, Marilyn Putnam, Carol Kizziah, Brad Bunin, Patti Unterman, Ray Castor, Hayden Curry, Chris Cunningham, Mervin Cherrin, Christie Rigg, Walter Warner, Anthony Mancuso, John Larimore, Barbara Hodovan, Pauline Porreco, Amy Ihara, Toni Ihara, Linda Allison, Stephanie Harolde, Robyn Samuels, Carol Pladsen, Keija Kimura, John O'Donnell, and Glenn Voloshin.

Our special appreciation to two partnership experts for suggestions for improvements to the second edition—Roger Pritchard, a Berkeley, California small business advisor, and Attorney Elisse Brown of Oakland—who helped us make this a better book.

And finally, maniacal thanks to our favorite two sharp-penciled accountants, Bernard "Bear" Kamoroff, author of *Small-Time Operator*, and Malcolm Roberts, Berkeley, California's reigning tax wiz.

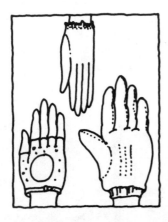

To Our Readers

This book can be of great help to you and your business associates. The advice about forming a partnership is as sound as we can make it, after much study of, and experience in, the area. Many knowledgeable people have reviewed these materials, and we have included many of their suggestions for change and clarification. But advice will not always work. Like well-meaning recommendations of all kinds, some of the advice we present here may not be helpful. So here are some qualifications. If you have access to a lawyer's or accountant's advice and it is contrary to that given here, be careful. Be sure you trust the lawyer or accountant; perhaps you can check his or her opinion with another expert. But also, remember that the individual characteristics of your problem can often better be considered by someone in possession of all the specific facts. Partnership laws and procedures vary somewhat from one state to the next and it is impossible to guarantee that every bit of information and advice contained here will be accurate. However, most of the basics of partnership law are the same in all the forty-nine states (all except Louisiana) which have adopted some form of the "Uniform Partnership Act." Please realize, too, that laws and regulations, especially those having to do with taxation, do change. It's your responsibility to check all material you have read here before relying on it. And finally, please pay attention to this general disclaimer—of necessity, neither the authors nor the publisher of this book makes any guarantee as to the uses to which this material is put. Thank you, and good luck!

Contents

(*Starred sections contain specific partnership agreement clauses.)

Introduction   1

Interlude I   5

Chapter 1: Getting Started—Choosing a Legal Form   9
    A. Introduction   10
    B. The Sole Proprietorship   11
    C. Partnerships
        1. Partnerships and Taxes   13
        2. The Rights and Responsibilities of Partners   13
        3. Personal Liability for Partnership Debts   14
        4. Partners' Relations to One Another   16
        5. Partnerships and Paperwork   17
        6. Other Things You Should Know About Partnerships   17
    D. Can You Do It All Yourself?   26

Chapter 2: Getting Your Business Started   31
    A. Introduction   32
    B. Short Form Partnership Agreements   32
    C. Naming Your New Enterprise   34
    D. Permits and Licenses   35
    E. Federal Taxes and Forms   35
        1. Partnership Returns   35
        2. Employee Tax Forms and Rules   36
    F. State and Local Taxes — Forms   37
    G. Bookkeeping   38
    H. Budgeting   40
        1. The Budget   40
        2. Your Profit and Loss Statement   43
        3. The Balance Sheet   44

    I. Partnership Accounting 45
    J. Insurance 46
    K. Renting Property 47

Interlude II 49

Chapter 3: An Overview of Your Partnership Agreement 52
    A. Decisions About Your Partnership Agreement 53
        1. Common Matters Covered in Partnership Agreements 54
        2. Subjects Often Covered in Partnership Agreements 54
    B. The Partners and Their Relationships 55
      *1. Term of the Partnership 56
      *2. Partnership No-No's 56
      *3. Partnership Decision Making 57
       4. Does a Partner Have Authority to Borrow Money? 58
       5. Liability of the Partnership to the Public 59
       6. The Legal Rights of a Partner Against a Partnership. 60
       7. Partnerships that Aren't Partnerships 60
    C. Financial Considerations in a Partnership Agreement 61
       1. Contributions to the Partnership 61
      *2. Profits and Losses 64
       3. Ownership of Property 66
       4. Tax Matters 66
    D. Disputes, Mediation, and Arbitration 67
      *1. Arbitration 68
      *2. Mediation 69
    E. Expanding, Changing, or Ending a Partnership 71

Interlude III 72

Chapter 4: Changes, Growth, and New Partners 75
    A. Expansion of Your Business 76
  *B. Growth and Changes in Your Partnership Agreement 77
  *C. Addition of a New Partner(s) 78
      *1. "Dissolution" of the Partnership When a New Partner Joins 80
      *2. The Incoming Partner's Liability for Existing Partnership Debts 81
       3. A Tax Note for Incoming Partners 82
       4. Outgoing Partners 82
  *D. Making Changes When You Have Failed to Plan Ahead 83

Interlude IV 84

Chapter 5: Changes (II) — Withdrawal, Death or Expulsion of a Partner, and Actual Termination 87

   A. Introduction 88
   B. Buy-Out Agreements 89
      *1. The Right to Buy 90
      2. Conflicts Regarding Buy-Outs 91
      3. How Much is a Partnership Interest Worth? — Valuation Methods 92
      4. Varying the Buy-Out Price Depending on When, or the Reason, a Partner Departs 93
      5. Valuation Methods 94
      6. Payments to Departing Partners 101
      7. Other Provisions Concerning Continuity of the Business 104
   C. Transfer of a Partner's Interest 110
      *1. Assignment of a Partner's Interest 110
      2. Sale of a Partner's Interest 111
 *D. Expulsion of a Partner 111
      *1. A Partner's Bankruptcy 112
      2. Partnership Contract Note 113
   E. Termination of a Partnership 114
      1. Winding Up the Partnership 114
      2. Termination Agreements 115
      *3. Interest 115
      4. Dissolution of a Partnership by Court Action 116

Chapter 6: Partnership Taxation 117

   A. Introduction 118
   B. Partnership Business and Personal Income Taxes 118
   C. Using Tax Experts 119
   D. Definitions 120
 *E. Tax Consequences of Contributions of Property to a Partnership 122
      1. Contributions of Property 123
      2. Complex Tax Problems Involving Contributions 126
         Mortgaged Property 126
         Recapture of Past Taxes 126
   F. Tax Consequences of Contributions of Service to a Partnership 127
   G. Some Other Points Regarding Taxation of Partnerships 128
   H. Payment of Taxes 129
      1. The Partnership Tax Return 129
      2. Some Rules Regarding the Partner's Individual Tax Return 130
      3. The Partnership As a Separate Tax Entity 132
   I. Taxation and the Disposition of a Partnership Interest 133
      1. Sale of a Partnership Interest 133
      2. Retirement or Death of a Partner(s) 135
   J. Tax Aspects of Joint Ventures 136

Interlude V   137

Chapter 7: Limited Partnerships

   A. Introduction   141

      Summary — Legal Requirements to Form a Valid Limited Partnership   143

   B. How a Limited Partnership Works   144

      1. Determining the Return to Limited Partners   146

      2. A Few Other Points about Limited Partnerships   147

  *C. The Registration Certificate   148

      Amendments of the Registration Certificate   152

   D. The "Security" Aspects of Limited Partnerships   152

      1. Federal Regulation   153

      2. Limited Partnership Exemption from Federal Securities Regulation   153

      3. State Regulations   155

   E. Tax Aspects of Limited Partnerships   156

      1. Joint Ventures   156

      2. Corporation Look-Alikes   156

   F. Limited Partnership Agreements   157

      1. Introduction   157

      2. Sample Limited Partnership Agreement   158

      3. Sample Lawyer's Limited Partnership Agreement   163

Chapter 8: Some Styles of Partnership Agreement   170

   A. Introduction   171

  *B. A "New Age" Partnership Contract Between Two Authors   171

  *C. A Real Estate Partnership   173

  *D. A Quasi-Professional Consulting Business   176

  *E. A Small Production Business   180

Chapter 9: Drafting Your Actual Partnership Agreement   185

   Step One: Discussing What You Expect and Need From Your Partnership Business   186

   Step Two: Review and Resolve the Major Problem Areas That Should Be Covered in Any Partnership Agreement   186

   Step Three: Actually Preparing Your Agreement   187

  *Step Four: The Heading   187

  *Step Five: Partnership Identification and Date of Formation Clause   187

  *Step Six: State Identification Clause   187

  *Step Seven: Name Clause   187

  *Step Eight: Principal Place of Business Clause   188

*Step Nine: The Purpose Clause   188
*Step Ten: Term of Partnership Clause   188
*Step Eleven: Contribution Clause   188
   A. Equal Shares Contributed   188
   B. Unequal Shares Contributed   189
   C. Contributions of Property   189
   D. Contribution of Service   189
*Step Twelve: Management Power and Duties Clause   189
*Step Thirteen: Distribution of Profits and Losses Clauses   190
*Step Fourteen: Buy-Out Clause   190
   A. Right to Buy and Right of First Refusal   190
   B. Valuation Methods   191
   C. Payment Methods   192
*Step Fifteen: Dissolution and/or Continuation of Business Clause   193
*Step Sixteen: Dispute Resolution Clause   193
   A. Arbitration   193
   B. Mediation   194
   C. Mediation/Arbitration   195
Step Seventeen: Add Any Additional Clauses You Desire   195
*Step Eighteen: Signature and Date Clause   195
Step Nineteen: Check Your Work Carefully   196
Step Twenty: The "We're All Done and We Did it Ourselves and It Didn't Cost Too Much" Celebration Party   196
Step Twenty-One: Good Luck and Our Best Wishes in Your New Adventure   197

Appendix   199

   A. Additional Clauses for Partnership Agreements   200
   B. Additional Clauses for Limited Partnership Agreements   213
   C. Resources for Further Research   217
   D. Sample Partnership Termination Agreement   219

Introduction

Millions of Americans dream of opening their own business, being their own boss, and controlling their own economic destiny. Often this dream involves joining with a friend or several friends to pool good energy and scarce resources. There are many advantages to shared ownership of a business. The chemistry and karma of two, three, or more minds and souls working together can often produce exciting results. There's more energy and enthusiasm—and at least as important, more cash, skills, and resouces. And don't overlook the fact that it's a lot easier to arrange for time off when you have a partner than if you're the sole boss.

There is something perversely wonderful in many of us that prefers working 8-to-6 for ourselves than 9-to-5 for the Racafrax Corporation. But for all of those who dream of doing their own thing—and who hasn't?—only a relative small number will be committed (or nutty) enough to invest the love and labor necessary to get a small business off the ground. Those who do will almost inevitably go through a period when they feel like a toddler trying to cross a freeway, with survival depending on mastering quickly and competently all sorts of unfamiliar information and skills. One of the first choices that must be made is how to organize and operate the new business entity. Should it be a sole proprietorship, a corporation, or a partnership? If it is to be a partnership, how can a good, solid one be established with a minimum of hassle and expense?

If these are some of the questions going through your head, you have arrived at the right place. To put it another way, if you're seriously thinking about joining with at least one friend to open a business, this book is designed for you. After discussing the pros and cons of the other legal ways that you might want to organize your business, we explain what partnerships are, both legally, and in day-to-day operation, and show you how to create a partnership that will fit your needs like a glove, not like handcuffs. While we can't resist slipping in a few of our world views here and there, this is primarily a workbook. It is designed to give you the tools to do an effective job of creating a partnership that will be a solid legal entity, capable of meeting your needs both now and in the future. Being trained as lawyers, we are perhaps overly careful when it comes to dealing with such things as buy-out agreements, disposition of partnership shares at death, etc. But we've learned that taking the time to establish a sound legal structure in the beginning can make all the difference between founding a solid and lasting enterprise and watching your dreams blow away like feathers on a windy day, the first time your business experiences difficulty.

Both of the authors are members of partnerships and have learned that the legal documents and forms used in creating a partnership can't (or shouldn't) be regarded separately from the pragmatic realities of how partnership businesses work. So while we include a number of legal documents, as well as detailed instructions on how to use them, we also include examples and stories of how partnerships we know have functioned and what many acquaintances and friends have learned about life in the cold, cruel world where payrolls have to be met, taxes paid, and the coffee machine is useless unless you buy the coffee. If you're new to the world of running your own business, you will obviously need to learn lots more than how to do the legal paperwork necessary for creating your partnership agreement. For example, you will also need to understand some rudiments of bookkeeping, management, business licenses, insurance, and much more. We supply you with as much help in these areas as we can without losing our main focus of getting your partnership established. We also supply you with a comprehensive set of references to other materials that will pick up where we leave off.

Perhaps the most important decision you will have to make in organizing your business is whether you want shared ownership. Don't just assume that you do without considering the alternatives. For example, some individual entrepreneurs who like being the boss find that profit-sharing agreements with key employees will serve to meet their needs as well as or better than setting up a formal partnership or small corporation. If you do decide on joint ownership, there are really only two possible legal forms for the business to take—partnership or corporation.* We discuss the advantages and disadvantages of each form in considerable detail, but right here at the beginning, we want you to realize that there isn't nearly as much difference between these two ways of organizing your small business as you might think. Partnerships appear to be more intimate—indeed, they've been described as "perhaps the business equivalent of marriage."Certainly it's true that it's often easier to change spouses than it is to change business partners. But in most small corporations, exactly the same human realities are present, and you should understand that the legal organization of your business is not nearly as important as the trust, competence, and compatibility of the owners.

Idealistic friends have asked, "Do we really need a formal partnership agreement? Why bother with the paperwork if honesty, good faith, and trust are what really matter? Can't we just work on a handshake?"

Our answer goes something like this: We'd like life to be so utopian that nothing ever needed to be written out, but we've learned that effective business relationships depend in large measure on good planning, and attention to detail. Writing a common-sense partnership agreement is definitely part of this process, if for no other reason than it's a better way to record an understanding than the all too fallible human memory. Also, it should go without saying that there is so much in any business venture that cannot be foreseen that it makes obvious sense to try to anticipate what you can and reduce it to writing. Finally, there's nothing like sitting down with your prospective partners and discussing what your options and alternatives are to learn whether you really are in full agreement. You should definitely prepare for change. The statistics are that very few small businesses last unchanged for years. To the extent possible, you should plan for handling change from the start, not just wing it and hope.

---

*We also spend considerable time discussing limited partnerships, which in some circumstances can combine the best qualities of both.

What happens if your business is an immediate hit? We know of some partnerships that got into trouble because they made no plans to handle the great success they achieved. What happens if you lose money for a considerable period of time, or you need to raise capital for expansion, or want to move the business, or the partners get into a dispute, or one partner wishes to sell their share, or becomes disabled, or dies leaving a spouse or children? Putting together your partnership agreement can be a creative way to review your plans for these sorts of contingencies at the same time it gives you a chance to test whether you're comfortable working with each other around questions of money and power. If you aren't, you will save yourself immense future pain and trouble by bailing out now.

This book is divided into several parts. The first two chapters are concerned with choosing whether or not you want to establish a partnership as well as some general information valuable to any small business. Then we deal with the nitty gritty of the partnership agreement itself; in chapters 3 to 6 we discuss the basic problems that should be resolved in a partnership agreement and present various clauses you can use to handle them. In the next chapter we show you how to use a different type of legal structure, the limited partnership. In chapter 8, we provide several sample partnership agreements from different businesses we know, so you can see what a completed agreement looks like, and the variety of styles possible. Then it's hands-on time for you. In chapter 9 we take you step-by-step through the process of putting your partnership agreement together. As you use these materials, it will be up to you to decide how deeply you want to investigate your options in your partnership contract. If your partnership involves each partner contributing cash only, there isn't much reason to worry about partnership taxation (yet), but if you are involved in a more complicated agreement, where partners contribute property or services, you will need to consider tax consequences and may want to see an accountant. Reasoning similarly, a knowledgeable attorney may well be an invaluable aid to check your work after you have completed a preliminary draft on your own. The important principal to remember is that it's your agreement, and you and your partners should be in charge of designing it.

The 1986 Tax Reform Act distinguishes between the tax treatment of income received from "active" and "passive" activities. To oversimplify, receiving "passive" income can be less advantageous than receiving "active" income for several reasons. Because the income that most partners receive who participate in the partnership business is generally considered to be "active" income, there is no reason to belabor this distinction here. (We discuss tax issues throughout this book as appropriate, especially in Chapter 6.) However, if any member of your proposed partnership will not materially participate in the operations and management of the partnership business, please see an accountant before finalizing your partnership agreement.

One practical suggestion. As you read through the book, be gentle with yourself; a partnership agreement is not something you design between the soup and salad. There is no need to grasp every detail the first time through. Remember, you have a partner—or partners—and they may be able to help in areas that befuddle you. Start by reading the entire book to get a general overview of what's involved, making a few notes as to clauses or provisions that are particularly applicable to you. Then go back and focus on the areas of most concern. While it's important to be sure that your agreement is technically and legally correct, it is also crucial that your partnership agreement reflects the reality of the business you're in, and how you and your partner(s) want it to be organized and run.

A Personal Note

Before we get into the nitty-gritty of starting and operating a partnership, and drafting a partnership agreement, a few personal words are in order. Both of us grew up in the East, went off to college and emerged, like so many others, unsure about "what we wanted to do with our lives." We considered lots of choices and both drifted on to law school with the vague idea that law would give us some skills useful to making the world a better place. How we each became disillusioned with that dream is another story; the point here is that through all of our dreaming and planning, neither of us ever imagined that we would wind up as proprietors of small businesses, full-fledged members of the "free enterprise system." But that's what happened. We've experienced both great satisfaction as well as some very real pain in running our own shops. We have been through our "babe on the freeway" stage, have made most of the routine mistakes, as well as pioneering some new lulu's. Somehow, we have survived it all to realize that doing our own thing gives us both a sense of freedom and self-worth — hard to match in this increasingly bureaucratized world.

In the process of putting this book together, we talked to all sorts of people who have successfully created their own small business partnerships. Our intitial goal was to find out what sorts of legal documents they used and what sorts of legal and organizational problems caused—or saved—them the most trouble. Inevitably, however, we also heard a lot about the personal and creative side of all sorts of small partnerships. We have been told time and again about the satisfactions, and even joy, inherent in providing a process, or product, or service that genuinely interests the provider and benefits the consumer. We've also learned a lot about how people relate to—and often gain satisfaction from— the tough competition that is so much a part of the world of small business, where surivival depends on your offering something that people really want and need. And most of all, we have been reminded constantly that although money is important, it is not usually the most important reason that most people organize their own businesses. We found that integrity and creativity—even altruism—are alive and well in small business America.

The Story of the Chocolate Moose

INTERLUDE I

We'd like to introduce two friends of ours—people who we hope you will like too. We'll tell the story of how they set up a partnership, sharing some of the joys and trials they experienced. They may be like you—they're excited about setting up their own business, optimistic about success, and a little scared about embarking on a journey into uncharted waters. But also, like you, they're unique, distinct individuals. We've purposely chosen them to illustrate that while all partnerships share some common elements, they are also as different as the people who establish them. So, while our new friends' hopes and fears, dreams and worries, may overlap yours more than a little, we present them to you more for their value in illustrating the process of establishing a good partnership, and partnership agreement, than because we expect your business or agreement to mirror theirs.

First, meet Sara Curry, thirty-two years old with sparkling brown eyes, a slightly crooked nose from a bout with a baseball when she was six, a big smile, and a mop of curly red hair. Sara attracts both men and calories like a watermelon patch draws neighborhood kids. She's naturally ebullient, and even her times of depression seem (to others, not herself) to be full of vivacity. She took up running a couple of years ago, and the ten or twelve pounds she's been vowing to lose for a decade, while still there, has gradually become firm. In high school she felt chagrined when she heard a boy remark, "she's built for comfort, not for speed;" now she thinks—fine, so what's the hurry?

Now say hello to John, a six-foot-two playground-basketball player with deep blue eyes and a prominent dark mustache who at thirty-six still fantasizes playing guard in the N.B.A. John is as quiet as Sara is flamboyant and enjoys a few close friends and a room full of books. He was trudging through a Ph.D. program several years ago, before he decided the path to academic respectability was too burdensome for him, and the job possibilities too slim. He isn't into small talk, and it's only as you get to know him that you discover he often smiles, as if seeing much of life as a private joke. In contrast to Sara, who lives in a perpetual state of motion, one of John's principal characteristics is his talent for repose. And just as it would be an exaggeration to say that Sara falls in love with every marginally attractive man who walks through her door, and is frequently lost in a romantic haze, it's false to say that John has a "drinking problem," though it is true that now and then he falls into a bottle and doesn't surface for a day or two.

John and Sara have been friends for five years.* They live in Coeur D'Alene,

---

*It's best to confess here that Sara and John are fictional, although they have been drawn using bits and pieces of a number of real friends.

Idaho, where John is the manager of a natural foods store and Sara cooks at a truck stop. They met when each rented a room in a large old house and briefly enjoyed a romantic relationship. Their romance didn't survive (that's another story) but their friendship flourished. Gradually, each began to share their visions, hopes, and dreams with the other. They began to realize that they were growing older, and hoped that they were also growing up.

In the last year or so, John has begun to worry about his future. As he told Sara, "success may be an illusion, but failure is very real." Sara has never been known for being prudent, whether about love or money, but she, too, has come to the conclusion that she would like to gain some control over her economic destiny. Lately they've both been surprised at how often they wind up talking about money, having always seen themselves as dreamers, and lovers of nature and things of the spirit. Perhaps they are ready to pay more attention to the economic side of life because they understand that their present, low-paying jobs are intruding on their capacity to dream.

John often confided in Sara about his frustrations working for Herb, the owner of The Food Odyssey, a local natural food store. Many of John's complaints were fairly commonplace. He worked long hours, lavished lots of good energy on the store, and knew that he was not being adequately compensated. When he first started working at The Food Odyssey, it had been a marginal operation. John slowly learned the business, and to his surprise, discovered that he was good at running it. Under his tutelage, it blossomed and became quite profitable. He larned to handle the money side of the business, truly amazing for one who only a few years back could hardly balance a checkbook. Also, he found he had a knack for creating an attractive store, responsive to the needs of its customers. Herb tended to take all this for granted, and, although he had given John a few token raises, he had used the lion's share of The Food Odyssey's profits to buy himself a B.M.W. and ten acres of land in the country. In addition, Herb had cut back his own work hours to the point where most of the day-to-day decision-making fell on John's shoulders.

Sara's story had much in common with John's. After dropping out of college, she had gone through successive careers as a flower child, communal back-to-the-lander, devotee of one of the less memorable Indian Gurus, part-time jazz singer (not great), and full-time waitress (the boss said she talked too much, but she got good tips). Finally she taught herself to be a short-order cook. Preparing tasiy meals, it turned out, was Sara's true calling. Before long she had a devoted local following down at Greasy Al's truck stop next to the interstate. This was a local miracle of more than minor proportions; before Sara's arrival, the only people who ever pushed through Greasy Al's door were either new to the area or looking for the bathroom. While Sara could cook almost anything superbly, her desserts were most spectacular, and were so much in demand that Al installed a special counter and began selling her confections for take-out.

Al recognized that he had a good employee and raised Sara's pay several times, but in Sara's opinion, these increases didn't come close to approaching her fair value to the business. Finally Sara approached Al about a profit-sharing arrangement. Al just laughed and gave her a $.25 per hour raise. That was the day Sara decided to go into business for herself as soon as possible.

Gradually, as Sara and John's confidence in their own abilities grew and their trust in one another deepened, a dream began to take shape. Originally it took the form of a game called, "What if we started our own business?" which the two *friends played almost every Sunday afternoon over cups of strong tea and Sara's irresistible brownies. While the game had extremely flexible rules, it usually proceeded something like this: one of the friends would dream up a possible business and they would each fill in a few details. The winner was the person who could come up with the most compelling reasons not to start that particular business. As Sunday followed Sunday, and all sorts of possible ventures were rejected, two basic understandings became clear. First, both Sara and John realized that the game had become much more than amusement and both agreed that when they found a business that sounded good to both of them, they would go for it. Second, they narrowed down the type of business they would consider. It would have to be involved with food, so that they could capitalize on their mutual expertise in that area.*

As proof that they were really serious, they began doing research during the week, and quickly learned how much there was to starting a business. They checked rents, examined population growth figures, read books on how to run a food operation, talked to people who ran successful small businesses, and gathered financial information on loans, interest rates, etc. Each had saved a little money and Sara had inherited a few thousand dollars. Between them, they had a maximum of $25,000 to invest in the business. It sounded like a lot of money. "We're rich," Sara joked, "why don't we just go to Paris instead?" But they both knew their cash reserve could vanish at the bat of an eyelash with just a few bad business decisions.

Since neither wanted to start off deeply in debt, they decided that their business had to be one that could be started relatively cheaply. Several ideas had to be rejected, including a French Restaurant (too costly to open) and a gourmet delicatessen (involving the preparation of many different items, and the hiring of several employees). Ideas for a number of other food establishments were also put aside, both because they required an expensive liquor license, and would require John to work around booze, which was more temptation than he felt like dealing with.

Finally, one sunny Sunday in early April, Sara, beaming with enthusiasm, started their meeting with a pronouncement (accompanied by fourteen gestures and at least as many tosses of her head), "John, I have it! I really have an idea that is simple, affordable, will make us money, and above all, will be fun for us to do!"

"That's what you said about the gourmet burrito stand," John replied laconically. Recently he'd been getting discouraged about ever getting their dream off the ground.

"Well, maybe that wasn't such a good idea—but you have to admit that a concession called 'Low Rider Heaven' would be original. But John, this time I've got a much better idea. Let's do a bakery . . ."

"A bakery?" John interrupted in a disappointed voice. "You know we agreed last month that since there were already a couple of good bakeries in town, and you would hate to get up at four in the morning to bake the bread, it just wasn't practical."

"Don't interrupt," Sara said brusquely, and handed John another brownie. "I wasn't talking about your run-of-the-mill bread bakery, but about a chocolate bakery—we'd specialize in impossibly rich, outrageously wonderful, chocolate concoctions."

"You mean like chocolate decadence, truffles, chocolate cheesecake, and chocolate mousse?" he asked while chewing the last of the brownie.

"Yep, and you just thought up the name," Sara laughed gleefully.

"I did?" he asked.

"Sure," Sara said, *"let's call it The Chocolate Moose."* Her euphoria switched to earnestness. *"Listen John, I didn't just come up with this scheme all on my own. I read several articles in some food magazines about "Chez Chocolat," a chocolate store in Berkeley, California, that is fabulously successful, so successful that others are springing up around the country."*

John tried to play devil's advocate, but Sara's enthusiasm quickly prevailed.

"You know," John said, *"I really can't think of a thing wrong with the idea. We could start with a few wonderful things, use great ingredients and charge good prices. If we could rent a small storefront cheap, most of the cost would be for a couple of good ovens, a commercial refrigerator, and a few display cases. And you're right, no one sells any really good chocolate desserts within a hundred miles, yet every other person who walks down the street is a chocolate junkie. Best of all, you could handle the baking and I could run the store and the business end and, at least at first, we wouldn't have to hire anyone."*

"Don't forget about party catering," Sara added, delighted that John was excited too. *"We could get Max and Joan, or someone else if they're not interested, to help us when we get big jobs."*

"You know, Sara," John said, *"I think this is it. Between us we have enough money to get started and it should be the sort of business that won't devour us. If we close Sunday and Monday and get a few others to spell us now and then, we should be able to get away enough so we don't burn out."*

Sara smiled and said, *"Well, I only have one more thing to say."*

"What's that?" John asked.

"Put it there, partner!" Sara beamed, extending her hand to John.

"You're on, partner," John responded, extending his right hand to clasp Sara's and his left to grab the last brownie.

(A few hours later, Sara and John are in the middle of a fancy supper they have concocted to celebrate the launching of The Chocolate Moose.)

"Ah, er, Sara—I don't mean to put a damper on a good time, but I do have a few questions," John said.

"Sure, shoot," Sara replied easily.

"Well, you may think this is a stupid question, but what does it mean to be a business partner? Do we have to write out some papers and file them somewhere? Also, does being a partner mean that we have to share everything equally? And, if that's true, how do we deal with the fact that you have $5,000 more to invest than I do? Then there's this—my uncle Jim, who's an architect in Atlanta, told me that he heard that it's much better to organize a business as a corporation because you qualify for limited liability, which has something to do with what happens if our Chocolate Moose melts instead of multiplies. Also, I'm not sure about taxes. I'll have some other questions soon, I'm sure."

"Huh?" Sara frowned. *"Maybe our first move has to be to get a lawyer and let her worry about the partnership stuff."*

"At $75 an hour?" John gasped. *"No way! There must be some place where we can get some good information about how we can set up our partnership agreement and all the legal stuff. Once we know what's involved, we can decide if we need a lawyer or not—and if we do, how we can keep the cost down."*

"Okay with me," Sara said, passing John another piece of chocolate pie. *"You worry about the business end, and all the paper work, and I'll get started on the food—what we should sell, how much we need to charge, and what I'll need for equipment; we can meet back here next week and see where we are."*

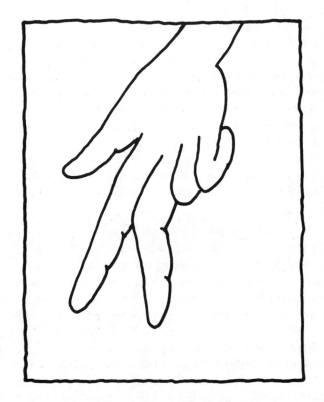

Chapter 1:

Getting Started — Choosing a Legal Form

A. Introduction

Okay, it's time to get serious. Whatever your great idea—a store, a product, a service—you're ready to get your business organized, or, if you have already started in a small way, to deal with the changes that expansion inevitably brings. As part of this process, one of your first decisions involves which legal form of business organization to choose. To do this sensibly, you will need to understand the consequences of choosing one rather than another.

There are only four common forms of business ownership in use today—sole proprietorship, partnership, limited partnership and corporation.[1] Here at the beginning, we discuss the legalities and practical realities of each broad category, to assist you in choosing the organizational form that best suits your needs. If you're absolutely sure you want a partnership, and understand the legal basics of what a partnership is and what partners have committed themselves to, you can skip this chapter and proceed directly to the chapters explaining how to create a partnership agreement.

COMMON SENSE NOTE: Before we consider the details of why one form of business organization is better (or worse) than another, let's establish several basic principles. First, the most important attribute of any shared business is the competence of the co-owners and the trust they have in one another, not matters having to do with technical forms of ownership. Second, many of the problems involved in shared ownership are, in reality, the same no matter whether you choose a partnership, small corporation, or even a sole proprietorship with a profit-sharing agreement for key employees. Third, many of the differences between partnerships and large enterprises are not important for small business owners.

We do not mean to suggest that there are no important differences between the various kinds of business organizations. Indeed, the purpose of this chapter is to discuss these differences so that you can make an informed choice. However, when you finish this chapter, you will probably conclude, as we have, that the advantages and disadvantages of the various ways to organize your business are not as significant as many advocates of one or the other approach would have you believe.[2] For example, suppose you and a friend are co-owners of a radio repair business. It's clearly prudent to make provisions to cover what happens if one person quits or dies. A common method of handling this is to create a "buy-out" clause, enabling the remaining owner to purchase (usually over time) the interest of the departing owner. If the business is owned as a partnership, the agreement you devise will normally be included in the partnership agreement. if the business is a corporation, you'll put the provision in the articles, bylaws, or other corporate agreement. But the practical reality will be the same.

& & &

---

1. Some states have distinct subcategories of these four, especially partnerships. For example, there's a creature called a "mining partnership" used in mining and oil ventures in some states. Corporations, too, have been broken into subgroups for some special purposes in many states (i.e., professional corporations, non-profit corporations, close corporations, etc.). In addition, corporations with 35 or fewer shareholders can elect S corporation tax status, which means that gains and losses are taxed directly to the shareholders and are not taxed at the corporate level.

2. Some businesses that are subject to extensive government regulation are not suited to the informality of partnerships. We doubt these businesses are the kinds our readers are considering—they're such enterprises as banks, insurance companies, utility companies, or motor carriers. (Not that we'd mind owning a bank these days!)

Partnerships date to the beginning of recorded history. References are made to partnerships in the Babylonian Code of Hammurabi, approximately 2300 B.C. The Jews, around 2000 B.C., a pastoral not commercial people, evolved a form of landsharing or grazing partnership called a "shutolin." Later, commercial Jewish partnerships evolved from the trading caravans.

B. The Sole Proprietorship

An extended discussion of sole proprietorship is outside the scope of this book which is designed for people who want the advantages of shared business ownership. *Small Time Operator*, by Bernard Kamoroff, is an excellent source of more information on this subject. Quite simply, the main advantage of a sole proprietorship is that there is only one boss (you); thus potential conflicts are eliminated, unless you argue with yourself. The disadvantages stem from the same reality as do the advantages—there's only you as owner and boss. If you get sick, or want time off, or simply want to share the responsibility of decision-making with someone else, you are likely to be stuck. Deciding to be the only boss is often a question of personal temperament. Lots of people like, and need, to run the whole show and always chafe in a partnership situation, while others want, or at least appreciate, the resources and strengths, from cash to comaraderie, that co-owners can bring. The best advice we can give you here is that old bromide—know thyself.

In deciding whether or not a sole proprietorship will work, business owners are often inclined to choose a more complicated form of ownership because they want or need to involve key employees in the future of the business. While it may make great sense to allow important employees to become either partners or stockholders, you should know that this is not the only way dedicated and talented employees can be encouraged. A profit-sharing agreement within the framework of the sole proprietorship may well be a better way to go, at least until you see if you and the key employee(s) are really compatible over the long term.

Example: Eric is a self-employed architect. He gets a big job and hires Frank and Samantha to help with the drafting. Half-way through the job, things are working so well that Eric decides to bid on an even larger job. He knows that to complete this job successfully, he will have to depend a great deal on his two assistants. Eric first considers making Frank and Samantha junior partners. However, because he has only known them for a few months, and because Samantha is pondering moving to the other side of the country in a year of so, Eric decides that it makes more sense to put off the partnership decision and offer each 10 percent of his profit on the deal, over and above their regular salary.

Example: Susan decides to open a sandwich shop near a busy college campus. She wants her friend, Ellen, to work with real enthusiasm, but because money is short, can only pay her a modest salary to start. To insure Ellen's continued dedication, Susan offers her a bonus of a profit-sharing agreement under which Ellen gets 25 percent of all net profits.

NOTE: Profit Sharing: There can be many forms of profit-sharing agreements. Unfortunately, there is no good layman's guide in this area. Your best approach is probably to write about something that makes sense to you and then have it reviewed by a lawyer and/or an accountant. Be sure that your advisor is experienced with small business realities, and sympathetic to profit-sharing plans.

C. Partnerships

Most people have a common sense understanding of what partnership is — the partners are in it together, all-for-one and one-for-all. In a rough way, this is true, but it's obviously desirable to have a much clearer understanding of what's really involved — what you're committing yourself to when you decide to establish a partnership.

The legal definition of a partnership is "an association of two or more persons to carry on as co-owners of a business for profit." [3] The concept of a partnership is very broad; for example, the I.R.S. definition of a partnership includes:

> . . . *a syndicate, pool, joint venture or other unincorporated organization through which . . . any business is carried on . . . and is not . . . a corporation or trust or an estate [or sole ownership] . . .* Internal Revenue Code Section 761(a).

It's not required that you use the words "partners" or "partnership," or create a written agreement, to become a legal partnership. If you simply join with other persons and run a jointly owned business, you have created a partnership. Use of the words "partners," or "partnership" will, however, insure that you are involved in a partnership. For example, if there is a question whether a person is an employee of a sole proprietorship, or a partner, calling him or her a partner will probably be determinative. Here are some other partnership basics:

● The Uniform Partnership Act, abbreviated "U.P.A.", has been adopted (often with some slight modifications) in all states except Louisiana. The U.P.A., in essence, provides the rules for partnerships that haven't created their own rules. In other words, you can vary or alter most provisions of the U.P.A. if you choose to do so.

● As a practical matter, partnerships should always be formed with a written partnership agreement. You should know, however, that oral or handshake partnerships are often legal, although highly inadvisable.

● Partners do not have to share ownership equally. You can agree on any percentage of individual ownership or distribution of the profits that you want. Thus, one partner could own 80 percent of the partnership and four more could own 5 percent each.

● Partnerships can be organized for all sorts of purposes. They can sell products or services just as they can mine, manufacture, or operate as agents. Professional partnerships, however, are subject to special rules set down by the profession. Usually the most important of these is that everyone in the partnership be a member of the profession.

---

3. Uniform Partnership Act (U.P.A.) Section 6(1). Legal scholars have expended considerable energy trying to determine whether a partnership is an "aggregate" or an "entity" — i.e., is it a legal thing separate and distinct from the partners or is it simply a continuation of the partners. Well, like light, which is a wave or a particle depending on how you view it, a partnership is sometimes a separate thing, and sometimes it isn't. We'll explain this a bit more throughout this section, but as an abstract question, frankly, it doesn't make any difference to you which it "really" is.

• Partners don't normally receive salaries per se; commonly, they get either a percentage of the profits, or a guaranteed return, depending upon their partnership agreement. However, it is common for partners to take on an agreed-upon monthly amount from the business — commonly called a draw — against their yearly partnership share.

In Roman law (for instance, the Code of Justinian), there were provisions allowing partnerships that were very similar to our contemporary law. The Romans also evolved the rules of agency, which are the foundation of much of modern partnership law. As the Romans put it, "Qui facit per alium facit per se," — he who acts through another acts for himself.

Roman law considered the element of voluntary choice of associates as the essence of partnership, and "delectus personas" — choice of persons — remains a crucial element of partnerships.

• Partners, as well as the partnership itself, are personally and individually liable for the legal obligations of the partnership.

Okay, so much for a thumbnail review of what a partnership is. Now let's look at several areas that will be important to you in more detail. Because many readers will also be interested in the possibility of forming a small corporation, we've included in this discussion a comparison between some of the legal aspects of a corporate vs. partnership approach. The discussion of small corporations will be expanded in section F of this chapter.

1. PARTNERSHIP AND TAXES

Partnerships are not liable for federal or state income taxes. Any profits or losses from the partnership "flow through" the partnership to the individual partners. Thus, taxes on partnership profits are paid only by the individual partners (see Chapter 6, Partnership Taxation). What this means is that there *cannot* be double taxation of partnership profits, once at the partnership level, and then a second time when partnership profits are distributed to the individual partners. Under the 1986 Tax Reform Act, partners' income or losses may be, for I.R.S. purposes, either "active" or "passive." If all partners materially participate in the operations of the business—which is certainly the rule for most small business partnerships—partners' income will be considered active. As is explained in Chapter 6, Section D, it's generally desirable to have income be treated as "active," if possible.

2. THE RIGHTS AND RESPONSIBILITIES OF PARTNERS — *OR* ONE PARTNER CAN BIND ANOTHER

Each partner has full power to speak for and represent a partnership within the "normal course of business."[4] This makes it obvious why trust is so vital in a partnership. One partner can obligate the other partners, even if they never in fact authorized him/her to do so. Indeed, in many circumstances, a partner can bind a partnership even when the other partners told him/her not to. For example, Al, Fred, and Mike are partners in a printing business. They discuss buying an expensive new press and vote two to one against it. Fred, the disgruntled loser, goes out and signs a contract for the press anyway. Since this is within the "normal course of business," Fred's act binds the partnership.[5]

It is legal to limit the powers of any partner in the partnership agreement.[6] However, those limits probably won't be binding on people outside the partnership who have no actual knowledge of them. Outsiders are entitled, legally, to rely on the "apparent authority" of a partner, as determined by the customs of the particular trade or business. When Fred bought the printing press, the manufacturer — as long as it had no knowledge of the partnership's limits on Fred — could rely on his "apparent authority," i.e., a partner of a printing business can reasonably be expected to have the authority to buy a press. If Fred, however, sought to bind the printing partnership on a deal to open a chain of massage parlors, an outsider probably wouldn't be able to rely on his signature alone as binding the partnership.

3. PERSONAL LIABILITY FOR PARTNERSHIP DEBTS

Another crucial partnership legal principle is that each partner is personally liable for all partnership debts and obligations that cannot be paid by the partnership itself. Partners are *not* liable for the personal, non-partnership debts and obligations of the other partner.[7] Partners are liable for any money damages that result from the negligence of another partner, as well as damages that result from any frauds or other intentional acts done in the ordinary course of partnership business. For example, suppose Jane and Alfonso are partners in a retail flower business. Jane has no money; Alfonso is rich. The partnership just opened and the partners haven't gotten around to buying insurance yet. While Jane is driving the flower delivery van to pick up flowers (i.e., on partnership business), she hits and severely injures a pedestrian who sues and gets a substantial judgment. If the partnership doesn't have sufficient assets to pay off the pedestrian's judgment, Alfonso is personally liable for any unpaid amount. If he doesn't have enough money to cover it, his personal assets — with the exception of the few protected by state debtors' exemption laws — can be seized to satisfy the judgment.

Incidentally, a "silent" partner — one who's membership in the partnership is not revealed to the public — is every bit as liable for partnership debts as any other partner. However, a "sub-partner" is not. A "sub-partner" is a person who agrees with one member of a partnership to share in that partner's profits. This is a separate agreement,

---

4. Section 9 U.P.A.

5. Unless the seller of the press *knew* Fred had no actual authority to order it in the partnership name, which is both unlikely and hard to prove.

6. §18(e) U.P.A.

7. If one partner is having financial problems outside the partnership, her creditors can seek to get at her share of the partnership business. This can result in obvious problems as far as disrupting the business is concerned, etc.

14

and does not, legally, involve the sub-partner in the partnership.[8]

A REMINDER! We recite these rules of partnership responsibility not to discourage you from entering into a partnership, but to alert you to the fact that like any human endeavor, there are risks to be acknowledged and dealt with. As a practical consideration, while limited liability does give stockholders of a small corporation considerable protection, some of these risks are also present if you elect to form a small corporation. By use of insurance (see chapter 2, section G) and other common sense business practices, many of the potential partnership risks can be minimized. The fact that there are so many functioning partnerships in the United States is probably the best proof that the risks need not be prohibitive.

---

8. Sub-partnership agreements can be tricky. If you're interested in pursuing one, see a lawyer.

4. PARTNERS' RELATIONS TO ONE ANOTHER

Partners are "fiduciaries" toward one another. This bit of legal jargon means that they owe complete loyalty to the partnership, and cannot engage in any activity which in any way conflicts with the partnership's business. One court put it, "the rule of undivided loyalty is relentless and supreme." Another wrote, "Many forms of conduct permissible in a work-a-day world for those acting at arm's length are forbidden to those bound by fiduciary ties . . . Not honesty alone, but the punctilio of an honor the most sensitive, is thus the standard of behavior."[9]

Here are a couple of examples of judicial application of partnership fiduciary duties:

Fred and Tom agree to be partners in one real estate purchase after which the partnership will be dissolved. In the course of conducting negotiations for that purchase, Fred learns of another real estate buy, a real bargain. Legally, Fred cannot simply wait until the partnership expires and purchase the second property himself. He has a fiduciary duty to tell Tom any valuable information he learned while acting on partnership business.

Fred decides to buy Tom out of the partnership. The rule of caveat emptor (let the buyer beware) does not apply. Fred must act in complete good faith, including *volunteering* any significant information about the partnership and its worth which he's aware Tom does not know. Thus, if Fred knows that a big order is in the works from a major corporation and Tom doesn't, Fred has the duty to tell him. If he doesn't, the buy-out deal can be legally rescinded.

There is voluminous litigation on the rights and duties of partners to each other — sad evidence that partnerships can go sour. Here are some representative "no-no's" which a partner cannot legally do. Notice that common sense indicates these are not ways in which honest people customarily deal with each other:

● A partner secretly obtaining for him/herself an opportunity available to the partnership.

● The diversion of partnership assets for personal use.

● The refusal of one partner to distribute partnership profits to other members of the partnership.

● The failure of a partner to disclose any and all "material facts" affecting the business to the other partners.

CAUTION! The courts often rule that those who've seriously discussed a partnership must adhere to the same exacting standards of good faith that bind partners, even if an actual partnership agreement is never signed. Just when this "partner-like" responsibility arises isn't totally clear, but once real negotiating begins, that probably means there are fiduciary duties involved. Since you'll have to trust your partners, eventually, it makes sense to start building that trust by full disclosure and square dealing right from the start.

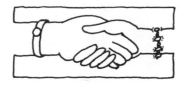

---

9. *Meinhard v. Salmon,* 164 N.E. 545 (1928).

In medieval England, the legal affairs of merchants were administered separately from the "common law" courts (the main English courts, where law was so extremely complex as to mock their name). England, which then, as now, depended heavily on trade, did not subject its merchants, and especially foreign traders, to the expensive and tedious forms of common law. English partnership law thus evolved from the realities of how merchants did business with most basic partnership principles being codifications of the customs of trade. Eventually, this codification became known as "law merchant."

Partnership lawsuits were handled in informal businessmen's courts, as the Court Staple,[10] first given official sanction by the "Statute of the Staple" in 1353. This law proclaimed that justice was to be done to foreign traders according to the law of the staple (or "law merchant"), from "day to day and hour to hour," (i.e., speedily).

5. PARTNERSHIPS AND PAPERWORK

As you will see further on, the technicalities of setting up most partnerships are not difficult. Once you agree on your basic partnership agreement, that's pretty much it as far as legal paperwork is concerned, aside from the paperwork involved in running any business — tax forms, accounting records, etc., etc., etc. As partners pay taxes themselves on their individual partnership income, the only partnership tax return required is a once-a-year-one for informational purposes.[11] Except for applying for a federal identification number, no papers need be filed with any bureau, department or agency to establish a partnership or keep it going unless the partnership operates under a fictitious name (a name other than those of the partners). For example, if Johnson, Olivier and Simmons call themselves Ace Electric, they will have to meet state requirements for all businesses operating under a fictitious name.

6. OTHER THINGS YOU SHOULD KNOW ABOUT PARTNERSHIPS

Joint Ventures (Partnerships for a Single Purpose)

A joint venture is simply a partnership for a limited or specified purpose.[12] If you and Joe go into the construction business together, that's a partnership. If you and Joe agree to build a house together, that's normally a joint venture. Common examples of joint ventures are natural resource projects — drilling for oil, or a cooperative mining venture.

10. A staple was a trade fair.

11. Of course, partnerships have to get resale permits, file payroll returns, etc. if they have employees and deal with all the rest of the bureaucratic procedures that go with starting a business (see Chapter 2).

12. The term comes from "joint (ad)venture," a concept often used in the days of sailing vessels.

Joint ventures are governed by partnership law and should be defined in an agreement, just like any partnership. Indeed, except for the fact that the agreement should state that the venture is a specifically defined one, the same issues and problems must be resolved in a joint venture agreement as in a partnership agreement.

Complexities of Partnership Law

As we've indicated earlier, partnership law, as it's studied in law school, can get pretty complex. This is partially because lawyers have an institutional bias toward the esoteric and convoluted, and partially because lawyers commonly focus on partnership law at the point that people are already engaged in a nasty dispute.[13] In a sense, their job is to put Humpty Dumpty back together again, while your only job is to keep him (your partnership) from falling off the wall in the first place. You do this by designing a sound partnership agreement and then by following it in good faith.

However, and this is important, if for any reason your partnership does begin to disintegrate and you can't resolve your problems yourselves,[14] or you suffer business problems and are sued, you will need a lawyer. We don't pretend to deal with the almost endless complexity involved in partnership litigation here.

"Partnerships" That Aren't Partnerships

Just as it's important to know what qualifies as a partnership, it can be crucial to recognize a "mock" or "phony" partnership. Many people have been burned when a so-called partnership turned out not to qualify legally.

Tax scam partnerships are particularly vulnerable to being ruled invalid by the I.R.S. Sometimes — especially to try to lower tax liability — it can seem to be very desirable to turn a sole proprietorship into a partnership. For example, Daniel and Marie live together. Daniel is a poor artist who makes very little from his paintings (ah, but he has his dreams); Marie runs a profitable dress store and pays substantial taxes. Can Daniel and Marie legally declare they are now in a partnership to run the dress store and, for tax purposes, each report half the store's profits as their separate income, thus significantly lowering the total amount of tax paid? As you might expect, if the purpose of a partnership is only to evade or reduce taxes, the I.R.S. won't recognize it. There must be some genuine sharing, either of management and control of a business, or investment in it, for there to be a tax-valid partnership;[15] the partnership can't exist solely in bookkeeping terms.

The I.R.S. traditionally takes a close look at any partnership involving family members or relations.[16] (Since Daniel and Marie aren't married, the I.R.S. won't be suspicious because of their legal relationship — but it might notice they live at the same address.) The basic rule is that in order for there to be a partnership, each partner must actually contribute something — either money or service (or both) — to the partnership.

---

13. Being involved in litigation, in the American legal system, is truly a horrible experience — emotionally exhausting and financially draining. Ambrose Bierce's definition of a litigant says it well. "A person about to give up his skin for the hope of retaining his bones."

14. As you'll see, we recommend an arbitration clause in all partnership agreements, to help keep you out of the clutches of lawyers and courts even if there is a falling-out among the partners.

15. *I.R.S. v. Tower*, 327 U.S. 290 (1946).

16. Defined under Section 704(e), Internal Revenue Code.

> In Europe, as in England, partnership law evolved from the customs of the merchants — so civil law regarding partnerships is similar to ours. Civil law recognizes a "societas," the equivalent of our general partnership, and a "societe en common dite," the equivalent of our limited partnership.

Enterprises not primarily designed to make a profit also fail to qualify as partnerships. Such an endeavor is either a "nonprofit corporation," if it is incorporated, or an "unincorporated association" if it isn't. This latter sort of group includes religious, charitable, educational, scientific, civic, social, athletic and patriotic groups or clubs, and trade unions and associations.

Another area of some confusion — as to whether or not a true legal partnership exists — involves the intentions of the people doing business together. To have a partnership, each person must volunteer to be a partner, they can't be drafted against their will. However, intention to be a partner can be implied from the circumstances of a business operation. For example, if three people, who have no other business relationship, each inherit one-third of some real estate, or a business, they do not automatically become partners, because they have never agreed to do business together. If they then proceed to run the business, or develop the land together, they've become partners, even if there is no written partnership agreement.

However, not every active joining of interests makes people partners (either for tax purposes or legally). Here are two examples taken from regulations of the Internal Revenue Service:[17]

1. Mere co-owners of property are *not* partners, even if they lease the property and share rents, provided they do not *"actively"* carry on a business on or with the property;

2. The mere sharing of the expense of a project does *not* "automatically" create a partnership or joint venture. For example, if two adjoining landowners construct a ditch merely to drain surface waters from their property, there is no partnership for tax purposes.

In general, receipt by a person of a share of the profits of an (unincorporated) business indicates that person is a partner in the business. The complexities of business relationships, however, can make application of this rule murky. For example, if Al loans money to Jane and Joan's partnership business, that alone clearly doesn't make him a partner.[18] But suppose Al is worried about Jane and Joan's business sense, so he imposes some controls along with his loan (i.e., requires some new inventory controls or the installation of a time-clock for employees). Does this render Al actively involved in the management of the business, and hence a partner? The answer is — it might. The I.R.S. takes the position that when a lender imposes "excessive controls" on a loan, he or she becomes a partner. Just what are "excessive" controls isn't generally defined — so be wary.

---

17. Treasury Regs. Sections 1.761-1(a)(1); 301.7701-3(a).

18. Unless the loan is really a disguised ownership investment in the business; a key factor here is if a definite time is established when the loan is due. If not, the "loan" looks like an investment.

Limited Partnerships

A limited partnership offers a way for people to invest money in an unincorporated business and still gain limited liability protection. In some circumstances, this device combines the best attributes of both partnership and corporation. Here is how it works. A limited partnership is an entity that has at least one partner who runs the business (the general partner) and in addition, other partners whose only role is to invest in the partnership business (the limited partners). Limited partners have no management powers. Because of this, their income from the limited partnership business is "passive" income. As the name indicates, limited partners do have limited liability for partnership debts or losses — that is, they are financially liable only up to the amount they invested in the partnership. The general partner (or partners) functions like partners in any other partnership, with management powers for the business, and is usually personally liable for any business losses or debts.

Limited partnerships are normally used to raise money without having to engage in the intricacies of creating a corporation and issuing stock, although it must be pointed out that limited partnerships themselves can develop into fairly complicated animals (see chapter 7). Limited partners are investors, not full co-owners and co-managers of a business. In this sense, they are akin to shareholders in a corporation. Limited partners can normally assign their interest in the business freely, unlike general partners.

WARNING: The offering or sale of limited partnership interests involves the sale of a "security;" federal and state securities laws must be checked and complied with, when applicable.

We discuss limited partnerships in detail, including sample agreements and the applicability of securities laws in chapter 7. Here, we just want to alert you to the existence of limited partnerships and the important uses to which they can be put.

Example: Anthony and Janice plan to purchase run-down houses, renovate them, and sell at a good profit. All they lack is the cash to make the initial purchases. To solve this minor difficulty, they first create a partnership between themselves and then establish a series of limited partnerships with others who are willing to put up money for a share in the venture. Janice and Anthony decide that they need $100,000 more than they have to get started and proceed to include ten limited partners in their enterprise, each of whom puts up $10,000.

The return offered limited partners is defined by the limited partnership agreement. Often, limited partners receive a set return on their investment (assuming the venture makes money); thus their investment is similar to making a loan except it normally doesn't have to be repaid if the partnership business fails. There are, however, a number of other options, including giving limited partners a percentage of the profits for a specific period of months or years, or even forever.

Limited partnerships can also be a useful means of raising money to expand an existing business, especially at times when other sources of money are tight and interest rates are high.

Example: Judith and Aretha have a small picture-frame shop that has just begun to prosper after a couple of years of short rations. Believing that the time is now right to expand, the two women spot a much larger store in a much better location, but they don't have the money they need to finance the move and the larger inventory that it will entail. To solve this problem, they create a limited partnership, offering investors a 5 percent interest in the total profits of the store for the next three years as well as the return of the invested capital at the end of that period, in return for $10,000. They sell four of their limited partnerships, raising $40,000. As Judith and Aretha's original partnership agreement did not provide for limited partners, they must rewrite it along the lines discussed in chapter 7.

Limited partnerships involve more legal formalities than do general partnerships. In addition to securities laws, limited partnerships are subject to other state controls, principally registration. Normally, a limited partnership must file a registration statement with some government agency. The partnership and limited partnership agreements must be disclosed, and the names and addresses of all partners and limited partners listed. Failure to comply with state registration requirements can subject the partnership to serious penalties, and cause the would-be limited partners to lose their limited liability status. Fortunately, it's not difficult to comply with the registration requirements; thousands and thousands of limited partnerships are formed each year, and the forms for registration are routine. Also, every state (except Louisiana) has adopted the Uniform Limited Partnership Act, which standardizes both substantive law and the registration procedures.

Small Corporations

A corporation is a legal person — an entity which exists separately from any of its owners. A corporation is created by filing the proper papers — Articles of Incorporation — with state officials. Once this is done, stock certificates are printed and stock in the corporation sold, or with many small corporations, distributed to the founders. The corporation is owned by its shareholders, who — like limited partners — have limited liability for the corporation's debts or obligations. Normally, the most that shareholders can be liable for, or lose, is the amount of their investment.

Corporations, as we know them, have evolved in the last hundred and fifty years as the major organizational form through which large-scale international capitalism does business.[19] Because corporations seem to be such a grown-up, big-time way of doing business, some people just starting a small business are convinced that they, too, need a corporation — or at least, that there must be great advantages to doing business in

---

19. Theoretically, large corporations are run by their shareholders, but this is a capitalistic fiction. Large corporations are occasionally, sporadically, and rarely seriously supervised by a Board of Directors, and actually run by the corporate officers and managers who, within very broad limits, are answerable to no one. An excellent analysis of this state of affairs is found in Galbraith's, *The New Industrial State.*

corporate form.

The truth is that for new small businesses, forming a corporation isn't necessarily wise; indeed, in many situations, the corporate form of doing business provides no real advantage over a partnership and sometimes can be disadvantageous.

Let's review some of the pros and cons that are conventionally listed when it comes to corporate ownership. Some of this material intentionally repeats points that we have already touched on earlier in this chapter, because we feel that it is extremely important that they be clearly understood.

"Advantages" of the Small Corporation:

- Stockholders of a corporation are not liable for corporate debts, if the corporation is adequately capitalized and corporate formalities are followed;
- Corporations have "eternal life." This means that if one of the principal people in a small corporation dies, the corporate entity continues to exist;
- The formalities of corporate existence (paperwork, tax forms, etc.) encourage some people to maintain better records and to engage in organized management practices;
- In some situations, the corporate form allows you to pay less tax. This occurs in situations where corporate profits are less than $75,000 per year and the profit is retained in the corporation from one year to the next. If this is done, lower corporate tax rates result in savings, as compared to having this money taxed directly to the partners. When you realize that after most small corporations pay deductible salaries and fringe benefits to owner-employees and deduct other business expenses, gross receipts even in the range of several million dollars are commonly reduced to a small taxable amount.
- Psychologically, it's sometimes easier to raise capital by selling stock than by establishing a limited partnership;
- Corporate retirement plans are available to business owners;
- Corporate stock can be more easily transferred to third parties than an interest in a partnership can.

"Disadvantages" of the Small Corporation:

- Increased paperwork and costs associated with preparing it. Just filing the initial incorporation papers costs $300-$500 in some states. If you hire a lawyer to set up your corporation, total costs can easily exceed $2,000.
- Double taxation of profits, paid to shareholders in the form of dividends, unless S corporation status is elected which involves even more paperwork.
- Tax rates for corporate profits over $75,000 are higher than individual rates, which means that as compared to a partnership, a corporation with profits at this level pays more.
- Most states have rules making it reasonably simple to operate as a small or "closely held" corporation. However, these same rules contain numerous restrictions on how many shareholders the enterprise can have (e.g., often its 35, with some additional people exempt from being counted), how shares can be sold (usually public sales are prohibited), and many more. What all this really amounts to is that if the corporation stays truly small, the restrictions aren't normally difficult to comply with. But if it starts to act like a large corporation (i.e., sell stock to the public), all sorts of cumbersome restrictions apply.

• When a corporation is ended and appreciated property is distributed to shareholders, the gain in value is taxed both to the corporation and the shareholders. This means that it can potentially be more expensive from a tax point of view to wind up a profitable corporation than a partnership.

Realities:

Okay, enough of the textbook approach. Let's go beyond the "theoretical" advantages and disadvantages of organizing your business as a corporation and return to the thesis with which we began this chapter, that for small, beginning businesses, there often isn't all that much difference between choosing a small corporation or a partnership. First, let's look at "limited liability" of stockholders (as opposed to partners). In some situations this is not as significant as many people believe. Why? Well most small business people with common sense, whether incorporated or not, will have insurance to protect them from the most obvious sorts of liability claims (i.e., insurance protecting restaurant owners from claims filed by customers who become ill). A corporation's "limited liability" is obviously no substitute for business-liability insurance, since "limited liability" doesn't protect the assets of the corporation from being wiped out.

Okay, but what happens if the business loses money, as lots of new ventures do? Doesn't limited liability protect individual shareholders from having personal debts taken as part of a corporate bankruptcy or liquidation? Yes, but here again, limited liability protection may be less valuable than it first appears. Why? Well, because to borrow money or get any significant amount of credit extended in the first place, the individuals who own the small corporation are very likely to have to pledge their personal credit in addition to that of the corporation. Lenders and creditors are well aware of the rules of limited-shareholder liability for corporate debts, so it has become a matter of common practice to require the owners of a new small business (whether incorporated or not) to guarantee personally any loan or extension of credit made to the business. Although it's certainly possible to think of a situation where the limited liability — that comes with incorporation — has in fact shielded the shareholders' personal assets when partners would have been liable, it is more likely that you are less able to escape from personal responsibility for the debts of your business just by choosing one legal form over another.[20]

Second, regarding taxation, let's take a minute to cut through some myths. You may have heard that partnerships enjoy an advantage over corporations because corporate income is taxed twice (both to the corporation and the individual shareholder), while partnership income is only taxed once. While this is true in theory, it is often meaningless in practice. Small corporations can avoid double taxation in two ways. First, they can pay out most of what would otherwise be corporate profits in the form of salaries and bonuses (rather than in dividends). This is easy to do because the principal corporate employees are normally the owners. As long as salaries aren't completely unreasonable, the I.R.S. has no objection. Money paid in salaries, bonuses, social security, health plans, and other fringe benefits, is a business expense for the corporation and is thus not taxed to the corporation. Another advantage of what amounts to dividing income between two tax entities (the corporation and the employee-owner) is that profits retained by the corporation in the form of inventory, or cash for future expansion, etc. are not taxed to

---

20. Limited liability is particularly valuable in a situation where a small business is engaged in any sort of activity that may generate damage claims and law suits and where for whatever reason insurance coverage is unavailable, or too expensive.

the business owners on their personal returns (as would be the situation with a partnership), but are taxed to the corporation.[21] This can result in an actual tax savings for corporations. This is because corporations are only taxed at a 15% rate for the first $50,000 of profit and 25% for the next $25,000 as opposed to the higher tax rate most individuals must pay.

The second common way to avoid double taxation is to elect federal "S corporation" status. An S corporation is permitted to function like a partnership for income tax purposes. This means that an S corporation doesn't pay income taxes; only the shareholders do. Another advantage of S corporation status is that individuals can apply losses from an active business against other income on their individual returns. This can be important if you expect a new business to lose money in its first years.[22]

Although a small corporation can use S corporation status to attain a similar income tax status to a partnership, doing so does involve filing a timely form with the I.R.S. to come out in the same place that a partnership is in automatically. The question is often asked, "Why form an S corporation if you can attain the same tax results with a partnership?" The answer is that sometimes people desire one of the other attributes of incorporation, such as limited liability.

Finally, there is one other tax advantage to using a corporate rather than a partnership form of business. A corporation can establish a tax-deductible pension and/or profit-sharing plan for all its workers, including working shareholders and/or managing owners. A partnership pension plan is only tax deductible for employees, not for partners themselves. However, this difference, too, is often more apparent than real, since partners are eligible for Keogh, I.R.A., and other individual retirement plans which tend to equalize tax treatment. Also, there are restrictions on the amounts put in owners' pension and profit-sharing plans that sub-chapter S corporations can adopt.[23]

In sum, incorporation will probably not lower the taxes, or convey significant tax advantages to most new businesses. However, if you wish to return earnings in the business from one year to the next, a corporation usually offers tax advantages up to $75,000. Sometimes people decide that it's simpler to start their small business as a partnership and change it to a corporation should the tax realities make it beneficial to do so.[24] If all partners agree, this will not be difficult to do.

A third difference between corporations and partnerships involves the fact that corporations have "eternal life." In theory, this means that once a corporate charter is issued, the corporation lasts forever, and business continuity is thus assured. Partnerships, on the other hand, automatically dissolve when any one partner withdraws or dies. But again, when we look behind theory, we find that the day-to-day truth of what

---

21. There are limits as to how much a corporation can retain. Very generally, this is normally $250,000, plus money needed to meet the reasonable needs of the business.

22. We don't discuss S corporation status or the other tax technicalities of organizing a small corporation here, at least in part because they are so well-covered in Anthony Mancuso's books, *How to Form Your Own California Corporation, How to Form Your Own Texas Corporation, How to Form Your Own New York Corporation* and *How to Form Your Own Florida Corporation* (see back of this book for order information). The federal tax discussion in these books is applicable in all states. Mancuso very competently illustrates how most potential tax problems can be either avoided or competently handled.

23. I.R.C. Section 1379(d)

24. Because of the impossible number of permutations of our tax laws, it is impossible to generalize as to whether the corporate form will offer tax savings or will result in more tax without examining the details of the particular business. Talk to a good tax accountant.

happens when a principal owner of a small business dies is similar, whether a corporation or partnership is involved. If one of two co-owners of a small corporation quits or dies, the survival of the business is no more assured than if a partner dies, no matter what the law book rules on "survival" of the corporation. Small businesses survive because of the energies and capital of their owners; take away half the work and cash from a business, whether owned in corporate or partnership form, and it may well not survive.

Thus, if you're creating a small business with a few owners, you should think out what you'll do if one of the owners quits or dies, no matter what business form you choose. How is that owner (or his/her inheritors) to be compensated for his/her interest, while still preserving the business for the remaining owners? How is the value of that interest to be calculated? How can the owners be assured that they will have adequate cash to buy out a departing owner? We discuss methods of resolving these problems in chapter 5. Our point now is simply that you don't avoid any of them by creating a corporation.

Easy transferability of corporation shares to third parties is another "advantage" often cited for the corporate form of ownership. A partner's interest cannot be transferred without the consent of all partners unless, as is rarely the case, the partnership agreement expressly allows for free transferability of interest. But is free transferability really much of an advantage? The answer is clearly "no," for two reasons. First, when it comes to small closely held corporations, state law often restricts the right of a shareholder to freely transfer shares. Second, and even more important, the stock of most small corporations is extremely difficult, or even impossible, to sell. This is because the shares of small corporations are not listed on stock exchanges, and there is no regular market where they can be bought and sold. Even if the business is doing well, a potential buyer will probably be more interested in purchasing profitable business assets (e.g., a building, patent invention, etc.) rather than corporate shares.

Even in situations where the shares in a small corporation can be readily transferred to a third party, there can be drawbacks. In any small business, all depends on the efforts and skills of a few people. If one of the owners/managers can summarily transfer their interest to any third person, the corporation (and the other owners) is obviously vulnerable should the new owner have no ability to help the corporation, or be unacceptable for any number of other reasons. To protect against this happening, the articles of incorporation — or the bylaws — of many small corporations, commonly restrict the right of any owner to sell his/her interest to a third person, and provide that the remaining owners have the option to buy out the interest of any departing owner just as is done in partnership agreements (see Chapter 5, Section C). So again, the realities of running a small business dictate that certain very similar steps to be taken, no matter what the legal form of the business.

We suspect that the real reason why most people starting businesses choose either the corporate or partnership form of legal organization has more to do with style than substance. Just as the day-to-day realities of marriage and living together (especially where the living-together couple has written out an understanding of their business affairs) are not greatly different, so you should also realize that running a small business as either a corporation or a partnership is not nearly as different as you have probably been led to think. Whether or not you and your friends choose one form of organization or the other will have little to do with how you operate your business day-to-day. Probably, the main real difference between the two is that a corporation involves more paperwork, formal meeting requirements, fees, etc., while a partnership requires little formal work after the initial agreement is drafted. For this reason, we personally prefer the partnership form for use in starting most small businesses, recognizing the possible advantages of forming a corporation for tax reasons if the business becomes extremely successful later. Assuming the partners all agree, a partnership can, legally, be turned into a corporation at any time. As we've said, the paperwork is a hassle, but not really an obstacle. However, and this is important, we recognize that some business owners, investors or creditors, prefer the increased formality that goes with a corporation; this is a perfectly valid reason to form one.

D. Can You Do It All Yourself?

So far, so good. You've decided, tentatively, that a partnership is the best legal form for your business. Now you're ready to draw up a partnership agreement. By reding this far, you've already demonstrated that you're unwilling merely to turn all decision-making over to a lawyer. But does this mean that you can and should do everything yourself? Our answer in many cases is "yes, *but.*" First, the "yes." In the next chapters, we discuss partnership agreements in some detail and supply you with the sample clauses and agreements you will need to set up your partnership.

Now, the "but." Even though you can do all the work yourself, there are situations where an experienced lawyer[25] or tax expert can be of great assistance. This is particularly true for complicated tax matters. As we mentioned in the Introduction, the 1986 Tax Reform Act distinguishes between income received from "active" or "passive" activities. If, after you've read this book, any partner has doubts regarding the proper classification of his income, see a tax specialist. Suppose, for example, that you are setting up a partnership to run a restaurant and you are contributing a building you already own. Do you transfer it outright to the partnership? Lease it? Rent it? How is depreciation on the building to be apportioned? If one partner has a much higher income than the others, can all the depreciation be alloted to him? This, as we discuss in Chapter 6, Partnership Taxation, can become complicated in a hurry. Unless you understand the applicable tax rules yourself, it's probably wise to consult an experienced tax person.

---

25. Ambrose Bierce defines a lawyer as "one skilled in circumvention of the law."

Of course, many, if not most, people starting small businesses won't be in a complicated tax situation. All partners most definitely actively and materially participate in the business, usually up to their eyeballs. Even so, any new partnership business venture will involve a number of choices, some complicated. The fact that you are competent to make most, if not all, of these decisions doesn't mean that you would not benefit from the advice of an experienced financial or legal friend.

After you've done the work to set up your own partnership, and work out the substance of your agreement, it can sometimes make sense to hire an expert for a couple of hours to review your work with you. When is this advisable? Really, it depends on how complicated your business and partnership agreement is and how much time and effort you have expended on your agreement.

If your business arrangement is relatively straightforward, and you're confident you've covered the basic problems in your partnership agreement, why pay lawyer's fees merely to get an authority-figure's stamp of approval? Even if you do use an expert, it is best not to dump the whole problem of creating your partnership on the desk. Remember, it's your business. Use this book and other available resources to figure out how to structure your partnership, and seek professional help only for the few areas you can't resolve unaided or want to have double-checked.

If you decide you need a lawyer, how do you find one?[26] What "type" of lawyer do you need? This can pose a real problem if you don't have a lawyer you trust or know a good friend who does. There are an awful lot of lawyers out there these days and the mystique the profession once had (or at least wanted to have) has become badly tarnished. The most important attributes your lawyer can have are your trust and that he or she is competent in small business law. Competence is sometimes hard to judge. Fancy office trappings, three-piece suits, and solemn looks don't guarantee it — although they will insure high fees. Also, just because a lawyer has a big reputation for winning accident or divorce cases, doesn't mean he or she knows small-business law. On the other hand, it hardly makes sense to avoid paying high fees if, instead, you end up paying to educate an inexperienced lawyer. It can also be true that a young, hungry lawyer will work for a much more reasonable rate, and his or her interest and energy will prove preferable to the indifferent efforts of a burned-out "expert."

Personal routes are the traditional — and we think still the best — means for locating a lawyer. If a good friend found a lawyer he/she liked, chances are, you'll like him/her, too. Small business people are almost always willing to share experiences and if you can't get a referral from a trusted friend, talk to some business people who run businesses that you respect. If this doesn't produce good results, here are some other alternatives.

• Be cautious when dealing with bar associations' referral panels and those run as a private business. There's often a charge for referral. While lawyers are supposed to be screened as to their specialty, in some areas this is perfunctory. So don't assume a bar association is some sort of seal of approval. Question the lawyer and make your own judgment, just as you would if you got the referral in any other way.

---

26. Some very cautious folks would advise you'll need more than one attorney. Since each partner has their own interest, they would argue, you'll need separate attorneys. However, in most cases, we doubt if such near-paranoid thoroughness is really needed. If one partner is clearly the "driving force" of a proposed partnership, and he or she suggests a lawyer to draft or review the partnership agreement, the other partners might want a second view.

● Talk to people you know who run successful small businesses. Most people who are smart enough to run a profitable business that you respect are usually also smart enough to have found a competent lawyer and accountant to help them at a reasonable cost.

● In dealing with lawyers, don't be intimidated. Lawyers who act mysterious and say, "Place the problem in my hands," (for a large fee, natch) are either faking it and don't really know how to handle your problem (common) or are people who find it impossible to live without the "me-expert, you-peasant" approach to life (at least as common).

● When talking to a lawyer, you should explain that you want to create as much of your own partnership agreement as possible and see the lawyer's role as a consulting one. You should emphasize that you are not planning to turn all your business problems over to an expert, and want to make key decisions yourself. At the same time, make it clear that you want to lay the foundation for a continuing relationship in which you call on the lawyer as needed. If a lawyer or accountant can work with this approach, you're off to a good start. If not, try another lawyer.

HINT: When making a first appointment, agree in advance on a one-hour consulting fee. Talk your problems over with the lawyer and see how open and knowledgeable he or she is. If the first hour goes well, you may want to talk about establishing a continuing relationship. If you have any doubts, go home and think about them. Even if you have to pay several consulting fees before finding the right person, it will be vastly better than ending up with someone you don't like.

Partnership law was slowly merged into the conventional English legal system, but has always retained the flexibility of its practical roots. First "equity" courts took on partnership cases: equity courts evolved from the tradition that the King, acting through his Chancellor, could do justice on an ad hoc, individual basis, without the limits of the common-law rules. Then, under Lord Coke (in the 1600s) and Lord Masefield (1700s), the common law courts themselves consciously began to change and develop streamlined procedures for dealing with commercial disputes.

The roots of law in the United States are English (except in Louisiana, where law is based on the Napoleonic Code). After the American Revolution, the states passed laws which "received" the English common law as American law, except where the state specifically varied it. That received law included English partnership law, the basis of our current law.

& & &

Further Research

In the appendix at the back of this book, you'll find a list of research materials on small business operation and organization in general and on partnership law in particular. These materials may well provide you with answers to problems too detailed or intricate to be covered in the text. Before you give up and put all your unsolved problems in the lap of a lawyer, consider doing further research yourself. Lawyers, after all, are experts at recycling information and charging large amounts for the service. In reality, the lawyer (often the secretary or a paralegal assistant) is often doing no more than opening a book of legal forms or information and copying out the answers. Even in some complicated tax matters, many lawyers do little more than check the standard reference sources. Why can't you do this for yourself? Often you can if you know where to look, hence the appendix.

Some zealous souls may wish to go beyond the list of resources we provide and do their own legal research. Why not? There is nothing particularly hard about reading law books (boring, yes; hard, no). The most convenient places to find law books are local law libraries. In most states, there are county law libraries, free to the general public. Also, the law libraries of many law schools can be used for research by members of the public, particularly if you courteously explain your needs to a librarian. Unfortunately, legal resources are arranged following a different code than the Dewey Decimal or Library of Congress system followed in public libraries. For an excellent exploration on how to conduct your own legal research, see Elias, *Legal Research: How to Find and Understand the Law*, Nolo Press.

Here are a couple of general hints for the intrepid legal researcher. Each state has its own partnership laws and partnership cases. All the states, except Louisiana, have adopted the Uniform Partnership Act, but most have made at least some changes. Start by reading your state's version of the Uniform Partnership Act. The annotated version will provide you with excerpts and citations (references to) relevant judicial decisions. There are also useful legal encyclopedias, arranged by topic, and form books (collections of sample legal forms, including partnership forms). Your law librarian should be able to direct you to many of these.

In the second half of the twentieth century, the regular civil courts have become over-complicated, over-expensive, and slow, slow, slow. As a result, practical business people have increasingly abandoned them as a sensible place to resolve disputes. As in the middle ages, business has come to rely increasingly on what amounts to a private court system. Thus arbitration, and more recently mediation, clauses have become increasingly popular in business practices. Having an arbitrator render a decision is normally inexpensive and fast. It remains to be seen whether the civil court system will respond to this challenge by modernizing its old-fashioned rules, procedures, and language. There are some signs that this is happening, as some larger states are beginning to make arbitration a part of their system. Also, several states have passed "plain English" statutes, requiring standard legal documents — such as leases, insurance contracts, etc. — to be phrased in clear, everyday English, not legalese.

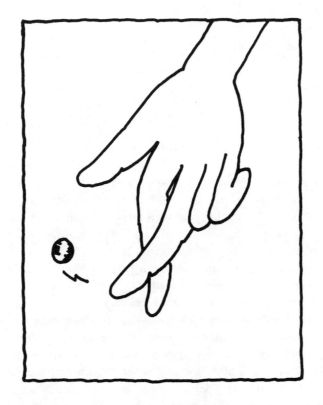

Chapter 2:

Getting Your Business Started

A. Introduction

The principal focus of this book is on assisting you in drafting a sound partnership agreement. There is obviously a lot more involved in getting your business going than working out that agreement. To emphasize this, and share with you some of the realities we've learned about running a small business, we devote this chapter to a brief review of some of the other necessities, and formalities, you'll have to cope with. Those of you who've already lived through the excitements and distresses that attend the birth of a new enterprise may prefer to skip to the next chapter which contains an overview of your partnership agreement.

Sad to say, many peoples' businesses flounder because their owners refuse to see that where there's some paperwork — and there's often quite a bit of it — there's a serious responsibility to keep good records and attend to detail. Yes, it is generally true that keeping books is a drag, especially in the beginning before you get the hang of it. And, yes, it's understandable that the basic urge that propels so many people to drop out of corporate America and "do their own thing," is accompanied by a profound dislike for and distrust of government forms and regulations. Unfortunately, this desire to be free of bureaucratic restraint commonly manifests itself in a refusal to deal seriously with the many ways that government intrudes on a small businessman's life.[1] It's an understandable impulse, surely, but it's self-defeating. Nothing brings government into our individual or business lives faster than the showing of too obvious contempt for their bureaucratic rules and games. Also, we've found many government employees are helpful, if they're treated as human beings, not adversaries.

It's up to you — right here at the beginning — to make a conscious decision that you are going to master all the permit applications, tax forms, and other permission slips that are part of any small businessman's life. If you don't want to follow regulations, meet deadlines, keep good books, and pay attention to a thousand other details (many of them obnoxious), don't start your own business. It's really that simple.

CAUTION! What you will read here is a shorthand version of what the average small business person will have to contend with to start and operate his or her business. For a far more comprehensive review of what's involved, we highly recommend *Small Time Operator* by Bernard Kamoroff. Prospective partners should also consider drafting an initial business plan that assigns a dollar value to each partner's personal assumptions regarding the future conduct of the partnership business. *Start Up Money: How To Finance Your New Small Business* by Michael McKeever (Nolo Press) shows you step-by-step how to do this, including methods for estimating income and how to obtain financing.

B. Short Form Partnership Agreements

As we put these materials together, we began to realize that there was quite a gap between starting a partnership with a handshake and signing a detailed partnership agreement. However, nature being what it is, it's simply too easy to put off doing a comprehensive job and end up with nothing in writing at all. So, with some trepidation, we include a couple of short form agreements that say little more than the fact that the partnership has been established and that there is more to come. Why the trepidation?

---

1. Bob Black's tongue in cheek definition of "Libertarianism" is "all the freedom money can buy." Unfortunately, most people starting a new enterprise aren't wealthy enough to be libertarians, although with proper attention to detail, many may get there in the future.

Well, we're a little afraid that some people will try to substitute the short agreement for a longer one and use it as an excuse not to design something that will work over the long term. **So, let us take a sentence to emphasize that a short agreement is no more than a stop-gap device and should never be used for longer than one to three months.** If you can, it's preferable to draft your final, complete partnership agreement right at the start. But if you do decide to take your time, a short-form agreement is preferable to nothing in writing at all. Here are two sample short-form partnership agreements.

Partnership Agreement

Arnold Presnor and Imogene Grange agree as follows:

1) That as of July 1, 19 _____ they are partners in a business to be known as Acme Illusions. Acme Illusions will operate an interior design business in the greater Dallas, Texas metropolitan area;

2) That Arnold Presnor and Imogene Grange will each contribute $5,000 to get the business going and will be 50-50 partners;

3) That all initial decisions regarding business location, advertising, prices, etc., will be made jointly;

4) That neither partner will obligate the business for any debt in an amount more than $200 without the other's consent;

5) That within two months from the date of this agreement, a formal partnership agreement shall be prepared which will cover what happens if a partner dies, or quits, as well as partnership decision-making, a dispute resolution mechanism, etc.

Partnership Agreement

Olga March, Randy Graham, and Bill Obie make the following temporary partnership agreement with the express intention of replacing it with a detailed agreement prior to _____ , 19 ____ . The partners agree:

1) That they are equal partners in the Happy Clam, a seafood restaurant to be located on the waterfront in Baltimore Maryland;

2) That Olga and Randy will each contribute $25,000 to refurbish an existing restaurant which has been known as Toni's Terrific Tostadas;

3) That Bill obligates himself to serve as chef of the new restaurant for two years in exchange for his one-third share;

4) That all major business decisions involving getting the new restaurant operational will be made by Olga and Randy and all decisions having to do with the kitchen, including the menu, food ordering, hiring kitchen assistants, etc., will be made by Bill;

5) That the formal partnership agreement which will be drafted prior to _____ , 19 ___ will include clauses covering the following matters:

- *The purpose of the partnership business*
- *The terms of the partnership*
- *The contributions made by each partner*
- *Distribution of profits and losses*
- *Management powers and responsibilities*
- *Admission of new partners*
- *Provisions for continuing the business if a partner departs, dies, etc., including valuation and buy-out terms*
- *Arbitration*

[A third sample short-form agreement is provided in Interlude Two]

C. Naming Your New Enterprise

It's your baby and you can pretty much call it what you want. You can legally do business in the name of one partner (Smith Lumber Company or Ricardo's Hamburgers) or all the partners' last names (Smith, White and Vanderweigh Lumber Co.). If you use all the partners' last names, registration of the name is not required. However, it may well be that you want to organize your partnership business using a fictitious name (Two-by-Four Lumber Company) or at least not use all the partners' names, etc. State law or local ordinances normally require registration of a fictitious name, but this is neither a complicated or particularly expensive procedure. It involves filing a single registration statement, often colloquially referred to as a "d/b/a" (doing business as), and in many states, publishing a series of brief notices in a newspaper of general circulation. Contact your city or county clerk, or tax and license office, for more information.

WARNING! Who gets the right to continue to use the business name in case the partners split up can become very important. An obvious example is a name used by a successful rock band. If your business name will have real value in the marketplace, be sure your partnership agreement solves this potential problem. Also, putting your own name on a business can cause problems if you sell out — you may have sold the right to use your own name for that type of business.

NOTE: A partnership cannot legally hold itself out to be a corporation. This means that you can't use Inc., Ltd., Corporation, Incorporated, or Foundation after your name. However, terms that don't directly imply that you are incorporated, such as Company (Co.), Associates, Affiliates, Group, and Organization are normally okay.

As far as titles the partners take for themselves, you are legally free to let your imaginations loose. You can call yourselves partners, managing partners, or Dukes, or Barons for that matter. Denis's law firm has but three partners, all of whom are "senior partners."

D. Permits and Licenses

Many businesses require one or more state and/or local permits and licenses. Sometimes the individual members of the partnership must be licensed (lawyers, doctors, architects, etc.), while in other situations the business itself must have a permit to operate (restaurants, bars, massage parlors, movie theaters, etc.).

You will probably know the rules as to whether the individuals in your business must be licensed, but may not be so sure about what sort of permission slips the business itself will need. Talk to others in the same field and then pay a call on your local city and/or county authorities. Many counties have business libraries (and librarians) which can be quite helpful. Use your business sense. If you're in the food business, be sure you know about health rules. If your business makes noise, find out about anti-noise ordinances. In all cases, make sure you understand how local zoning ordinances apply to you. For example, the fact that you find a commercial location doesn't mean that you can carry on any sort of commerce there. You may be too close to a school to sell liquor, or your type of business may require more parking than is available, etc.

In most situations, it will be wise to get your licenses and permits in the name of your new business. This does away with the possibility of any conflict later should you and your partners get into a spat. We have seen nasty situations where one partner got all permits and licenses in her name, and then later — after falling out with the other partners — refused to execute documents so that the partnership business could operate. In another situation, we witnessed a partner trying to use her supposed control of the licenses and permits as a lever to take over the business and drive the other partners out. The partnership agreement should define who controls these licenses in the event the partnership breaks up.

E. Federal Taxes and Forms

1. PARTNERSHIP RETURNS

Each partner is required to report and pay tax on his or her share of partnership profits whether they are distributed to the partner or held in the business. While the partnership itself is not taxed, it must file an "informational" tax return each year, listing all partnership income, expenses, assets, liabilities, and a reconciliation of the capital account (ownership, equity) of each partner (see chapter 6, Partnership Taxation).

2. EMPLOYEE TAX FORMS AND RULES

If your partnership will have employees — not counting the partners themselves — you will regularly need to prepare and file a number of forms. It's no fun to keep the records necessary to do this, but even less fun to have federal or state officials hassling you — or imposing substantial penalties — for failure to do so.[2] The I.R.S. publishes a pamphlet (I.R.S. 454) entitled *Your Business Tax Kit* which you will find helpful. You will need to do the following:

(1) Get an Employer Identification Number, as described above. The I.R.S. publishes a pamphlet (Circular E — Employer's Tax Guide) that you will find helpful. And don't be fooled by the name. You need a number whether or not you have employees.

(2) Get each employee to fill out I.R.S. Form W-4 or W-4E. These forms are used to determine the amount of income taxes to be withheld from the employees' wages;

(3) Comply with minimum wage requirements and other federal wage and hour requirements. For more information contact the Department of Labor's regional office nearest you or write the Department of Labor, Washington, D.C. 20210, and ask for information on the Fair Labor Standard Act.

(4) Set up procedures to withhold federal income tax and social security tax (F.I.C.A.) and other required withholdings (see §F below) from wages paid to each employee. Social security taxes are withheld at a certain percentage of each employee's earnings. The partnership is required to make matching social security tax contributions for each employee. Circular E mentioned above contains the rules and dates. If you're running an eating or drinking establishment or anyplace else where tips are expected, also ask about special rules on employee tips.

(5) Prepare and file a quarterly withholding return (I.R.S. Form 941) for each quarter of the calendar year, setting out all social security and federal income taxes withheld from each employee's wages and the partnership's matching social security contribution. Rules for how often you send money to the government depend on how much tax is withheld. Contact the I.R.S. for more information.

(6) Each year the partnership must furnish each employee with three copies of a form entitled "Wage and Tax Statement" (I.R.S. Form W-2), if income tax has been withheld from any of that employee's pay checks. In addition, the partnership must send a copy of each employee's W-2 form to the I.R.S. along with an I.R.S. Form W-3, Transmittal of Income and Tax Statements.

In addition to Federal income taxes, an employer must deal with the Federal unemployment insurance bureaucracy. The Federal Unemployment Tax (F.U.T.A.) is paid by the partnership and is not deducted from the employee's wage. See Form #940, the "Employer's Annual Federal Unemployment Tax Return."

& & &

---

2. We know of more than one business that was physically closed down, assets seized, the doors padlocked by the I.R.S., after repeated failures to comply with employee tax laws.

F. State and Local Taxes and Forms

(1) Most states will require that your partnership file for and receive a State Employer I.D. Number.

(2) Almost all states require an employer to pay state unemployment insurance and disability insurance taxes. Contact your state department of employment for forms and instructions.

(3) Most states require employers to carry worker's compensation insurance. Premiums normally depend on the number of workers and type of job. Your state department of employment can give you more information.

(4) All but nine states have a state income tax on wages and require income withholding. This means you as an employer must keep records, withhold the money, fill out forms and file them on time.

(5) States that have personal income taxes impose tax and reporting requirements on the partnership similar to those in federal law.

(6) In all but five states (Alaska, Delaware, Montana, New Hampshire, and Oregon), a partnership business must collect sales tax from your customers and remit the tax to the state unless they are in a business that is sales-tax exempt (e.g., food, in most states). Depending on your state and your dollar volume, forms must be filed and money remitted either monthly, quarterly, or annually. But before you can do this, you have to get a permit (called a "resale permit" in many states). This often requires making a deposit, which can be substantial. Since the deposit is normally based on your anticipated income, it pays to make a conservative estimate.

There are all sorts of other forms you may have to file, and taxes you will have to pay, depending on where you live and what you do. For example, some states, like Washington, have a "gross receipts" tax, while others, like Michigan, have a business-income tax. In addition, many states have special taxes in certain industries such as hotels, loggers, chain stores, and dozens more. Contact your state tax people for details in your area and be sure to see *Small Time Operator*.

In addition to health, safety, and zoning permits mentioned earlier, most cities and counties require one or more business licenses. While these are commonly graduated, based on the gross receipts of the business, it is really just one more tax.

G. Bookkeeping

By now it should be obvious that every small business needs a knowledgeable person to keep the books, fill out the forms, and keep the bureaucrats out of their hair. Good books are not only important for dealing with the outside world — they are absolutely essential to you. Without an efficient, simple accounting system, it can be difficult to know even the most basic things, such as whether you're making money or losing money.

For example, our friend Carol, who was a partner in a small consulting firm, realized — after many months in business — that employing a funky bookkeeper/accountant was a big mistake. The record keeping was so haphazard that the partners couldn't obtain solid facts as to how to allocate overhead to their different projects. Since their bidding on various projects depended in part on their own overhead and other administrative costs, they were at times unable to determine the proper bid to insure a job obtained would be profitable. Here are some bookkeeping suggestions and hints:

(1) Try to do your own bookkeeping only if you both enjoy it and have a knack for it. If you don't, you are likely to end up both doing a bad job and hating it — not a sensible combination. If your partnership has no employees, your task will be simpler; but even so, keeping good records involves lots of work.

(2) Start by understanding how business records are kept. If you don't know how simple accounting works, learn. Through hard personal experience we've been convinced that you should adopt a good system from the start and stick to it. Don't start with a shoe box and a vague plan to take a bookkeeping course next year. No system, no matter how clever, will benefit you if you don't understand it. In brief outline, you will want to be sure that your bookkeeping system will produce the following information:

• An up to date summary of how much cash you take in from all sources (sales receipts, register tapes, charge account records or whatever);

• A record of expenses (a business checkbook may be adequate if you're starting small and pay everything by check.) Before long, though, you will probably want a more formal expense ledger which will also allow you to keep track of cash and accounts payable.

• A record of accounts payable. This will often take the form of a purchase journal which will show when shipments have been received, when money is due, and what's left for future acquisitions.

• A list of accounts receivable, when due, how much overdue, etc.

• An employee ledger listing hours worked, compensation, money withheld for taxes, etc. Again, we recommend *Small Time Operator*.

(3) Consider a two-tier system of involving experts in your financial record keeping. Many small business people we know follow some version of it at a very reasonable cost. Here's how it works. First, hire a competent bookkeeper to actually set up your books, make necessary entries each week (or day), and prepare your routine tax forms. You don't need an accountant to do this and shouldn't have to pay accountant's fees. Most small businesses can start with part-time bookkeeping help; if you ask around you will find lots of small bookkeeping services that will provide you with the hours you need at a reasonable cost.

Next, coordinate your bookkeeping arrangements with those of an accountant who specializes in small businesses. Talk to friends and choose your adviser carefully. You will want to avoid both slipshod operators and large expensive firms that specialize in big business. Your accountant's role is primarily one of a tax advisor. A good advisor will almost always be able to make tax savings suggestions that will more than pay for the services. Your accountant should check the system that your bookkeeper sets up in advance to be sure that it is compatible with the system (often computerized) that is used for the preparation of your tax returns. Many small business people we know only need to sit down with their accountant a couple of times a year, thus minimizing this expense.

NOTE: Keep your books simple and keep them honest. Keeping good books doesn't mean that you need a paperwork system appropriate to an international conglomerate. As in so many other aspects of running a small business, accuracy and simplicity should be your talismans. A few years ago, Steven, a friend who was a recent graduate of Harvard Business School, came to New York City and met a talented and extremely unconventional artist — call him John. They decided to go into the business of manufacturing and selling plexiglass furniture. John was to design the furniture and oversee its construction in his loft in Soho. Steve, as befits a graduate of H.B.S., set up all sorts of fiscal controls and records — double entry bookkeeping, elaborate inventory controls, the works. John refused to pay attention to any of it; he continued to go his very merry way, designing furniture and talking to people, convincing them, as he convinced himself, that each piece he made was a marvel, and a bargain, even at its seemingly hefty price. As the business prospered, mostly because of John's salesmanship, Steve eventually realized that the bookkeeping and paperwork he'd established might be necessary for General Motors, but was far more elaborate and cumbersome than their small business needed. He greatly simplified their system and is now fond of noting, only half in jest, that the one thing you have to have to run a small business successfully is sufficient income (and a conscientiously maintained checkbook). In fact, he knows that more is required, but he does make a good point — complicated bookkeeping methods won't help if no one buys your mousetrap. Before we leave the subject of books, let us refer you to a little book that both of us have found to be inspirational. It's *Honest Business: A Superior Strategy for Starting and Managing Your Own Business*, Random House, by

Michael Phillips and Salli Rasberry. This is no ordinary business book, but one that emphasizes the personal side of an enterprise. For example, in the area of bookkeeping, the authors give the following unconventional advice:

> No single element defines the distinction between an honest business and one that is not than the issue of open books. Somebody who is new to business and enthusiastic about it will usually bring out whatever pieces of paper pass for their books to show a curious visitor without hesitation. Yet 99 percent of the people in the general business world will have a reaction of total terror at the possibility of some outsider seeing their financial records.
>
> Having open books means letting anyone look at your business records, expecially your financial statements and the details necessary to understand them. 'Anyone' includes employees, customers, suppliers and curious bystanders.

H. Budgeting

While in the planning stages of any new venture, the discussion eventually and inevitably turns to finances. Inadequate funding, can be a cause of the failure of small businesses. Also, perhaps surprisingly, as we discuss in a minute, there are real perils to having too much initial capital. Often it's not easy to know how much you really need to start a small business. To determine the amount for yourself, a careful examination of projected expenses and income is imperative.

1. THE BUDGET

This projection gives you an idea of what it will take to set up shop. Initial expenses include:
- Down payment on purchase of business property (or a deposit on the lease);
- Furniture, fixtures, and remodeling costs not absorbed by the lessor;
- Purchase or lease of necessary machinery and equipment;
- Opening inventory (some of this will be on credit terms, but many suppliers will not give much credit to a new business with no established credit history);
- Installation fees and deposits for telephone and utility service;
- Office and store supplies (including stationery, receipt books, pens, paperclips, etc.);
- Taxes and licenses;
- Professional fees (architects, designers, business consultants, attorneys, accountants);
- Initial advertising and promotion.

Here is how you can set up your budget worksheet:

Living Expenses for Partners for 1st 3 months
(including Regular Monthly Payments, Household Operating Expenses, Food, Personal Expenses & Tax Expenses for average months)

_____

Deposits and Prepayments—1 month's business rent or mortgage
(the 1st three are in operating costs, below)

_____

   Telephone and Utility deposits & installation

_____

   Sales Tax deposit

_____

   Business License & Permits

_____

   Insurance Premiums

_____

_____

Real Property Improvements—Remodeling Expenses

   Furniture, fixtures and equipment, including signs (indoors and out)

_____

41

Labor for installation of above _____

_____

Inventory

Service, delivery charges, supplies _____

*Merchandise (approximately 65% of
this should be invested in opening
inventory)* _____

_____

Miscellaneous

Professional Fees _____

Advertising and Promotion _____

Business Travel Expense _____

_____

*Total Operating Costs for Three Months
(from Projected Profit and Loss
Statement)* _____

Reserve to Carry Credit Accounts _____

*Cash on hand to set up cash register,
petty cash, etc.* _____

TOTAL ═══════════

Before we go on and examine an estimated profit-and-loss statement, let's take a moment to leaven our calculations with a little common sense. It may seem obvious that partners starting a new enterprise need enough money to get it off the ground, but in our research we have been constantly struck by two phenomena:

● Many people have made small business work with very little capital to start with. Hard work, creative marketing, and an excellent product or service are important. We have found that lots of money, a flashy store or office, and high salaries are no guarantees of success. People who start small have one enormous advantage—low overhead. They are not burdened by the necessity of covering a hugh capital investment;

● People who invest a lot of money in a business to start with (i.e., a fancy restaurant and bar) often seem to be trying to make up for their lack of small business skills by throwing money at the problem. However, this approach is often counterproductive. Most small businesses go through an inevitable (and healthy) learning stage in which a number of the orginial business assumptions must be modified. If a business is over-capitalized it can be difficult to do this for several reasons, including the fact that the money may have already been spent in the wrong place.

In their book *Honest Business: A Superior Strategy for Starting and Managing Your Own Business*, Michael Phillips and Salli Rasberry have some wise words to say about the over-capitalization phenomena.

> When you start and run a business with the primary goal of serving people, you will be more effective by starting with minimum capital. Minimizing your capital requires maximizing other business components such as quick response to the market, attention to details, and innovation.
>
> The idea of starting with small capital is opposite from the prevailing view of most graduate schools of business, and from the advice almost universally given by small-business writers. The most commonly stated reason given for the failure of small businesses is that they are under-capitalized.
>
> Nonsense! Undercapitalization is the prevailing excuse for insensitivity to the real needs of the market. Too much capital is often a more serious problem than too little.

NOTE: We don't mean to suggest that you don't need money to get started. As everyone will tell you, you do. But don't go overboard—a better mouse trap, a tastier brownie, or more efficient bookkeeping service, and a lot of hard work have launched many a successful partnership.

Now, let's return to our forms and have you set up your estimated monthly profit and loss worksheet.

2. YOUR PROFIT-AND-LOSS STATEMENT

You can set up your Estimated Profit-and-Loss worksheet like this for each month:

Total Sales Month #X
(excluding sales taxes) _____

Cost of Sales < _____ >

Gross Profit _____

Expenses:

  Operating Expenses:

    Salaries _____

    Payroll Taxes _____

    Advertising _____

    Auto and Travel _____

    Supplies _____

    Telephone and Utilities _____

    Other _____ _____

Fixed Expenses:

    Depreciation _____

    Insurance _____

    Rent _____

                                     _____

Total Expenses (see budget worksheet)

                                     < _____ >

*Net Income (before taxes
and partner draw)* _____

NOTE: A worksheet is only as accurate as the information the partners plug in. We have learned that it's wise to err a bit on the conservative side. The art of drafting profit and loss statements is fully explained in *Start-Up Money: How to Finance You New Small Business*, McKeever, Nolo Press. This book provides a far more detailed and sophisticated approach to financing a small business start-up than we have room for here. For example, it shows you how to do a cash flow analysis. This is an essential tool for retail and manufacturing businesses, especially. It allows you to figure out whether you will actually be paid enough real money fast enough by your debtors to keep your suppliers and other creditors from pulling the plug on you.

---

3. THE BALANCE SHEET

This worksheet is useful to answer two basic questions. Are you solvent? If so, by how much? This is determined by subtracting what the business owes from what it owns, to determine net worth. Partners can use a beginning balance sheet as one tool to indicate the state of their business at the start. Subsequent balance sheets are useful to monitor business activity.

A Balance Sheet looks like this:

===

Date: _____

Current Assets

    Cash _____

    Accounts Receivable _____

    Inventory _____

                                       _____

Fixed Assets

    Real Estate _____

    Furniture and Equipment _____

    Less: Accumulated depreciation < _____ > _____

Other Assets _____

TOTAL ASSETS _____

Current Liabilities

   Notes payable within 1 year _____

   Accounts Payable _____

   Accrued Expenses _____

   Taxes Payable _____ _____

Long-Term Liabilities

   Notes payable after 1 year _____

   Others _____

TOTAL LIABILITIES _____

NET WORTH
*(assets minus
liabilities)* _____

[Liabilities + Net Worth = Assets]

NOTE: A worksheet is only as accurate as the information the partners plug in. We have learned that it's wise to err a bit on the conservative side.

I. Partnership Accounting

There are two methods commonly used in partnership accounting — the cash method and the accrual method. For cash accounting, you simply list, in the appropriate ledger, expenses and income as received. If you don't actually take money in, or pay it out, you don't list it. This method of accounting is commonly used for service businesses.

Retail businesses and other businesses with significant inventories normally use the "accrual" method of accounting. With accrual accounting, income is reported as received, or spent, when the item or obligation involved is created or received, regardless of when the actual cash shows up or goes out. In other words, when you ship merchandise to a customer, and bill him, that bill is "income" right away under the "accrual" method. Likewise, it's an expense *when* you order some supplies, not when you actually pay for them. The accrual method of accounting is generally required for income tax purposes when a business regularly buys and sells goods. Otherwise, a partnership can elect whichever accounting method it will use.

J. Insurance

We mentioned in chapter 1 that it is wise to purchase insurance against obvious risks because partners do not enjoy limited liability. If someone slips on your linoleum, or eats a bad oyster, or walks under your ladder at the wrong moment, the partnership and all general partners can be sued. If the partnership assets are insufficient to pay the judgment, the partners can be made to pay out of their own pockets.

Example: Al and Melody establish a housepainting partnership called Bright Spot. They unwisely use a sprayer on a windy day and end up getting dark red paint on ten automobiles parked in a lot which neighbors the building they are painting. Unfortunately, since none of the cars are red, Al and Melody have to face up to paying for the ten cars to be repainted. Several are fancy cars needing fancy paint jobs, and the total bill comes to close to $20,000. Faced with this disaster, Al disappears and Bright Spot goes broke. Melody is liable to pay the whole $20,000 from her own personal funds.

What sort of insurance you should buy is directly related to where the risks in your business fall. In addition to normal fire and theft coverage, it's an excellent idea to get a general liability policy which will cover normal sorts of accidents, such as someone falling on your front steps. Beyond that, you will have to think about the details of your own business. An architect, a dress designer, and a fish store are obviously going to need different sorts of protection. We are by no means insurance freaks, but we do believe that a reasonable amount of product liability insurance makes sense in many businesses, if it can be purchased at a cost that isn't prohibitive. In others, you may not think the risk is severe enough to justify the cost of the insurance. However, if your business uses any vehicles, you will want to be sure they are adequately insured, even if they belong to an employee. (This is required by law in most states.) If an employee driving her own car gets into an accident on partnership business, you may be sued.

One of us recently purchased some business insurance. We started by getting leads from other small business people as to knowledgeable brokers. We called these people and asked each to stop by our office for a *short* talk. Then we asked for bids. They varied considerably as to both amount and details of coverage. We have been happy with both the broker and the coverage we chose.

K. Renting Property

Rent can be one of the larger expenses for many small businesses. While it's essential that you locate your new enterprise in an advantageous place, it's also important that you not obligate yourself for so much rent that you jeopardize the future of the business. Here are a few lessons that the small business people who have helped us put this book together have learned:

● Figure out your minimum space needs and then really shop around. For some people, even minimum needs will be fairly costly (e.g., a specialty food shop that has to locate in an expensive neighborhood). For others, minimum needs can be pretty funky — that is, they can start their operation in a small store front or garage. We ran Nolo Press out of an attic for years and used the rent savings to print more books.

● Assuming that you do plan to rent commercial or retail space, be sure to get a lease that provides you with adequate security. Often small entrepreneurs rent a location fairly cheaply, on a short lease or month-to-month tenancy, only to have the landlord raise the rent as soon as they begin to prosper. Also, real estate prices have a way of rising fast in neighborhoods where small, creative businesses congregate. A few entrepreneurs, a few artists, and then — shazam — the media says it's chic and you' ve got Soho, Manhattan, or Venice, California.

We recently talked with some partners who'd opened a restaurant in a rundown neighborhood in San Francisco. The food was wonderful and people lined up to get in. Before long, two similar restaurants announced plans to open nearby. What happened? You guessed it — the landlord tripled the rent. Of course, some small businesses aren't particularly sensitive to location, and others plan to move fairly quickly from the start. but if you have the sort of business, such as a restaurant, where you're making a real investment in having people know where you are, plan ahead.

This is not a book on commercial leases, but here are a few things you should know:

● It's often easier for a tenant to end a lease then you might think. Why? Because of a legal doctrine known as mitigation of damages. This bit of legal gobbledygook means that if you do have to move out before the lease term is up, your landlord must try to rent the place to someone else. If he does so immediately (or often even if he could have), you're off the hook and normally you won't owe any damages for moving early.[3]

● Consider getting a lease for a couple of years and then an option (or options) to renew for a longer term. If, for example, you had a three-year lease with an option to renew for an additional three years at a slightly higher rent, you would be free to stay (or not stay) for the second period, depending on how things looked at the time. Obviously, if you are going to make major improvements to the building you will want to get a long-term lease.

● Landlords are sometimes reluctant to commit themselves to a long-term lease because they don't know how bad inflation will be. One way to handle this anxiety is to offer to tie automatic yearly rent increases to the consumer price index. For example, it might be appropriate to have your rent automatically go up each year at about two-thirds of the C.P.I. increase. Thus, if the C.P.I. goes up at a yearly rate of 5%, your rent would go up about 3.5%. We suggest that you bargain for a rent increase of less than the

---

3. This is a brief summary of what can be a complicated subject. If you face it, check the rules in your state. Often you can find a new tenant for the landlord to insure that he suffers little or no damage.

C.P.I. increase because many of the landlord's cost will be fixed and his costs are unlikely to be going up as much as the C.P.I.

● If the landlord promises to make improvements on the property to induce you to sign the original lease, make sure you get them in writing.

● If you need to modify the structure of your rented space in any way, be sure you have written permission to do so as part of the lease. This advice also applies if you plan to attach anything (called a trade fixture in lawyerese) to the building. A simple written statement from the landlord as part of the lease that you can detach it when you leave is all you need. If you don't do this, you may find that you have made your landlord an unintentional present.

REMINDER: Be absolutely sure that the location you choose meets all the zoning and other permit requirements necessary for your business before you sign a lease.

PARTNERSHIP AGREEMENT NOTE: Sometimes partners will still be formulating their written agreement when they find the perfect location and want to sign a lease. Perhaps the best thing to do in this situation is to slow down — simply wait to make any formal commitments until the partnership agreement is signed. But this is an impatient society and sometimes you do have to move quickly to be sure you get the right — any decent — location. If this happens, you may want to sign a short-form partnership agreement like those set out in section A. This will formally establish your partnership and will be a sound legal basis for leasing property in the partnership name.

The Story of the Chocolate Moose

INTERLUDE II

Let's take a moment and see how things are going for John and Sara. Three weeks have passed since they agreed to start their bakery and a lot has happened. Sara has found a downtown store that used to be occupied by a seedy cafe, one that couldn't even compete with Greasy Al's. Because the store's been empty for over a year, the rent is reasonable. It'll need a lot of work, but fortunately Sara and John have a couple of carpenter friends who do good work relatively cheap. The kitchen isn't quite ideal, but with the addition of two secondhand commercial baking ovens and a large refrigerator, it will be adequate to start. The zoning in the area permits a bakery; Sara has talked to the city health people and has been briefed on all health regulations, none of which seem difficult to meet. The building department has approved the preliminary remodeling work.

In the meantime, John has been working on business matters, including the building lease, the partnership agreement, insurance, bookkeeping, etc. Today the two friends are meeting to review their progress and see what they need to do next. As he listens to Sara's detailed report on the store, John feels elated. It's becoming a reality.

"It's gonna work, John, it really is!"

"Why, I never had a moment's doubt," John answered with a slightly mocking laugh. "I can see it now, a chain of Chocolate Mooses, spreading across America, trips to Paris . . ."

"Anyway," Sara interjected, "at least I'm not going to be stuck in that lousy diner all my life."

"I thought I was the realist," John laughed. "Okay, time for my report. I've done some research on how we should organize our business. We can either set up a small corporation or do a partnership. They're pretty much the same for our purposes. Since the corporation is more trouble and expensive to get going, and requires more paperwork to maintain, I think we're better off starting as legal partners. All that a partnership requires is a contract—a partnership agreement between the two of us which sets up what we've agreed to."

"Does that cover what happens if one of us wants to do something else in a few years?" Sara asked.

"Sure—it can cover buy-out agreements and anything else we want to include, such as what happens if one of us dies, or wants to quit, what our shares are, and our work obligations, etc."

"Okay, where do I sign?" Sara responded cheerfully.

"I'm afraid it's not quite that simple, m' dear."

"Why not? We're friends, aren't we? We can work it out without a lot of wherefores and wherevers."

"Sure—or at least I hope we can. But it's risky being too casual about it. For example, we agreed we're 50-50 partners, right?"

"Right."

"Wrong," John continued, "or at least we should discuss it. You're going to contribute $15,000 and I can only raise $10,000. What do we do about that? I thought it would be fair if you took a larger percentage of the profits, say sixty percent, for the first year or two, and then we could share everything equally."

"Mmmmm . . . how about for the first two years?" Sara asked.

"Why you capitalist, you! One year!"

"Okay," Sara laughed, "eighteen months!"

"Fair enough," John concluded.

"Hummm," Sara mused. "Yeah, I guess it would be better to hash everything out and then write it down. How do we go about it?"

"I though I'd use this book I just found on partnership agreements by Clifford and Warner to come up with a working draft.* I feel we should treat this seriously. When I complete a draft which I'm reasonably sure is legal and fits our needs, we'll go over it together carefully and see what changes we want to make."

"One thing I've been thinking about," Sara said, "is how we should get paid. If we invest all of our savings in the business, we'll have some problems when it comes to our rent and food bills. We'll need to begin drawing a salary right away."

"Well, one way to do that," John replied, "is to have the partnership provide a monthly draw for each of us—either so much per week, or per hour, or whatever we decide. Even if we don't take in a fortune at first, we should have a decent amount left over after we've paid our initial expenses. We can use that to pay our salaries. We'll start out taking only a minimum until we can afford the life style to which we aspire."

"That makes sense," Sara agreed. "Hey, what happens if the business gets going well and one of us wants to split? I haven't forgotten about your fantasy about living in Europe. What happens if the business is a great success and you want to pull out? I don't want you to sell your half of the business to some stranger."

"That's a problem, alright. I think we can include something in our partnership agreement that gives us the right to buy each other out if one of us decides to leave."

"But what if we don't have enough money?"

"We can write it up so that the person who's going to stay in the business can buy the other out over several years."

"Okay. Well, there's obviously a lot we still have to work out after you've written the preliminary draft. In the meantime, though, I think we'd better sign the lease and start our remodeling so that we don't risk losing the place to someone else."

"Suppose we do? It's not the only location in town and I don't think we should get caught in a fear and greed mentality. We're going to set up a good business and lots of people will want to rent to us."

Sara smiled, waiting for John's instinctive "don't fence me in" response to play out. John caught her look and instinctively understood. "Okay, you're right. The location is good and we both like the building. Let's make an offer to lease the place for a year with an option to renew the lease yearly for five more years. That way we'll be protected for six years, but if we want to close down or move, we can

---

*You didn't think we'd let them get their partnership information anywhere else, did you?

get out of the lease at the end of any of those years."

"But won't the landlord want to raise the rent?" Sara asked.

"Most likely—that's the nature of the beast. But if inflation continues, we'll want to raise the prices of our brownies every year, too. Why not suggest that the rent can be raised every 18 months by half the amount the cost of living goes up? If the consumer price index increases by eleven percent, our rent would go up five and a half percent."

"Do you think the landlord will go for that?"

"We won't know unless we ask. Remember, the place is empty now and he's not getting any rent."

"Well, it's okay with me, but do we need to be official partners before we sign the lease?"

"Well, technically we have been partners ever since we shook hands—you don't need a written agreement to start a partnership. But you're right—I do think we should put something in writing in the form of an interim agreement. Why don't you take a look at the one I drafted last night."

PARTNERSHIP AGREEMENT

Sara Holcombe and John Shalakatinsky make the following agreement:

1. That they are partners in a bakery to be called "The Chocolate Moose." Their goal is to make the best chocolate desserts in _____ County at the same time that they make an adequate living and allow each other the opportunity to live a sensible and fulfilling life. Or in other words, both recognize that although work is an important part of life, it isn't the only thing in life.

2. That a formal partnership agreement that will specifically cover partnership shares, division of work responsiblities, what happens if a partner wants to quit, or dies, or if there is a dispute, is to be prepared by John prior to March 1, 19 ____ .

3. That until the formal agreement is signed, all significant decisions involving the partnership shall be made by both partners jointly. This includes leases, equipment purchase of more than $100, establishing bank accounts, etc.

DATE _____

_____
SARA HOLCOMBE

DATE _____

_____
JOHN SHALAKATINSKY

Sara finished reading it. "Where's the pen?" she asked. "Now, if you'll get started on the full agreement and the lease so that we can take over next week, and then arrange for the carpenters to start, I'll get started on my recipes."

"Don't forget the truffles," John interjected. "We have to have tip-top truffles. And are chocolate chip cookies enough of a gourmet item? And . . ."

"And don't meddle," Sara interrupted unceremoniously. "You may be the head honcho when it comes to the business end of things, but I'll not have you telling me how many chocolate chips to put in the cookies!"

Chapter 3:

An Overview of Your Partnership Agreement

A. Decisions About Your Partnership Agreement

In this chapter, we look more deeply at decisions involved in actually drafting a partnership agreement. Commonly, that agreement gets worked out between the heady day when you first realize that you're going to take your dream seriously and the even headier day when you open for business. Perhaps right now you're barely past the initial excitement stage, just realizing that you are entering one of the busiest and most exciting phases of your life, or perhaps you have already started business in a small way and feel a little anxious about not taking care of your partnership contract. In either situation, what do you do? Where to start? If you're like most of us, you'll find yourself going in several directions at once, and making time to set up your business as a legal entity won't be easy. It's our job to lay out the details you need to understand how to establish your partnership as simply as possible, but you will have to commit yourself to some hard work.

Legally, your partnership starts when you agree that it does. As we noted in chapter 1, a legal partnership can be based on an oral agreement, or can even be implied from the operational realities of a business. But for obvious reasons, implied or oral agreements are such a lousy idea that henceforth we will assume that you will adopt the common sense approach of putting your partnership agreement in writing. Many states' laws effectively compel partnership agreements to be in writing. For example, under the New York "Statute of Frauds," any partnership agreement must be in writing if:

1. The agreement is to last for more than one year;
2. Real property is involved;
3. An arbitration clause is included;
4. There are guaranteed payments to a partner, etc.

A written partnership agreement is effective when it is signed, unless the agreement itself specifies a different date. (As we've mentioned earlier, full fiduciary partnership's loyalty is owed prospective partners even *before* the partnership legally exists.)

This brings us to a point worthy of emphasis. **Partnership agreements are simply contracts that express your understanding, your decisions, regarding how you want your business relationship to work.** There is a body of law — primarily the Uniform Partnership Act (the U.P.A.)[4] — which establishes most basic legal rules applicable to partnerships, such as the date a partnership commences. However, almost all these rules can be varied — if you decide to do so — by an express statement in the partnership agreement. As we proceed, we discuss not only what the standard rules are, but how you can alter them if you wish.

Let's agree on some basics. Your partnership agreement legally does not need to be (and should not be) a gobbledygook-filled monstrosity stuffed with abstruse lawyer language. It should be clearly written, in plain English, to express the decisions you've made. Throughout this book, we will supply you with sample clauses that you can use as written, or adapt to meet your needs. Don't be afraid of making changes if they will better express what you've agreed on. If you make a lot of changes, you may want to check your work with an expert to be sure that you haven't somehow created an agreement that could pose serious problems of legality or interpretation. Frankly, though, if your agreement is

---

4. Adopted in all states except Louisiana; in most states, however, there are some variations, usually slight, between the state Uniform Partnership Act, and the original "uniform" act.

clear to you, and expresses everything that you and your partners have agreed on, subsequent trouble over its technical correctness is unlikely.

1. COMMON MATTERS COVERED IN PARTNERSHIP AGREEMENTS

What's normally covered in a partnership agreement anyway? Let's start with an overview. Take a look at the list below which gives numerous subjects which can be included. You don't have to pick definite clauses or make any final decisions regarding what you'll cover in your agreement yet; that can come later. But some things may be clear from the beginning. For example, you may decide that you want a concise agreement that isn't burdened with some of the subjects on this list, such as "expense accounts" or "accounting rules," etc. Indeed, we suggest that for most starting small businesses, only the real basics (we've starred * those we consider most important on this list) need be covered in the agreement.

2. SUBJECTS OFTEN COVERED IN PARTNERSHIP AGREEMENTS

* Name of the partnership (and names of individual partners)
* Term of the partnership (indefinite, or for a set, limited time); and date started;
* Purpose of the partnership; the type of business to be conducted;
* Personal business goals of the partners and partnership;
* Cash and property contributed to start the business;
* What happens if more cash is needed;
* Skills to be contributed (hours to be worked, work duties of partners, management roles, possible other business activities, etc.);
* Distribution of profits;
* Losses (how divided);
* Salaries, guarantees, or drawing accounts;
* Withdrawals of contributed assets/capital by a partner;
* Duties of partners, acts expressly restricted or authorized by partners;
* General management provisions (power to borrow money);
* Expense accounts;
* Accounting and check signing rules and procedures;
* Disputes (rule by majority voting, provision for arbitration or mediation, etc.);
* Sale, assignment, etc. of a partnership interest;
* Admission of new partners;
* Expulsion of a partner;
* Continuing business if a partner withdraws, dies, becomes disabled, or retires;
* Determining value of a departing partner's interest, provisions for payment of that interest;
* Dissolution, winding up, and termination.

If the partnership is a joint venture (remember, this is a partnership with a specific, limited purpose, such as building one house), there will usually be some additional matters that should be covered in the agreement, including:

- Extent of the venture;
- Staffing, control of hiring;
- Conflicts of interest;
- Management control and buy-outs;
- Application of tax laws;

In the rest of this chapter, we discuss some of the basic problems that are handled in virtually all partnership contracts — for example, initial contributions to the partnership, and distribution of profits. We present sample clauses that you may find useful in your agreement. As we've said, our own preference is for simplicity — so here we try to stick closely to the real fundamentals. As you read through this overview material, grab a pencil. If you see something that makes sense, mark it so that you will remember to discuss it with your partners. Also, when it comes time to draft your agreement, it'll be a real help if you've already marked the clauses you want.

B. The Partners and Their Relationships

The rights and powers of partners can be defined in your partnership agreement with any degree of specificity you desire. Indeed, some partnership agreements contain pages and pages defining the authority, duties, and restrictions on partners. We suggest that this type of endless detail is usually not helpful, and can even signal serious mistrust between the partners. Remember, trust is the central requirement for any partnership, and no number of legal clauses can compensate for its absence. So, while it is important to carefully define the basic rights of the partners, vis-a-vis each other, it doesn't make sense to produce something as thick as the Manhattan phone book and as complicated as the Federal budget.

In the absence of a specific limitation, any partner can bind the partnership by decisions made in "the ordinary course of partnership business."

Example: Herb, Frank, and Connie own a record store. Herb, a country music freak, gets carried away and orders four times as many Hoyt Axton records as can normally be sold. Frank and Connie disagree, but the partnership (and each partner) is liable to pay the bill.

While the rights and duties of the partners between themselves are primarily controlled by the partnership agreement, that's not necessarily true for other people dealing with a partner. After all, outsiders usually don't have any idea what's in the partnership agreement. So, in the above example, even if Herb, Frank, and Connie's partnership agreement specifically limited the number or type of records that a partner could buy, a third party wouldn't be bound by this unless they had actual notice of the provision. To translate this into lawyer lingo would be to say that an outsider can legally rely on the "ostensible" or "apparent" authority of a partner. Generally, this is authority that's been demonstrated by the partner in the course of the business, or authority that's normal in similar business partnerships.

NOTE: We don't mean to suggest that partners usually violate their own agreements; we only want to tell you what usually happens when they do.

1. TERM OF THE PARTNERSHIP

Many partnership agreements do not contain a term for their duration;[5] in that case they last indefinitely, until one partner departs, or dies, etc., or all agree to dissolve the partnership. Often this is the wisest approach. You may decide, however, you want to limit the partnership term to a set period; after all, the partners can all agree to continue it, if they then agree on it. Here are some sample clauses:

> *The partnership shall continue for a period of _____ years, at which time it shall be dissolved and its affairs wound up.*
>
> or
>
> *The partnership shall be continued for a period of _____ years; after that time, the partnership may be dissolved by a vote of _____ % of the partners.*

[Particularly suitable for large partnerships.]

2. PARTNERSHIP NO-NO'S

We have now learned rules that would seem to indicate that one partner has considerable authority to bind the partnership. Does this mean that one partner can bind the other(s) no matter what they do, unless there is a specific clause prohibiting the particular activity in the partnership agreement, and it's brought to the attention of someone dealing with the partner? No, it doesn't. There are some things that the Uniform Partnership Act says that a partner can't do, and members of the outside world are presumed to know a partner can't do them "in the ordinary course of business." Here is a list of the actions which are not legally binding for a partner to take without partnership approval *unless* the agreement specifically provides otherwise:

- Convey one's interest in the partnership to another person;
- Convey one's interest in any partnership property;
- Mortgage or otherwise subject partnership property to a lien because of one's personal debts or borrowing;
- Attempt to dispose of specific partnership property (rather than one's own interest in the partnership) through one's will;
- Assign partnership property in trust for creditors or on the assignee's promise to pay the debts of the partnership;
- Dispose of the goodwill of the business;
- Do any act which would make it impossible to carry on the ordinary business of the partnership;
- Confess a judgment (i.e., agree to a judgment for the other side in a law suit);
- Submit a partnership claim or liability to arbitration or reference.

We think that it's sensible that these acts not be authorized in a partnership agreement. However, if you disagree and want a single partner to be able to mortgage property, or take any of the other listed steps, you will have to state this expressly in your partnership agreement.

---

5. The term of a partnership should be coordinated with dissolution provisions. Be sure to check chapter 5, section (B)(5)(b) on dissolution before adopting your final "term" clause.

Some partnership agreements contain additional restrictions on a partner's authority. These restrictions are often not binding on the rest of the world — again, unless they have actual notice of them. For example, members of the partnership can include a clause in the partnership agreement to the effect that:

> *The following acts may only be done with the consent of a majority of the partners (or, by unanimous consent of the partners, etc.).*
> *a. transferring, compromising, or releasing any partnership claim, except upon payment in full;*
> *b. borrowing money in the partnership's name;*
> *c. signing partnership checks over the amount of $ _____ .*[6]

This list could be continued, and altered to suit the specific needs of any particular partners and business. These types of restrictions are perhaps advisable for some large partnerships, but most are unnecessary for small ones. Their main purpose is to define rights between partners in case one acts improperly. If you have so little trust in your prospective partners that you think this sort of clause is necessary, you should seriously question whether that partnership is advisable at all.

3. PARTNERSHIP DECISION MAKING

Our next task is to understand how a partnership can make decisions where there is a desire to have everyone consulted. Often, this is done democratically, with each partner having one vote. The Uniform Partnership Act calls for this approach even if there hasn't been an equal contribution of assets to the partnership by the partners (unless the agreement provides differently). We believe it's usually wisest to adopt a one-partner, one-vote approach; it's more attuned to the all-for-one, one-for-all attitude that's the spiritual basis of a partnership. However, some situations — or some people — call for a different approach. If you do want to do it differently, you have to spell it out in the partnership agreement. Partnership voting is not a mechanical matter, but a reflection of how the partners feel about each other, and what each is actually contributing.

Example: Stephanie, Susan, and Maria decide to set up a modeling agency. Stephanie contributes $20,000 to starting the business and will work full-time. Susan contributes $10,000 and will work only occasionally at the business. Maria will contribute only $500 and will work half-time. Obviously, Stephanie is contributing the most to the business. Should she nevertheless have just one vote, i.e., a total of one-third control in the partnership? That's up to the three partners. If Stephanie feels she does not want to risk subjecting her interest to possible out-voting by the two other partners, and all three agree that's fair, here are two possible clauses to solve her problem:

> *No. 1. Each partner shall participate in the management of the business; in exercising the powers of management, each partner's vote shall be in proportion to her interest in the partnership's capital.*

---

6. In reality, requiring more than one partner for check signing often causes delays and can lead to partners pre-signing blank checks. If you do want to impose limits on check signing powers, discuss these with your bank as soon as possible.

This clause leaves Maria without any significant say in the management of the business, since she contributed such a small amount of capital. It might well be fairer to proportion voting rights *"according to each partner's share of profits,"* since they (presumably) reflect all contributions to the partnership, i.e., ongoing services as well as initial capital.

Another method is simply for the partners to agree on the proportion of voting power, or management control, they believe is fair. Thus, a clause could be drafted stating:

> *No. 2. In the management, control, and direction of the business, the partners shall have the following percentages of voting power:*
>
> | | |
> |---|---|
> | *Stephanie* | *60 percent* |
> | *Susan* | *20 percent* |
> | *Maria* | *20 percent* |
>
> *Except as specified in their agreement, all major decisions may be made by a majority of the total percentage of votes possible.*

NOTE: Both these clauses leave Stephanie in complete control. Her problem has been solved; but if she adopts a course of action that Susan and Maria don't care for, there's little they can do but resign and try to liquidate the partnership. This often isn't easy to do, unless (as we advise) specific clauses have been included in the partnership agreement covering what happens if any partner leaves (see chapter 5).

Clauses involving the control and management of a partnership can get very detailed — down to specifying just when office meetings should be. If you want that kind of precision, examine the clauses in the Appendix, section A closely. One common sense approach is to require joint partnership decision making only for fairly major concerns. Of course, how you define major and minor will depend on the personalities of the partners and the type of business. Some partners do this by adopting money as a yardstick to define the authority of each individual partner (i.e., all decisions involving the expenditure or potential expenditure of more than $1,000 shall be discussed and voted on by all partners) while others handle this in some other way (i.e., all decisions as to what jobs to bid on, the design specifications, and the amount of the bid shall be unanimously agreed to by all partners).

Another approach, which can work well for small partnerships, is to require all decisions to be unanimous; i.e., every partner has veto power. Sample clause:

> *All partnership decisions must be made by unanimous decision of all partners.*

TAX NOTE: As explained in Chapter 6, it's generally desirable to have all partnership income be "active" under I.R.S. rules. This requires that each partner "materially participate" in the business, which is defined as "regular, continuous and substantial involvement in partnership business operations." The "Management Powers and Duties" Clause in Chapter 9, Drafting Your Actual Partnership Agreement, expressly states that all partners "materially participate" in the business.

---

4. DOES A PARTNER HAVE AUTHORITY TO BORROW MONEY?

It is not uncommon for a partnership to borrow money either to get started or expand. Normally, the lender will insist on the signature of all the partners. Banks are particularly careful about this.

Some lenders, however, will not be so fussy; so, the question arises — does one partner have the power to borrow money and obligate the partnership to pay it back without the express approval of the other partner(s)? This is something that should be covered in your partnership agreement. We recommend that unless there are special circumstances in your business that compel a different approach, you should adopt a partnership agreement that requires all partners to approve all loans. It's simpler that way.

There is a risk here that you should be aware of. No matter what the partnership agreement states, partners — in what have traditionally been called "trading partnerships"[7] — have the apparent authority to borrow money or execute loan notes on behalf of the partnership.[8] "Trading partnerships" are, as the name states, those directly involved in trade, like merchants selling a product. Examples of "non-trading" partnerships include "service" businesses like law firms, theaters, banks, real estate enterprises, or farms. Partners in "non-trading" partnerships traditionally do not have the apparent authority to borrow money on behalf of the partnership.

WARNING: What all this means is simply that in many partnership-small businesses, e.g., any retail one, this is yet another danger if you have an unreliable partner. Without actual authorization, this partner can borrow money and leave you and the other partners stuck for the loan.

5. LIABILITY OF THE PARTNERSHIP TO THE PUBLIC

Standard legal rules of responsibility are applicable to partnerships. For example, partners must perform any services provided to the public competently, or the partnership can be liable for negligence. Competence means a partner must use the level of professional skill, care, and diligence generally applicable in the profession or trade. This standard generally applies to all partnership enterprises whether they're set up to fix teeth, cars, toilets, or hot tubs. Thus, if one partner (or an employee of the partnership) in a pest control business inspects a house sloppily and doesn't spot termites in the roof, the partnership is liable for any loss that results from the negligence.

The partnership is also liable for "any wrongful act or omission of any partner acting in the ordinary course of business of the partnership where loss or injury is caused to any person . . ." (Section 13 U.P.A.). Thus, if a partner negligently injures a pedestrian while driving a car on partnership business, the entire partnership is liable for the pedestrian's damages. Similarly, the partnership is generally liable for intentionally wrongful acts — deceit, assault, trespass — committed by a partner during the course of partnership business.

---

7. The distinction between "trading" and "non-trading" partnerships has, one commentator states, "haunted" partnership law for generations." The U.P.A. does not make this distinction; however, it doesn't outlaw it, so the courts in many states still adhere to it.

8. Unless the lender in fact knows that the partner in a "trading partnership" does *not* have power to borrow money for the partnership.

The conventional way to protect against most business risks is to buy liability insurance. As we indicated in chapter 2 Section G, we're no great fans of insurance. Often you pay a relatively high cost for protection against occurrences that are highly unlikely. However, insurance protection against traditional sorts of negligence lawsuits — someone allegedly slips and falls in you store and sues for hundreds of thousands — is normally a sensible idea. It's a relatively inexpensive form of insurance. Whether you want insurance against other risks such as professional incompetence or intentional injuries, is often a more difficult choice and depends to a large degree on who you are and what you are doing. For example, legal and medical malpractice insurance has become so costly that some lawyers and doctors no longer purchase it, but choose to accept the risk that if they're sued for malpractice, they'll have to pay legal defense costs themselves — and, if they lose the case, they'll have to pay the judgment from their own assets. While this approach may make sense for podiatrists and copyright specialists, it might be too risky for brain surgeons and trial lawyers.

NOTE: Deciding whether or not you need insurance by asking an insurance agent for a recommendation is a little like leaving it up to a car dealer to add on all the optional equipment he or she sees fit. A better approach is to talk to people in similar businesses and compare how they have solved the liability/insurance dilemma. Once you decide on the insurance you want, shop around — rates will vary considerably.

6. THE LEGAL RIGHTS OF A PARTNER AGAINST A PARTNERSHIP

You should realize it is at least theoretically possible that — despite your good intentions — you and your partners will end up having a spat. It would be best to settle your dispute following a mediation-arbitration approach. (See section D of this chapter.) However, if for any reason a compromise approach fails, you should know that partners do have some formal legal rights, vis-a-vis, their partnership. These include:

● The right to an accounting of the partnership assets, i.e., an examination of the books by an outside accountant.[9] (Accountings are generally paid for by the partnership itself, but if a lawsuit results, a court has the right to apportion the cost of an accounting as it decides is fair.)

● A right to a legal action for dissolution of the partnership under certain circumstances.

● A legal action for an injunction to restrain illegal partnership acts, and the appointment of a receiver to handle partnership assets.

● Ordinary breach of contract actions.

7. PARTNERSHIPS THAT AREN'T PARTNERSHIPS

Here's one more area of possible partnership danger — the possibility of you being held liable as a member of a partnership you are not legally part of. This liability arises if it "reasonably appears" to members of the public that you are a member of the partnership when they take some action relying on their belief that the partnership exists.

---

9. Periodic accountings are often provided for in partnership agreements. See Appendix A for specific clauses.

For instance, you and two acquaintances investigate forming a partnership, and even have partnership stationary printed, with all three names on it. Then you decide, for whatever reasons, to back out. Later, someone is stiffed by the partnership and sues you, too, for his bill claiming, on the basis of the letterhead and statements made by the continuing partners, he believed that you were involved and relied on this in dealing with the partnership. Is this enough for him to prevail against you? Maybe — maybe not; it'll depend on what a jury decides. Certainly, this can be enough to cause someone to sue you. Who needs that worry? We discuss this whole issue in more detail in chapter 5 when we discuss withdrawals from a partnership. For now, the point is simple — if you discuss a partnership that you don't actually join, be sure that there is no chance that you will subsequently be "held out" as a member of the partnership. If stationary or cards have been printed, destroy them. If third parties have been informed about the partnership, write each to inform them of the true state of affairs.

C. Financial Considerations in a Partnership Agreement

Love of money may not be *the* root of all evil, but few would deny that it's high on the list. Yet, as we remind you not to forget what really matters in life, we must also state we've learned that a sensible regard for money is essential for a partnership business to work. Money is funny stuff; conflicts over money can destroy a partnership with astounding speed. It's essential that you reach a real understanding of how you'll handle money matters, and then pin that understanding down in your partnership agreement. Here we discuss the most basic financial matters involved in a partnership agreement. But, don't stop with this coverage. Check the clauses in the Appendix, section A to see if they're a help. Most of all — think carefully about how money applies to your business situation. **Be sure you cover those things that are important to you.**

1. CONTRIBUTIONS TO THE PARTNERSHIP

Practically speaking, your partnership will need some assets to commence business — the initial contributions by yourself and your partners. In the simplest situation, each of you will contribute cash only. If this is what you have done, a clause based on one of the following should be used, or adapted, in your partnership agreement. (Also see the clauses in Appendix A regarding consequences of failure to make a contribution.)

Equal Shares Contributed

The initial capital of the partnership shall be a total of $_____ . Each partner shall contribute an equal share amounting to $_____, no later than _____, 198 ___.

Unequal Shares Contributed*

The partnership's initial capital shall consist of cash to be contributed by the partners in the following amounts:

Name	Amount
_____	_____
_____	_____
_____	_____

Each partner's contribution shall be paid in full by _____, 198 ____.

It is also common for partners to contribute property (either real or personal) as well as (or instead of) cash to a partnership. Or, a partner can sell property to a partnership. These situations can range from the simple to the highly complex. In simple situations, the major matters to be covered in the partnership agreement are the value the partnership puts on the property contributed and the conditions, if any, placed on its transfer to the partnership. Following is a sample clause that can be used, or adapted, when a property contribution is to be made (and, of course, this clause can also be combined with either above example, where appropriate).

Contribution of Property

_____shall contribute property valued at $_____, consisting of _____ (if the property is complex, you can add "more particularly described in Exhibit A, attached to this agreement.")

[If more than one partner contributes property, repeat this clause for each partner.]

NOTE: A partner can loan, lease, or rent property to the partnership, as well as contribute property to it. Loaning (etc.) property to a partnership can be particularly appropriate where one partner possesses an item that the partnership wants to use — for example, a valuable set of antique restaurant furniture — but does not wish to donate it to the partnership and it's too expensive for the partnership to buy.

In some cases, one or more of the partners will receive an owner's (partner's) interest in the business at least in part because of a promise to donate personal services to the business (i.e., a designer). Here's a clause covering the contribution of services:

---

* A separate issue to consider when unequal cash/property contributions are made is whether interest is to be paid on those contributions or extra contributions can be treated as a loan to the partnership.

Contribution of Service

_____ shall make no cash or property contribution at the commencement of the partnership. _____ shall donate his/her full work time (or, ____ hours per week) and energies to the partnership for a period of _____, [and for those services he/she shall be entitled to _____% of the profits of the partnership, as specified in Paragraph ____.]

In many cases, the partners contributing cash want the "service" partner to contribute labor to eventually equal their cash contribution. A standard way to do that is to require the service partner not to receive a share of the profits, or to receive a lesser percentage share, until his or her cash contribution equals that of the partners who made theirs upfront. Here's a clause for that:

Contribution of Profits from Service Partner

Should (name)'s share of the profits exceed $_____ per _____, (he/she) shall contribute the excess to (his/her) capital account in the business until the total amount of (his/her) capital account shall equal the separate capital contributions made by _____ and _____.

Clearly, this type of clause is subject to many possible variations, depending on the precise financial circumstances of the partnership.

Tax Aspects of Contribution

Contributions to a partnership, especially property contributions, can become quite complicated. For example if property has risen substantially in value between the time the partner bought it and the time he contributed it to the partnership, does that partner have to pay taxes on this unrealized "gain" when the partnership assumes ownership of the property? The answer is generally no — but that the transfer will create subsequent tax obligations. However, if the transferred property is subject to a mortgage under the tax laws, there may well be a taxable gain to the contributing partner.

Here's another problem which can arise. If a machine which has actually appreciated in value is transferred to a partnership, how are tax matters like prior investment credits and depreciation to be handled? We discuss all of these tax questions in some detail in chapter 6, Partnership Taxation, and we provide clauses to deal with these problems there and in the Appendix. For now, we want to alert you to take extra care if your contributions involve property, especially appreciated property.

Existing Business Note

Problems with contributions can also arise if a merchant or businessman decides to take in a partner and the merchant's inventory will be legally transferred to the partnership. This type of bulk transfer must comply with provisions of your state's "Bulk Sales Act" unless — as is often the case — the new partnership assumes all the debts previously owed by the merchant.[10]

---

10. Uniform Commercial Code, Section 9-103 et. seq.

2. PROFITS AND LOSSES

If your partnership agreement does not state how profits and losses are to be divided, the U.P.A. provides that all partners share both equally, even if they contributed unequal amounts of cash, property, or labor to the partnership. If the partnership agreement defines how profits are to be distributed, but does not mention losses, each partner must contribute toward the losses according to his or her share of profits (Section 18a, U.P.A.).

If profits and losses are to be shared equally, it's better to state this expressly in your partnership agreement, rather than rely on the U.P.A. This will prevent any possibility of later disagreement.

Many partnerships will choose to divide profits and losses unequally. This can be done for all sorts of reasons, such as one partner contributing more work or more money in the partnership. There is no one formula when you want to give one or more partner a larger or smaller share — it's your business and you can divide the profits and losses any way you all agree is fair.

Here are two examples of how the distribution of profits and losses have been handled in partnerships we are familiar with:

> *1. The partnership's profits and losses shall be shared by the partners in the same proportions as their initial contributions of capital bear to each other.*

This agreement assumes that all partners work almost equally in the business — or that it doesn't matter if one works more than another. It is based on the idea that the partners consider the initial cash investment to be the most significant aspect of the business.

2. The partnership profits and losses shall be shared among the partners as follows:

Name	Percentage
_____	_____
_____	_____
_____	_____

This clause is straightforward enough, but what do you do if you want different allocations of profits and losses? In that situation, the following clause would be appropriate.

3. The partnership profits and losses shall be shared among the partners as follows:

Name	Percentage of Profits	Percentage of Losses
_____	_____	_____
_____	_____	_____
_____	_____	_____

Sometimes partners decide that a certain partner, or partners, are to receive a fixed payment, in addition to a share of profits, if any.[11] This is often done where one, or some, partners actively work in the business and others do not. Here is a sample provision for covering salaries:

4. Partners _____ and _____ are entitled to the following payments from partnership income before the determination of partnership profits.

Name	Amount
_____	$_____ per _____
_____	$_____ per _____
_____	$_____ per _____

WARNING: In some states, oral contracts for partners' salaries are valid; if no salaries are to be paid, it can be wise to state this explicitly:

No partner will be paid any salary or such other amounts that may in the future be decided on by unanimous consent of all partners.

---

11. Generally, payments to partners cannot be deducted as business expenses, no matter what they are called. If this area is of concern to you, see your accountant.

3. OWNERSHIP OF PROPERTY

Property owned by a partnership is held in the partnership name (Section 25 U.P.A.) Partners, however, are free to decide whether property used by the business will be partnership property or will be owned by an individual partner and merely used by the partnership (i.e., rented, leased, or used free). Unless an express contrary agreement is made, property acquired with partnership funds is partnership property.

Example: Phil and Louise are partners in a local parcel delivery business. Phil has two cars of his own which are occasionally used in the business. A simple agreement is written to have the partnership compensate Phil so much per mile for use of the cars. In this situation, there is no implication that the cars belong to the partnership. But now assume that Phil's cars wear out and the partnership buys a car with partnership assets that Phil once in a while uses on the weekends. This new car is clearly a partnership asset.

Property held in the partnership name can logically and legally only be sold and transferred by the partnership itself. There are advantages to this. Aside from protection against unethical partners, partnership property is *not* subject to attachment or execution to satisfy a creditor's individual claim against one partner.

If the partnership agreement or the partners haven't defined what's partnership property, here are the four factors courts look to in determining the nature of possible partnership property.

1. The source of funds used to buy it.
2. Was it purchased in the partnership name?
3. Was it used in the partnership business?
4. Was it reflected on the books as a partnership asset?

4. TAX MATTERS

As we've said, we discuss partnership taxation in some depth in chapter 6. There are, however, a couple of tax matters we want to make sure you're aware of from the start of your consideration of partnership contracts.

● The partnership does not pay taxes itself, but must file an "informational" partnership tax return.

● The accrual method of accounting **must** be used by partnerships "whenever inventories of goods are maintained."[12]

● No tax deductions are allowed to partnerships or partners for money paid or incurred to organize or promote a partnership (Section 709(a) 1976 Tax Reform Act).

---

12. I.R.S. Treasury Reg. Sec. 1.446-1(c)(2)(i). More about this in chapter 3, section I.

D. Disputes, Mediation, and Arbitration

Any well-drafted partnership agreement should make provision for what happens in the event of serious disagreement between the partners. Certainly, when you're starting your business, you don't envision disputes, but it would be silly to assert it could never happen. It's just common sense to work out your method for handling any serious dispute far in advance of any possibility of it occurring. A dispute-resolution provision is no substitute for the day-to-day give and take we all use to prevent small annoyances and disputes from turning into big ones, but is essential in the rare event that compromise proves to be impossible. If you have management provisions in your agreement, they should cover most of the day-to-day matters. Also, we found that sharing a civilized lunch and good wine before discussing partnership problems can work wonders.

No matter what sort of dispute-resolution provision you draft, no court will order a person to remain active in a partnership if he or she doesn't want to. In theory, you can sue a partner who breaches his/her contract and leaves the partnership for damages, but this isn't normally a very effective remedy. Lawsuits, as you should already know, are expensive, tedious, and emotionally draining, as well as rarely producing results in proportion to their cost. What this means is that if a partner wants out, it's best to be cooperative. Usually, the best way to do this is to plan ahead and set up a fair mechanism to allow any partner to leave. Then, if you or any other partner wants out, it can be handled without a lot of paranoia and hard feelings (see chapter 5).

Many disputes may be real, but not so serious as to require a partner to leave. Or, even if a partner does pull out, disputes can remain, over such things as the amount one's entitled to on leaving, or one's debts to the partnership, etc. In either situation — in order to avoid possible lawsuits and also to encourage a healthier attitude by all concerned in the event of a serious dispute — we suggest that an arbitration and/or mediation clause be included in all partnership agreements.

It's also possible to include a clause requiring counseling, good faith discussions, or other informal methods of resolving disputes. Personally, we're sympathetic to the motives partners have in including these provisions in their agreements, and are optimistic that in some situations, they may serve to remind the partners of their good faith commitments to one another if a dispute arises. However, we must also say that we are skeptical about the value of statements of good faith if they are used as a substitute for a good, tight mediation/arbitration clause. Why? Because obviously if all partners voluntarily want to use such informal means to resolve a conflict, they will go ahead and do it and end the problem. But if feelings get truly riled and one or more partners refuses to be reasonable, you will need more than a vague statement about good faith to negotiate a good agreement.[13]

Arbitration and/or mediation can be a very effective way to solve disputes. Basically, both involve using a private (non-court) structure to handle disputes. The advantage is that the institutional corruption of our court system is replaced by a procedure that is cheaper, more humane, and perhaps, most important, it is vastly faster. Even so, you may

---

13. For this reason, we're opposed to non-binding arbitration; it can often finally resolve nothing, only adding to costs and delays.

have problems regarding who controls and manages the partnership business during the arbitration process. Using either an arbitration or mediation approach or a combination of the two, you create in your partnership agreement your own rules of the game. It's probably the sad truth that by the time you have to rely on the arbitration clause in your contract, your partnership is in trouble, but it's far better than facing trouble with no structure to solve it.

1. ARBITRATION

Your agreement can provide for arbitration by various methods, from naming a trusted friend to selecting a group of three colleagues, etc., to arbitrate any dispute.[14] It can be wise to name a specific arbitrator, a person all the partners respect, in the initial partnership agreement. Legally, an arbitrator's decision is almost always binding. Even in the rare circumstance that the arbitration decision is appealed to a court, it will be enforced, unless the arbitrator is proved to have been blatantly biased, or crazy. Business and labor have used arbitration to settle disputes for years, at least in part because of the realization that getting a dispute settled quickly can be as important as who wins and who loses.

We include here two sample arbitration clauses you can add to any of the written agreements in this book. Remember, you can adopt this clause to your specific needs. The second clause requires a far more complicated arbitration process than the first.

NOTE: If you complete one of the agreements in this book and do not add an arbitration or mediation clause, any dispute that can't be solved informally may be taken to court.

ARBITRATION CLAUSE

1. Any dispute arising out of this agreement shall be arbitrated under the terms of this clause. The arbitration shall be carried out by a single arbitrator, who shall be _____ _____[or who shall be agreed upon by the parties to the dispute. If the parties cannot agree on the arbitrator, the arbitrator shall be selected by _____ _____(include any method you wish,[15] such as naming a person all agree, now, is fair, to be the arbitrtator, or to select the arbitrator. Any arbitration shall be held as follows.

2. The person(s) initiating the arbitration procedure shall inform the other partner(s) in writing of the nature of the dispute at the same time that he or she notifies the arbitrator.

3. Within _____ days from receipt of this notice, the other persons shall reply in writing.

4. An arbitration meeting shall be held within seven days after the other person's reply. Each partner shall be entitled to present whatever oral or written statements he or she wishes and may present witnesses. No person may be represented by a lawyer or any third party.[16]

---

14. One caveat: "professional" arbitrators, such as those from the American Arbitration Association, are relatively expensive. Check fees before you agree on any expert. Another caveat: selecting a friend can raise some real problems if the friend rules against you. It's a good way to lose a friend.

15. If there are more than two sides to the conflict, the appointment of arbitrators becomes difficult. If you can't get at least two of the sides to agree on one arbitrator, you'll probably wind up in court.

16. If you want to allow lawyers in the arbitration, you're free to do so by changing the clause.

5. The arbitrator shall make his or her decision in writing within five days after the arbitration hearing.

6. If the person(s) to whom the demand for arbitration is directed fails to respond within the proper time limit, the person(s) initiating the arbitration must give the other an additional five days' written notice of "intention to proceed to arbitration." If there is still no response, the person(s) initiating the arbitration may proceed with the arbitration before the arbitrator, and his or her award shall be binding.

7. The cost of arbitration shall be borne by the parties as the arbitrators shall direct.

8. The arbitration award shall be conclusive on the parties and shall be set in such a way that a formal judgment can be entered thereon in the court having jurisdiction over the dispute if either party so desires.

Dated: _____   *Signature:* _____

Dated: _____   *Signature:* _____

Here's a more complex varient of the preceeding clause. The disadvantage is that it's more expensive and cumbersome. The advantage is that each person gets to select an arbitrator. (In general, we recommend a single arbitrator.)

ARBITRATION CLAUSE

Any dispute arising out of this agreement or the partnership business shall be arbitrated under the terms of this clause. The arbitration shall be carried out by three arbitrators. Each person or side to the dispute shall appoint an arbitrator. The two designated arbitrators shall appoint the third arbitrator. The technical details of the arbitration shall be carried out as follows:

1. The person(s) initiating the arbitration procedure shall inform the other partner(s) in writing of the nature of the dispute at the same time that he or she designates one arbitrator.

2. Within _____ days from receipt of this notice, the other persons shall reply in writing naming the second arbitrator.

3. The two arbitrator designees shall name a third arbitrator within ten days from the date that the second arbitrator is named. If they cannot agree [Insert whatever you've decided upon].

4. An arbitration meeting shall be held within seven days after the third arbitrator is named.

[The balance of this clause is similar to the preceeding one, adapted to three arbitrators, i.e., a decision by a majority is binding, etc.]

NOTE: If you have an expulsion clause in your partnership, you might want to exempt that clause from arbitration. See Ch. 5 (D)(2).

2. MEDIATION

Mediation is a process where an outside party — the mediator — attempts to assist two parties, or sides, to a dispute to solve their own dispute, usually by reaching a mutually satisfactory compromise or resolution. Unlike an arbitrator, a mediator has no power to impose a decision. This means that if, even with the assistance of a mediator the parties can't resolve the matter, they are left with traditional legal remedies. Therefore, some partnership agreements have adopted a hybrid mediation-arbitration approach. A mediator-arbitrator is named, who has the final power to arbitrate the dispute and impose a binding decision only if mediation fails and the parties can't agree.

Many people feel that mediation is even more advantageous than arbitration because it does away with the adversary approach and encourages compromise. It can be especially valuable where the people involved in a dispute will have some form of continuing relationship, as is often the case for partners, or (even) ex-partners. The mediator's job is to assist the parties in seeing the other side, helping them to reach a compromise. By its very nature, mediation is an unstructured process, without formal rules of evidence, etc. Normally, if one person thinks something should be discussed, it is. Once the parties arrive at their own solution through mediation, the agreement is normally put in writing, and it then becomes as binding as a contract.

The most important decision in including a mediation clause in a partnership agreement involves deciding on the mediator.[17] You can leave this to be decided until a dispute occurs, but we feel it's usually better to decide who you'll have as a mediator at the beginning. However, sometimes this isn't feasible, if a dispute arises over a technical matter — for instance, the need for some complicated piece of machinery — you may well want a mediator who understands these technical issues. We know some lawyers who have been so repelled by the hostility and craziness of the adversary court system, that they have established legal practices devoted solely to mediating disputes. The experience these people have as mediators can be very helpful. Successful mediation is a skill; just being a decent, fair human being isn't always enough to make someone a good mediator.

Here's a clause you can use, or adapt, if you decide you want mediation of any disputes:

1. _____, _____, _____, [etc.,] the partners, agree that any dispute arising out of this agreement or the partnership business shall be resolved by mediation. The partners are aware that mediation is a voluntary process, and pledge to cooperate fully and fairly with the mediator in an attempt to reach a mutually satisfactory compromise of any dispute.

2. The mediator shall be _____.

3. If any party to a dispute feels it cannot be resolved by the partners themselves, he shall so notify the other partners, and the mediator, in writing.

4. Mediation shall commence within _____ days of this notice of request for mediation.

[The details of the mediation process could be provided in greater detail, but we don't feel this is either necessary or advisable — but, if you disagree, add whatever details you decide you want spelled out.]

5. Any decision reached by mediation shall be reduced to writing, signed by all parties, and will be binding on them.

6. The costs of mediation shall be shared equally by both sides to the dispute.

---

17. Whether mediators should have the ultimate power to decide a dispute if the parties can't is an issue that divides many mediation professionals. Some feel that giving the mediator that much ultimate power destroys the "voluntariness" of the whole process.

Combining Arbitration with Mediation

We believe it is a good idea to combine an arbitration provision with a mediation provision, just in case mediation doesn't work. For example, you could then state that if mediation proved unsuccessful after a certain period of time, arbitration, such as the one set out in the clause provided above, would be followed. A simpler method would be to state:

If the parties cannot reach a decision by mediation, the dispute shall be arbitrated by _____ (the mediator/arbitrator), whose decision will be binding.

E. Expanding, Changing, or Ending a Partnership

In addition to establishing sensible rules for you to live with during the life of your partnership, your partnership agreement should provide for what happens if changes occur. For example, you may want to expand and include new partners, or a partner may die, retire, or just get tired of the business and want to move to Java to lie on the beach for a few years. In your happy excitement at the beginning of your enterprise, it is easy to act as if nothing will ever change (except that you will all get rich) and neglect provisions for what will happen if it does. As John Kennedy might have said, let us tell you this about that:

1. Sooner or later (the statistics tell us that it's more likely to be sooner), your partnership business will either end, or change substantially;

2. A good ending for your partnership is at least as important as a good beginning;

3. Whether or not your partnership ends as happily as it began has a great deal to do with the provisions of your initial partnership agreement.

In chapter 4, we discuss clauses having to do with the expansion of a partnership; in chapter 5, we discuss clauses regarding a partner leaving. Here, in our overview chapter, we just want to alert you to the fact that these are basic concerns, essential for any well-drafted partnership agreement. For example:

1. What happens if one or more partners dies? How is his/her interest paid for? Must the business be liquidated?

2. What happens if one or more partners wants to leave the partnership and the other wants to continue?

3. Assuming that a provision is included in the partnership agreement providing for one partner to leave, what are the alternative ways that "buy-out" can be handled?

There are many other aspects of expanding, changing, or ending a partnership that you might want to cover in your agreement. As you go through the book and we deal with specifics, these matters should become a good deal clearer.

The Story of the Chocolate Moose

INTERLUDE III

"Watch out, partner, the paint on the sign by the front door is wet," John yelled from the kitchen, where he was helping to install the linoleum tile.

"Who ever heard of 'Chocolate Moose' with raspberry-colored antlers?" Sara asked, laughing, as she stepped over a couple of paint cans.

"I thought it was a cute touch," John responded. "After all, our fanciest product is the chocolate decadence with raspberry sauce."

"Merely one of our fanciest products," Sara said, "And speaking of raspberries, the first order of supplies will be here next Friday. Do you think we can get everything done by then?"

"I think so," John said. "All business stuff is taken care of We have the health permit, the sales tax number, the lease is signed, etc. I know this place still looks a mess, but if everyone who promised to help paint comes by over the weekend, it should be okay. But Sara, we still have to make time to go over the final partnership agreement."

"I know. I've been putting it off because there's so much other work to be done. Do you have some time now to go over the draft? Maybe it won't take as long as we think."

"Okay," John replied, "but be careful. I could be robbing you blind! Seriously, Sara, I put a lot of effort into this and it's really important that we go over the agreement very carefully. It's a little hard because everything's so great now, but I want us to make sure there aren't any recriminations later. So after we go over it today, we should both think about it some more and go over it again in a few days. Agreed?"

"Sure, I agree. Okay, where do we start?"

"How about going through my draft clause by clause. Here's the first part:

PARTNERSHIP AGREEMENT

John Shalikatinsky and Sara Holcombe agree that they are partners in *The Chocolate Moose, a bakery producing exquisite chocolate delights for the discriminating palate, and that this formal partnership agreement replaces the interim partnership agreement dated* _____ *19* _____ *, as well as all verbal partnership agreements between them. John and Sara further agree as follows:*

1. That the scope of their partnership includes The Chocolate Moose bakery, located in the city of Coeur D'Alene, State of Idaho, which will specialize in the preparation and sale of gourmet chocolate desserts (both wholesale and retail) as well as engaging in catering for parties, social functions, weddings, etc., and that the partnership specifically contemplates the possibility of expansion into the preparation and sale of other types of desserts throughout _____ County.

"It looks okay to me so far," Sara said. "I particularly like that nice touch about discriminating palates. I gather you limited the types of business we would engage in to making desserts on purpose."

"Yes—you know I don't want to run a huge business. by saying that we are only going to do desserts and aren't going to expand beyond the county, I wanted to make it clear what my priorities are. If you wanted to open a full-scale restaurant, for example, you would have to do it outside of our partnership, unless we both agreed to change the agreement. But at the same time that I wrote in limitations, I allowed for some expansions too. If our Moose produces a couple of offspring anywhere in the county, that would be part of the partnership."

"Okay by me," Sara said. "And what would we call the second shop, 'Daughter of Chocolate Moose'?"

"How 'bout Ms. Moose? Or Mousettes?" John put in with a laugh. "Harrumph! Now, if I can have your attention, let's go over the next few clauses."

2. That the Chocolate Moose shall be guided by several operating principals:

a. Only the best quality products shall be produced and only the highest quality ingredients shall be used. (We're committed to making the best desserts, not the most, or cheapest.)

b. Pricing shall be calculated to bring in a fair return on the partners' investment and labor. Because of the high quality of ingredients used and the cost of hand labor, this means that prices will be relatively high. So be it. But recognizing that many potential customers are not affluent, a discount schedule shall be prepared for senior citizens, the handicapped, non-profit groups and others who need it;

c. That the mental health of the partners shall be the number one consideration of the business. This means that after the initial frenzy of opening the store has died down, each partner will have at least two days off per week and each shall take at least a month's vacation each year. Should either partner feel he or she needs more time off for any reason, the other shall do his or her best to cooperate. The partner taking off extra time shall not be paid for his or her "leave of absence" unless there is a specific agreement to do so. However, each partner commits his or herself to making the business a high energy, high priority part of his/her life until it is securely established, which both agree will probably take at least two years.

d. That making a good profit is an important partnership consideration, but is not the only consideration.

3. That they are equal partners with one exception: As Sara has invested $15,000 in the combined enterprise and John $10,000, Sara will receive 60 percent of all net partnership profits and John 40 percent of the first eighteen months of this partnership agreement. After eighteen months of elapses, Sara and John will share equally in all future partnership profits.

4. That important partnership decisions will be jointly agreed to by both Sara and John. "Important decisions" are defined to include all decisions to expend, or obligate the partnership to expend in the future, any amount in excess of $500. "Important decisions" will also involve the pricing of products, significantly expanding the business, selling products other than chocolate desserts, hiring employees, or independent contractors, leasing or buying property, or moving the principal business location. "Important decisions" shall also include any decision that one or the other partners clearly states to be important.

5. That no new partners will be added to the partnership without the agreement of both partners;

"All that's fine so far," Sara said. "I really like your clause about the purpose of the business. Maybe we will be cynical old business people by this time next year and start substituting emulsifiers for eggs, but I want to record our optimistic feelings about what we're doing here at the beginning, so that we will both have something to hang onto on bad days. In fact, why don't we get the second clause printed up with big letters and hang it over the sink."

"Good idea. Let's really do it. Hey, I think I hear some of our volunteer painters. We're going to have to stop this process and get them organized. Why don't we meet early tomorrow morning and try to go through the rest of it?"

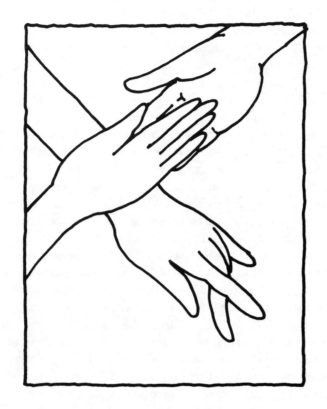

Chapter 4:

Changes, Growth, and New Partners

A. Expansion of Your Business

Your hope and dream is that your partnership business will prosper. Unfortunately, not even success comes trouble free. When your business does well, you'll inevitably have to face the opportunities and challenges of growth. These come in all shapes and sizes: hiring employees; hiring more employees; moving to a new store or office; adding a second store, warehouse, or factory; expanding into a related business; buying additional machinery; financing a larger staff or inventory; taking over an on-going operation, etc.

We want to say here at the beginning that there is more than one way to look at the possibility of increased business. Do you want to expand at all? Are the additional burdens that are bound to accompany expansion (at least for a while) worth it? We have friends whose consulting business grew rapidly, far beyond their original expectations. They just went along with the flow—and soon were mired in high overhead and innumerable problems arising from having many employees. What were their vacation policies, sick-leave plans, pension options, etc.? They grew more and more dissatisfied. Eventually they "down-scaled" their business to near its original size. They were a lot happier, even though they earned a little less. While these are personal, not legal matters, we believe that discussing your dreams and plans for the future of the business must be a part of the dialogue involved in creating any partnership. It is one excellent way for you to determine whether you and your partners are sufficiently compatible to press ahead.

Personal philosophy aside, we believe it is very important for new partners to discuss and review what they want to happen if business is terrific. Lawyers tend to worry about problems of failure or conflict. In drafting a partnership agreement they tell people to think about what happens if the business goes broke, the partners can't get along, or one of a hundred other disasters occurs. Being trained as lawyers, we are probably somewhat prone to disaster-mongering ourselves. But suppose your business goes well? Do you want to kick back and develop other interests, or redouble your efforts and become more prosperous? And how much income is sufficient before you feel satisfied?

While we believe you should talk about these matters, we don't feel that it's advisable normally to put specific provisions in your original partnership agreement that call for an expansion game plan—with one important exception. This has to do with a provision for the addition of a partner. The reason that there's not much point in incorporating details of how you'll handle future growth in your original agreement is that generally it's quite futile predicting the specifics of your business future. As Napoleon put it, "First you commit yourself, and then you see . . ." Whatever the future holds, it's almost surely going to be different from what you think it will be now.

As a practical matter, any specifics that you put in your agreement now aren't likely to be of any use in legally binding a partner. For example, if a couple of years down the road your partner doesn't like the way the business is expanding, all the contract clauses in the world aren't likely to make him more cooperative. Courts will not issue orders compelling a partner to live up to a contract clause agreeing to work productively for expanded business. How could such an order be enforced? Remember, the essence of partnership is *voluntary* cooperation. If ever you and your partner(s) come to a fundamental conflict about the direction(s) your partnership business should take, it's time to go your separate ways. A well-drafted partnership agreement can help you by containing provisions governing a split-up of the partnership, but it can't make you continue to work together productively no matter how detailed it is. (See the next chapter for details on ending a partnership.)

COMMON SENSE NOTE: Sometimes partners feel that is worthwhile to place a section in their partnership agreement in which they do talk about their purposes for being in business, their hopes for the future, etc. This can make sense if it's done in the spirit of sharing intentions so that there is a written record of the shared understanding, and not as a binding legal provision. In the second interlude, John and Sara do this as part of their partnership agreement for The Chocolate Moose.

B. Growth and Changes in Your Partnership Agreement

Some types of business growth will necessitate a change in your partnership agreement. For example, the addition of a new partner, as discussed in the next section, necessarily entails revisions of (at least) the contributions, and distribution of profits, provisions of your agreement. Also, the admission of a partner may necessitate changes in the partnership agreement in other ways. For example, in a business we know, a former employee became a partner, "purchasing" a partnership capital interest. Since he had no actual cash, he paid for this purchase by having part of his weekly salary deducted. All this was put into the agreement admitting him into the partnership.

Growth of your business may require other changes in your partnership agreement. You and your partners may decide that the expanded business should be run differently than the original business. Or perhaps additional cash contributions will be required, and you decide that for some reason they will be made in proportions different from those originally agreed to. And *significant* change in the structure or operation of your business should be reflected by a change in the partnership agreement. We don't mean you should become fussy. Significant changes are just that and should be relatively unusual occurrences. Just what amounts to a significant change is up to you to decide, although some changes, such as an alteration in the distribution of profits a partner receives or assets he contributes, i.e., extra capital or labor, would seem to be patently "significant."

One way to avoid having to make numerous technical changes in your partnership agreement every time your business changes or expands is to define your business purposes fairly broadly in the original agreement.[1] Thus, three partners who plan to start a consulting business to provide specialized advice on the employment problems of county governments in Colorado might well want to consider what happens if they do well. Perhaps the next step would be to do consulting for governmental entities generally in fields other than employment and outside of Colorado. If this is the situation, it would make sense to draft the original partnership agreement to define the business as consulting in the public sector and leave out the words "employment," "county governments" and "Colorado." Another way to deal with the same problem would be to include both definitions as to the scope of the business. That is to say, you might draft something like this:

> *The original purpose of our partnership business is to provide high quality consulting services to county governments in the State of Colorado concerning employee relations. However, it is also contemplated that in the future, general consulting services will be offered to governmental units at all levels within and without Colorado.*

NOTE: There are exceptions to the general rule that it's wise to define a partnership agreement broadly. If you specifically decide you want to engage in a limited enterprise—such as a one-time joint venture—be sure to draft your purpose clause tightly so that if your enterprise expands, this clause must be specifically changed. And if it's contemplated that a partner will also work in a related business, you'll need to exclude that type of business from your "purpose."

C. Addition of a New Partner(s)

Now let's take a look at the one problem of growth that definitely should be handled in the original partnership agreement — the addition of a new partner, or partners. Growth of a partnership business often leads to the opportunity, or even the necessity, of expanding the partnership itself. There can be a near-infinity of reasons for expanding a partnership. To name a few of the more common reasons:
- a desire (or need) for the new partner's contribution of cash;
- the skills contributed by the new partner;
- the need for additional management or to retain key employees;
- the desire to expand your business to locations or customers offered by the new partner.

Expanding your partnership will require a revision of your partnership agreement to spell out your arrangement with your new partner(s). However, the rules to follow for addition of new partners should be set out in your original partnership agreement. It's obviously risky to wait until expansion is suggested to resolve the partnership's rules about including new partners. The Uniform Partnership Act (section 18 (e)) specifies

---

1. Also, it serves as a legal limit vis-a-vis the partners. If one partner acts clearly outside the partnership-defined purpose, then the partnership and the partners are not responsible. Obviously this sort of legalism is a poor substitute, at best, for choosing trustworthy partners.

78

that unanimous consent of all partners is required to admit a new partner. We strongly suggest that your partnership agreement state that a decision to add a new partner must be unanimous. Indeed, most partnership agreements do so state, either specifically or in a general clause requiring unanimous decision on all major issues. If you allow a majority to prevail on such a vital issue you can be left with a bad psychological situation if a new partner is brought in over the objections of at least one existing partner. It's hard to imagine a better way to guarantee future discord. Here is a simple clause that can prevent this type of problem:

> *The addition of any new partner, or partners, to this partnership may be done only by unanimous agreement of all existing partners, on such terms and conditions as they agree upon.*

NOTE FOR LARGE PARTNERSHIPS: You may want to modify the rule of unanimity when it comes to new partners if you are setting up a partnership with a lot of members. We know of some collective businesses, for example, where there are fifteen, twenty, and even thirty partners. In this situation, it may make sense to admit a new partner if 80 percent of the old partners approve. Other collectives or large partnerships such as big law firms, retain the requirement of unanimous consent for admission of a new partner.[2] These enterprises rely on peer pressure to prevent one or a few partners from thwarting the will of the majority too often. Also, large partnerships almost invariably have expulsion provisions in their agreement, so a partner who consistently, or arbitrarily, stands alone to allow a new partner to be admitted may find himself rejected. Here's a clause where less than unanimity is required to admit a partner:

A new partner may be admitted to the partnership with the written approval of _____ (partners holding 75% of the capital interest of the partnership; or, 80% of the votes of the partners, etc. or whatever you decide).

1. "DISSOLUTION" OF THE PARTNERSHIP WHEN A NEW PARTNER JOINS

Most changes in the composition of a partnership, for whatever reason, cause a technical "dissolution" of the original partnership. This generally means that each time a partner is added, or leaves a partnership, it is legally "dissolved."[3] A "dissolution" of a partnership need not imply the sort of negative consequences that we associate with the term "dissolution of marriage," (i.e., termination of the relationship). A partnership "dissolution" is simply the legal term used whenever a change occurs in the membership of the partnership even though the business may well continue much as usual. In other situations, of course, the "dissolution" of a partnership may signal a much more fundamental change, up to and including the partnership ceasing to do business.

Legally, from the moment of "dissolution" of a partnership business, no *new* partnership business can be undertaken. The partners only have legal authority to "wind up" the business as rapidly as feasible.[4] In the case of the addition of a new partner, the "dissolution" of the old partnership is normally not a problem, except as regards closing out an old set of books and starting another. The business itself might go happily on. If you want additional clarification of this, you can add the following to the clause governing admission of a new partner:

Admission of a new partner shall not cause dissolution of the underlying partnership business, which will be continued by the new partnership entity.

---

2. One food collective we know of invites prospective partners to work for the enterprise for a couple of weeks. At that time a vote is taken to determine whether they will be accepted into the business. If they are, the hours they have worked are credited toward their buy-in amount. However, if they are rejected after the other partners get to know them, they are paid at the going rate for their work.

3. Section 31 U.P.A., except for certain provisions on "assignment of interest," Section 27 U.P.A. [See chapter 5, section C(1).]

4. Sections 30, 33, 35, 37 U.P.A.

2. THE INCOMING PARTNER'S LIABILITY FOR EXISTING PARTNERSHIP DEBTS

Most of the issues that must be dealt with when a new partner is welcomed to your family are the same as those that were resolved in your original partnership agreement—who gets what, who contributes what, who does what, etc. There are few new legal issues to be dealt with. However, one important additional matter must be resolved. Will the incoming partner be personally responsible for the existing debts of the partnership? Under the Uniform Partnership Act (Section 17 U.P.A.), a new partner is personally liable for partnership debts incurred *before* he became a partner, up to his share (i.e., contribution to) of partnership property.[5]

EXAMPLE: If Raul contributed $50,000 when he joined Elaine and Beverly in a partnership to produce pet food at a time when the two women already owed $100,000, Raul's maximum liability for the pre-existing debts would be $50,000.

This rule can be varied by the partnership agreement. Thus, Beverly and Elaine could agree to release Raul from *any* liability for existing partnership debts, or—at the other extreme—Raul could assume full personal liability for all existing debts. But to do this, Raul must "clearly assume" such liability. Here are two provisions for handling this problem, the first limiting the incoming partner's liability, the second imposing maximum liability.

_____ *(incoming partner)* _____ *shall not be responsible for or assume any liability for any debts of the* _____ *(name of partnership business)* _____ *incurred on or before* _____ *, 19* _____

or

_____ *(incoming partner)* _____ *hereby expressly assumes full personal liability equal to the personal liability of each of the partners in the partnership of* _____ *(name of partnership business)* _____ *for all partnership debts and obligations whenever incurred.*

Certainly you hope that existing debts will be an academic problem, your business sufficiently profitable to pay debts from operating revenues. But this isn't a certainty. Indeed, one reason to bring in a new partner is precisely because you need more cash. This is one situation where our general advice—plan ahead and get your partnership agreement in writing before you start the business—is impractical. Why? Because it's impossible to know what sort of debt situation you will face two years from now. You could put a clause in your original agreement saying that all new partners must be ready to assume personal liability for all partnership debts, no matter when occurred, but what good does that do? What if the only suitable person you can find balks? Some sort of custom-tailored clause regarding a new partner's liability for existing debts is so likely to be necessary that there's no point in trying to anticipate the problem before you face it, if you ever do.

---

5. Of course, once someone becomes a partner, he or she has unlimited personal liability for partnership debts incurred *after* his/her admission to the partnership.

3. A TAX NOTE FOR INCOMING PARTNERS

If a new partner receives a capital (i.e., equity) interest in a partnership in exchange for services rendered, or to be rendered, to the partnership, he or she is immediately taxable for the fair market value of the interest received.[6] This can be a real problem for newly admitted partners to professional partnerships, because the new partner will probably receive an interest in the (taxable) assets of the partnership, including accounts receivable and earned—but unbilled—fees.

EXAMPLE: Phillip and Betty operate a successful accounting firm. They decide to invite Janice, who has worked for them for years, to join their partnership because she is a good worker and a good friend, but also because they fear that if they don't give her a better deal, she will open her own competing business. Janice receives one-quarter ownership interest in the partnership. The partners calculate the fair market value of this interest to be worth $50,000. Although Janice does not receive $50,000 cash, just her ownership interest in the business assets (i.e., fixed assets, accounts receivable, unbilled fees, and good will), the I.R.S. takes the position that she has received (ordinary) income amounting to $50,000 which is subject to income tax. In sum, Janice will be out-of-pocket a substantial amount, because she received her partnership ownership interest.

4. OUTGOING PARTNERS

We discuss the problems caused by a departing partner in the next chapter. Here we just want to remind you that it's not unusual for the admission of a new partner to a business to coincide with the departure of another partner, so the two occurrences often overlap.

---

6. The interest received must be "without substantial risk of forfeiture" for this tax rule to apply. Cases where there *is* a substantial risk of forfeiture are somewhat rare—they include instances where the partnership property has already been liened by a creditor.

Problems caused by the departure of a partner are usually much more complicated than admission of a new partner. Unless the new partner directly purchases the departing partner's interest it must be valued and arrangements must be made to pay off that amount. Specific clauses for how this is to be handled should be in the original partnership agreement, so be sure to check the next chapter carefully. Also, remember that outgoing partners remain personally liable for all debts of the partnership incurred up to the time they leave. An incoming partner may or may not assume personal responsibility for those debts. Either way, this doesn't release the leaving partner from potential liability to existing creditors. If all the partners (including the new one) are broke, creditors of the old partnership can still come after the departed partner.

EXAMPLE: Al and James are partners in A-J Auto Body Repair. Al leaves, selling his partnership interest to Peter, who assumes personal liability for all existing debts of A-J. On the date Al leaves, A-J owes $8,000 to Nifty Paints, a major paint supplier. The bill is never paid, and six months later A-J goes broke. Neither James nor Peter have any personal assets. Al can be held liable by Nifty for the full $8,000 owed. Of course, Al has a claim for this amount against Peter (who assumed that debt) but if Peter is broke it doesn't seem likely he can collect on it.

D. Making Changes When You Have Failed to Plan Ahead

Okay, so much for all the good advice about planning ahead. Suppose you didn't? How do you proceed if you have nothing but an oral-partnership agreement, or a written one that simply doesn't allow for the expansion of your business or the addition of a partner? Assuming that you and your partner have talked your situation over and are in agreement on future actions, now is the time to draft a comprehensive partnership agreement. If you can't agree on future plans, things won't be so simple; the fact that you have no written agreement including a procedure to handle disagreements will almost surely aggravate your problem. Obviously, if you can't at least agree on a mechanism to arrive at an agreement, there's little to be done except dissolve your partnership.

If, however, you do agree to expand and are full of new plans—in particular, the addition of a new partner—this can be an excellent time to review your partnership understanding. You may well want to replace your existing agreement with one that is both current and comprehensive. In a sense, you are in the same position as people adopting an agreement for the first time. One nice thing about a partnership—as opposed to a corporation—is that it can be changed easily at any time all partners agree. To clarify the situation, you could begin the partnership agreement with a general introductory clause, such as the following:

_____*(Names of old partners)*_____ *have been engaged in business at* _____*(location)*_____ *as a partnership under the firm name of* _____ *They now intend to admit* _____*(name of new partner)*_____ *to their partnership, and all the members of the expanded partnership desire to amend and clarify the terms and conditions of their partnership agreement and to reduce their agreement to writing.*

The Story of the Chocolate Moose

INTERLUDE IV

"Well, tomorrow is opening day," Sara said, scrunching up her crooked nose and trying to peel a speck of yellow paint off the tip of it.

"I don't believe it," John said. "You did an amazing amount of baking today. I just hope we sell half of it."

"Sure we will," Sara said confidently. "Look at all the people who have already come in to ask when we're opening. I'm really optimistic. If we can keep our energy flowing for the next couple of weeks, I believe we'll pull it off. By the way, how's the money situation?"

"Not bad actually. Maybe even a little better than we expected. We have a little over $8,000 left and we don't owe anyone anything. Since we don't have any established credit yet, everyone wanted to be paid up front."

"Did you go along with that?" Sara asked.

"Sure, but only after I demanded discounts for paying cash."

"And did you get them?"

"You bet. I learned at The Food Odyssey that no one pays both full price and cash in this world. Most everybody's operating on somebody else's money. The egg guy hesitated about giving us the discount and was adamant about not establishing credit until we'd made a couple of payments."

"So, what did you do?"

"I bought the eggs from his competitor for six percent less. Now the first guy wants to make us an offer we can't refuse."

"Nice, very nice, partner. Cheers!"

"Thanks, but you're putting the caboose ahead of the train, aren't you? Let's finish the agreement and then celebrate being partners."

"Okay—but we're already partners, you know, and besides, I've always felt that cabooses were discriminated against, being put at the end all of the time," Sara replied. Seeing that John was tired and not in a mood for bad jokes, she cleared her throat, hitched up her pants and said, "Okay, where did we leave off?"

"With Clause Six. That's the one you were worried about—the one that deals with buy-outs if one of us wants to leave the business for any reason. Here is what I suggest."

> If either partner leaves the partnership for any reason, whether he or she quits, retires or dies, he or she shall be obligated to sell his/her interest in the partnership and the remaining partner is obligated to buy that interest as set forth below.

"But, suppose one of us wants to sell out and we get a better offer from a third party?" Sara asked.

"I've included what I think is a fair way to decide what a partnership share is worth, if you read on, but I don't think that either of us should have to be stuck with a new partner chosen by the person who is leaving. If you want out, I would rather have the right to buy your share and then find a new partner myself if I want to. Also, remember, this buy-out stuff only comes into play if one of us leaves and the other wants to stay. If we both want to leave, we just sell the business and split the take. Bear with me for a minute and read a little further. Here's how we figure out how much a partner's share is worth."

> The value of a partner's interest in the partnership in the first two years of its existence shall be his or her ownership in the business; the value of the business shall be the sum of the following items, as of the date that value, is determined:
>
> 1. The credit balance in the business capital account(s), less all outstanding debts owed by the business;
> 2. All accounts receivable that are reasonably collectable and all unbilled but earned fees;
> 3. The current market value of all assets.
>
> All calculations as to the fair value of partnership assets, accounts, credit balances, etc. shall be made by Roger Pritchard, C.P.A.

"Wait a minute," Sara said, raising a freckled hand. "If I understand what I just read, it means that the business has no value over and above what it owns on the day one of us pulls out or dies. I thought the whole idea of this sort of deal was to pay the person leaving for the on-going value of the business. I mean, we've both done a lot of work already that wouldn't necessarily show up as a credit balance."

"Sure, Sara," John said, wandering around to the side of the kitchen where the newly made truffles had been tempting him. "But, here's my idea. You've insisted all along that we both should commit ourselves to the business for at least two years and not pull out before then. I agree—at least intellectually—but I do have my travel fantasies. So I thought that we should rig the agreement so that it would be against our interests to leave before the end of two years. Now look here. After two years, the deal gets much sweeter for the leaving partner," John said, grabbing a truffle while Sara read on.

> After two years from the date this agreement is signed, the value of a partner's interest in the partnership shall be 50 percent of the value of the partnership on the date of his or her departure from the partnership. The percentage shall be determined as follows:
>
> The net profits of the business shall be determined for the three fiscal years (two years if a partner leaves before the third year is completed) preceding the partner's departure. The average net profit shall then be calculated. From this amount, a figure representing a fair amount wage for both partners shall be subtracted. This shall be $18,000 per partner in the third year of this agreement and shall increase $1,000 per year for each fiscal year after that. This figure shall then be multiplied by six to determine the value of the business.

Sara looked up. "Let me try that out with some real numbers. She grabbed pencil and paper and began writing. "OK, suppose we made an average profit of $60,000 after expenses, then we subtracted the $36,000 wage figure. That would *leave us $24,000. According to your multiplier—6, right—that means that one person would have to pay the other close to $150,000. I think that's too much, you truffle-stealing monster. How about using a multiplier of three instead? I think if the buy-out was more than three times the yearly take I would just quit and buy another business."*

"Sara, you're forgetting that the surviving partner now owns the other's share too so the wage subtraction for that partner—his or her $18,000—would no longer be paid out."

"In a way it would," Sara replied, "because someone else would have to be hired. Still, I see what you're driving at. How about compromising at a multiple of four?"

"Done," John said, snatching one more truffle since Sara was appeased. "Now we have to decide on how the buy-out will be handled and we're about done with the heavy stuff. I suggest 25 percent down and 25 percent a year for three additional years."

Sara thought a moment. "I think that's fine, John, except maybe four years to pay off the balance so that the remaining partner isn't too burdened. If the business is expanding, it should be possible to borrow the money if necessary, but with interest rates the way they are, it'd be a lot cheaper to pay off out of income. Let me look at how you've written it."

> *Whenever the partnership is obligated or chooses to purchase a partner's interest, it shall pay for that interest 25 percent in cash and the rest with a promissory note. The note shall be dated as of the effective date of purchase, shall mature in four years, shall be payable in equal installments that come due monthly, shall bear interest at the rate of 8 percent per year; the first payment shall be made ninety days after the date of the promissory note."*

"I changed the interest rate to 8 percent, as well as changing the maturation of the balance of the buy-out from three to four years," Sara said, "so that I would get the feeling that I had some input into this agreement too. I'm sure we both want the business to survive—and cutting down on that interest has to help some.

"Okay by me," John said. "I'll add my initials next to yours. The rest of the contract is mostly stuff I took out of the book. The mediation-arbitration clause is important and so are several of the others. Why don't you go through them while I finish tacking down the carpet? Then if you have any questions, we can talk about them and get the agreement signed."

Sara read.
John tacked.
Sara made a couple of changes.
John grabbed another truffle.
Sara made a couple more changes.
John read everything one more time.
Both signed their names.
Both shook hands.
Sara kissed John.
John kissed Sara.
Sara slapped John's hand as she saw it edging again toward the truffles.

86

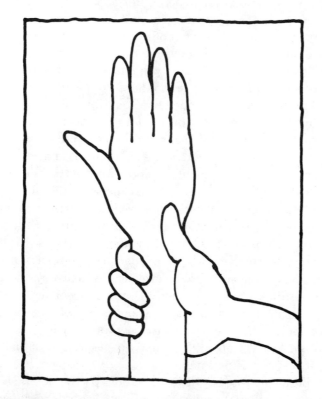

Chapter 5:

Withdrawal, Death, or Expulsion of a Partner, and Actual Termination

A. Introduction

This is very likely the most important chapter in this book and the one you are least likely to give adequate attention. This is because the problems caused by the departure of a partner are often hard to focus on at the start of a business. Everybody is up! What a downer to worry about disputes or buy-outs or valuation of the business. Unfortunately, ignoring these matters is foolish. Sooner or later you'll have to handle problems caused by the departure of a partner. Our experience in talking to many partners and former partners convinces us that it's likely to be sooner than you think. In a foot-loose age, very few jointly-owned businesses retain the same owners for more than a few years. And even if your partnership business does endure unchanged, eventually one of you will retire, or die, and you or your loved ones will have to deal with what to do next.

Do we have your attention? Good, because it's essential to set up a structure here at the beginning to handle what will happen when your partnership ends. There are several situations to consider. For example, what happens if one partner wants to quit? Remember, a partner can quit at any time. Or, what happens when a partner is expelled? Or retires? Or dies? Does the reason a partner quits matter in the sense that you would want to compensate someone more who left for a "good" reason such as illness, rather than for a "not-so-good" reason such as an extended vacation? And while we're inundating you with questions, what about these: How is the worth of the departing partner's interest to be valued? How is actual payment of that worth to be made? How can the remaining partners protect themselves against the problems they face if a partner leaves? If the business breaks up, who gets which assets—especially valuable business assets like customer lists or the business name?

Your solution to the problems raised by the departure of a partner should be covered *in detail in the original agreement*. This is the time to let yourself be a little paranoid. Imagine the worst situations or disasters you can. How would the partnership cope with these? If you wait until the problem actually arises, you are likely to end up in a fight. For example, if a partner leaves (and especially if he or she is expelled), there's likely to be a conflict over the worth of his interest, if you haven't already established a method to determine that worth. Not surprisingly, the departing partner rather regularly concludes that his/her interest is worth a lot more than the partners who remain do. Or, if a partner dies, his/her heirs will likewise often feel his/her interest is worth more than the partners say it is. Next, once you decide on how to value a partnership share, there's the question of payment. Departing partners usually prefer their entire payment in cash, immediately, while the remaining partners may face the destruction of the business unless time payments are allowed. A prior agreement on valuation eliminates these conflicts. Indeed, we've heard lawyers refer to partnership contracts as "divorce agreements signed while the parties are still in love."[1]

There may come a time when you mutually decide to end the partnership business. This doesn't necessarily mean you've "failed." In several partnerships we know of, substantial success lead to the eventual breakup of the partnership. For example, two friends of ours started a restaurant in Berkeley, California. Their first place was tiny, with delicious food and friendly service. The restaurant prospered sufficiently so the owners could move to a much bigger place which they later bought. When they continued to

---

1. This idea works so well that it is increasingly being used in the marriage area where antenuptial contracts are becoming more popular.

prosper, the owners began to realize that their dreams had begun to diverge. One now wanted to run an elegant vegetarian restaurant in Berkeley while the other dreamt of a stylish sea food restaurant in San Francisco. Both dreams held—so their partnership was terminated on a friendly, but business-like basis and two successful restaurants resulted.

As we have said, you should deal with the basic outline of how the termination of your partnership will be handled in your original agreement. On actual termination, however, there will inevitably be all sorts of details and fine points to be resolved, matters which haven't been foreseen. This means that when your partnership is terminated it is sensible to prepare a separate termination agreement—apart from, and in addition to, the provisions in the original partnership contract. We include a sample termination agreement in Appendix D.

Hopefully we have convinced you that planning ahead to handle a possible departure from the business is wise. Perhaps we have been a little severe. But the truth is that once you commit yourself to working out a good termination procedure, the actual details need not be difficult—picky and time-consuming, yes, but difficult, no. How do you do it? The first and most important step, after reading the rest of this chapter, is for all the partners to sit down and discuss what they want to happen if a partner leaves or dies, or trouble strikes. Don't worry about details or specifics at first—just get your opinions out. What happens if you lose money? How much of a commitment are you making—can you make? How do you resolve tensions and disputes if you're short of money? We have found, for example, that some people react to a cash shortage by belt-tightening, while others insist that you can't make money if you don't spend it, and conclude that more investment is needed. When you finish discussing money, move onto what happens if a partner quits or dies. As you'll see, there are several factors to consider in this area, the key ones being valuation of the business, and the method you adopt to pay the departing partner, or his heirs. Try looking at the question from the position of the partner who leaves, and then from the position of the remaining partners. It may help to use some real dollar figures, plugging them into the different valuation methods we propose later in the chapter. No two businesses are exactly the same and you will want to be sure that the provisions you adopt will work for you.

Honest dialogue is essential for the drafting of any partnership agreement. If you see a lawyer—and he or she's competent—all he/she can do is assist you to focus on the same issues, and suggest a variety of possible solutions. There's no magic, legal formula you can plug into to settle problems of valuation or pay-out. Indeed, we have talked to a number of partners who got perfectly legal, and very expensive, lawyer-drafted agreements that caused them nothing but trouble later. You have to come up with (or at least participate in drafting) your own solution. It must be one you can all live with. There is no easy substitute for understanding the legal structure that will serve as the constitution of your business.

B. Buy-Out Agreements

The first decision to make is whether you want to allow for the right, or at least the possibility, of continuing the business if one (or more) partners departs. Normally, remaining partners do want at least an option to continue the business. Otherwise, if one partner withdraws, the business will have to be liquidated. This usually means that much less money will be realized by all partners, as most businesses are worth far more as operating entities than they are as dead carcasses for sale to the highest bidder. Accordingly, a well-drafted partnership agreement normally contains provisions allowing the remaining partner(s) to purchase the interest of any departing partner.[2] There are four basic areas that you will wish to cover in your buy-out agreement:

1. Provisions requiring a departing partner (or his/her estate) to sell his/her interest to the remaining partner(s), or giving them the first option (at least) to buy that interest;

2. Provisions for determining the worth of the business;

3. Provisions for actually making payments to the departing partner;

4. Other provisions providing for continuity of the business.

TAX NOTE:

An additional benefit of a buy-out agreement involves death taxes.[3] Obviously, the interest of the deceased partner in a partnership business must be valued, for death-tax purposes. For many small businesses without a ready buyer, this isn't easy to do unless there is a buy-out agreement. If there is one, the I.R.S. will normally accept it when determining the worth of the deceased partner's interest, if it contains the following provisions:

1. The estate of the first to die is obligated to sell the business interest;

2. The remaining partners are either obligated to purchase the business interest of the deceased or are given an option to purchase it;

3. The agreement forbids each participating partner from disposing of his interest during his lifetime without first offering it to the other partners (at a price not higher than the estate sale price);

4. The agreement is the result of an "arm's length transaction," i.e., it cannot be a (disguised) gift.

---

1. THE RIGHT TO BUY

The first essential element of a buy-out agreement is a provision giving the remaining partners the right to buy the departing partner's interest. Often this is simply stated as a binding duty of both departing partners and partnerships, such as *"if any partner leaves the partnership, for whatever reason, whether he quits, withdraws, is expelled, retires, or dies, he shall be obligated to sell his interest in the partnership, and the remaining partners obligated to buy that interest, under the terms and conditions set forth below."*

---

2. Sometimes, buy-out agreements, especially when they are very complex, are prepared as separate documents. We see no reason for this additional paperwork in most cases. You should be able to keep the buy-out agreement succinct enough so it can be managed in your partnership agreement.

3. In a couple of states, there's a risk in buy-out agreements. In Alabama and Mississippi, buy-out agreements were held void in cases where one partner died, on the grounds that the agreement was "testamentory in character" and did not conform to the state laws on wills. *Gomez v. Higgins,* 130 Ala. 493, 30 So. 417(1901), *Thomas v. Byrd,* 112 Miss. 692, 73 So. 725(1916). If you are in these states, see a lawyer.

From a departing partner's point of view, there may be one significant drawback in this clause—the departing partner does not have the right to sell his/her interest to a third party. Even so, it is common that all partners decide at the start of the business that they do not want to risk having to take in new partners if one partner leaves. Most small businesses are so dependent on each individual partner's skills, trust, and cooperation, that they are simply not suited to the compelled introduction of a new partner. Of course, in many partnership situations, whether or not a sale can be made to a third party is not a real problem because there is no market (i.e., ready buyers) for the departing partner's interest anyway. Some partnerships, however, do decide they want to allow for the possibility of a partner selling his interest to a third person. If that person is acceptable to the remaining partner(s)—often a very big if—there can be real benefits from an outside sale. First, the sale price is determined by the marketplace, eliminating the complexities and inherent subjectivity of usual valuation methods. Second, the remaining partners don't have to come up with the money to pay for the departing partner's interest.

The standard method for resolving the question of whether a third party buyer is acceptable to the remaining partners is to give those partners a "right of first refusal." This amounts to an option to buy the departing partner's interest at the price and terms offered by a bona-fide outside buyer. Here's a clause for that kind of option (the bracket clauses are optional, allowing for more flexibility):

If any partner receives an offer, whether or not solicited by him, from a person not a partner to purchase all [or any portion] of his interest in the partnership, and if the partner receiving the offer is willing to accept it, he shall give written notice of the amount and terms of the offer, the identity of the proposed buyer, and his willingness to accept the offer to each of the other partners. The other partners shall have the option, within _____ days after that notice is given, to purchase that partner's interest [or designated portion of the interest] on the same terms as those contained in the offer. [The other partners may exercise this option jointly or individually. If more than one partner exercises the option individually, those partners shall share in the purchase of the selling partner's interest in the same proportion as their ownership interests in the partnership bear to each other.]

2 CONFLICTS REGARDING BUY-OUTS

Now let's examine what happens if two 50/50 partners can't get along, and each wants to buy the other out. Or, suppose there's a five-person equal partnership, and two factions develop (two on one side, three on the other) and each wants to buy the other out? How is it decided who has the right to buy? The answer is that it can't be decided, unless you've created some clause to resolve this question, or you work out some sort of compromise acceptable to all. If you haven't, and neither side will yield, the business will have to be liquidated, and the net proceeds distributed to the (ex) partners. In the case of a multi-member partnership, expulsion provisions may determine that the majority has the right to buy the minority's interest. In a two-person or even-member partnership, there's a real possibility of a deadlock. To prevent a forced sale, you could adopt one of the following methods to see who leaves and who stays:

1. One side (determined by a flip of a coin, or any other method you choose) sets a price for a half-interest in the business, and the other side gets to buy, or sell, at that price;

2. Each partner or group of partners can bid against the other for the business (i.e., a private auction), with the highest bidder buying the lowest bidder's share.

COMMON SENSE NOTE: In our experience, it's not that often that both partners or factions want to buy out the other(s). Usually, at least one partner wants out—and sometimes all of them do.

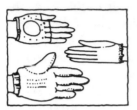

3. HOW MUCH IS A PARTNERSHIP INTEREST WORTH?—VALUATION METHODS

Let's start with a general summary of the law as to how much a partnership share is worth. It's not difficult. The departing partner—or his/her estate if he/she is deceased—is entitled to the "value" of his/her interest in the partnership business. That value, or more often the method for determining it, should be set in the original partnership agreement. If that hasn't been done, the Uniform Partnership Act defines the "value" of the business as its net worth on the date the partner departs. "Net worth" is simply the market value of all assets minus all liabilities. The departing partner's "ownership interest" is the same ownership percentage he/she held while an active participant in the partnership.

EXAMPLE: Assume that Lew, Wilbur, and George are equal partners in a car repair shop but they have never written a formal partnership agreement. Lew dies. His estate is entitled to one-third of the net worth of the repair shop. The value of the assets includes cash in the partners' capital account, fixed assets (such as tools, building, etc.), and accounts receivable; all liabilities are then deducted to determine the "value" of the business.

There are severe disadvantages to the U.P.A. method of determining and paying a departing partner's interest. First, the departing partner (or his/her estate) is due the full sum owed promptly; no payments over time are authorized. Few businesses have sufficient cash to make such a substantial payment, so the result can be a forced liquidation of the business at distress sale prices. Second, the U.P.A. method for determining value is rigid, and usually not very accurate. An on-going business is generally worth much more than its net worth; i.e. assets minus liabilities. For example, suppose the car repair shop we mentioned above has a net worth of $30,000, but profits have averaged $27,000 a year for the past ten years—and the partners haven't even had to be very active in working the business over that time? The business has "made it." Under the U.P.A., all Lew's estate is entitled to is $10,000, which seems clearly much lower than what the business is worth. Wouldn't you be delighted to pay $10,000 for a business that made you $9,000 a year?

Creating a fair method for determining the buy-out price of a partner's interest is one of the most difficult, as well as the most important, aspects of your partnership agreement. Usually the ownership percentage of a departing owner isn't hard to determine. That person has either a one-third or one-half share or whatever else is provided in the agreement. It's calculating the actual dollar value of that partnership interest that commonly poses problems. We'll present several different valuation methods shortly — but first, some general advice. No one method of valuation is inherently superior to others. It all depends on the nature of the business, and the partners' relationships and expectations. So, don't just pick one of the methods we present if it seems not to fit your situation. You can modify one, or blend two, or come up with your own method altogether.* Remember, the goal is to achieve a fair method of determining a buy-out price, and your own ingenuity can be used to the fullest. Your goal is to evaluate the factors that *actually* give your business value, and then to create a method for fairly calculating the total value of these factors. However, if you modify our agreement considerably, or write your own from scratch, you may want to check it with a lawyer (see chapter 1).

It can help to realize that determining the "real" value of a partnership business for buy-out purposes is often somewhat "artificial." This is because there isn't a marketplace, such as a stock exchange, where buyers and sellers engage in real arm's length transactions. And here is another important consideration. It's wise to structure the agreement so that the business is given the maximum chance to survive. If the buy-out price is too high, or the payment terms too onerous, the remaining partners may simply decide to liquidate the business, which means that the departing partner would receive his or her ownership percentage share of the net proceeds from a liquidation sale. Buy-out terms and price are clearly interrelated; often a somewhat higher buy-out price will be created in exchange for "low monthly payments" made by the remaining partners. Also, it's helpful — although often difficult with new businesses — to look at some earnings projections, and see how a buy-out method looks after you run some figures through it. If you're being bought out — or buying — in a couple of years, does what you would receive seem like a fair price if the partnership profits are $50,000 or $500,000? With a starting business like a service business (a repair shop, a consulting business, a hair-cutting salon, etc.) — which is without large capital accounts or substantial inventory — estimates of future income, profits, and worth will naturally be speculative. Therefore, it's often wise to state that the partners agree to review and revise the buy-out clause after a certain time — say two years — when there are solid figures on the specific performance of this one business.

4. VARYING THE BUY-OUT PRICE DEPENDING ON WHEN, OR THE REASON, A PARTNER DEPARTS

Here's one additional factor that you may want to consider along with any of the valuation methods we suggest. Does it make a difference why or when a partner departs when it comes to calculating that partner's share? Many partnerships have decided it does. For example, if a partner leaves during the initial stages of a business (whatever period you pick, often defined as one or two years), he or she is entitled only to the balance

---

* If you have an accountant you trust, see if he or she has any advice regarding valuation methods commonly used for your type of business.

in his or her capital account (i.e., his/her share of current net worth). After the initial period, a departing partner's interest is calculated by a method that more accurately reflects the actual operation and success of the business. Some partnerships adopt different prices (or different methods for calculating the price) for a departing partner's interest depending on the reason the partner leaves. For example, in a law firm we know, the buy-out price varies considerably, depending on whether the departing attorney:

1. Dies, becomes disabled, or retires over age sixty-five. This is the highest buy-out price (partially because insurance can cover much of the cost).

2. Quits to pursue some other non-legal dream, e.g., moves to Tahiti, or becomes a full-time flute player.

3. Quits, but remains a lawyer. This eventuality results in a lower buy-out price. If the departing partner remains active as a lawyer in the same county as his former partnership, the buy-out price is even lower.

All these different considerations may seem a little overwhelming when taken together. You may well be at the stage where you're ready to ask yourself — do we really want to bother with all of this? Or should we just hire a lawyer to do it for us? The answers are — yes and no. When the time comes to buy out a departing partner's interest, you'll be glad you took the time to resolve how to calculate the worth of that interest in advance. As any partnership lawyer can assure you, time and time again, it's disputes over the value of a departing partner's interest that lead to lawsuits and bitterness. And turning the whole problem over to a lawyer won't really solve your problem. Sure, your lawyer could say "okay, here's the method you should use." But a good one won't be that authoritarian. Instead, he or she will tell you to puzzle over the same issues and possible solutions we discuss here, and arrive at the substance of what you think is fair. It's your business, and no one else should decide how you determine what it's worth. This doesn't mean that you should never consult a lawyer, only that you should, at the very least, understand what's involved before you do.

5. VALUATION METHODS

The Set Dollar Amount Method

Under this plan, the partners agree in advance that if one partner departs from the partnership, the other(s) will buy out the share at a price that is agreed upon in advance and set out in the partnership agreement. Another variation is to require, in the partnership agreement, that the partners set a value to the partnership every year by a specified date. Assigning a set value in advance has the advantage of being definite, but may not be advisable for many partnerships. Why? Because the precise worth of any partnership business will fluctuate. So, the buy-out figure may become out of date and not reflect the current worth of the business. Establishing the set dollar valuation, made yearly, can solve this problem. A set dollar figure can be advisable when the primary value in the business is the energies of the partnership, with the business itself (name, good will, etc.) having little independent value. Such might be the case in a trading partnership (i.e., export-import, certain types of wholesaling, running a booth at a flea market, or a street stall). If this is the situation, a partner takes most of his or her share of the value on departure. Picking a low set-dollar value for that worth avoids spending time calculating the actual worth of assets already agreed to have little value. Another occasion to use a set-dollar buy-out amount is where the basic concern of the partnership is the preservation of the business and the members' relationship with each other. For example, we know of a two-man partnership that runs a trucking firm. Neither partner has immediate family to inherit his interest in the firm and both want to insure the business survives the death of a partner. So, they selected a lower estimate of the worth of their interest, to be used in the event either partner dies. This keeps the deceased partner's estate from getting involved in valuing the partnership interest, and means that the dollar value of this interest is both lower and known in advance. Thus, the payment itself is more easily accomplished. Here's a sample set-figure clause:[4]

> *The value of a partner's interest in the partnership shall be determined as follows:*
>
> *1. Within _____ [i.e., 90] days after the end of each fiscal year of the partnership, the partners shall determine the partnership's value by unanimous written agreement, and that value shall remain in effect from the date of that written determination until the next such written determination.*
>
> *2. Should the partners be unable to agree on a value or otherwise fail to make any such determination, the partnership's value shall be the greater of (a) the value last established under this section, or (b) the net worth of the partnership.*

Note that with this clause partners have to sit down yearly and work out the business' worth. This can help keep all partners up-to-date on valuation issues, and quite possibly diffuse disputes before they get really serious.

"Book Value" or Market Value Methods

Determining the "book value" of a partnership means calculating the worth of all partnership assets and liabilities as they are set forth in the partnership accounting books. This method has simplicity to recommend it, but little else. Often "book value" has little relation to reality. For example, the book value of real estate is generally its acquisition cost, not its current market value, which in inflationary times can be far higher. A somewhat more accurate method is to determine the current market value of all assets and liabilities of the business, which is basically what the U.P.A. provides. As we said earlier, this method fails too frequently to reflect the true worth of the business, especially one that's prospering, because it doesn't consider intangibles such as good will or the worth of the on-going business. It can be appropriate, though, for beginning businesses because

---

4. If you set the buy-out amount far too low, you are in effect making a gift to the remaining partners and there will be gift tax consequences. You do have some leeway, however, because it is always difficult to determine an exact valuation of partnership shares.

they have no reasonable way to estimate future success or profits. In some situations, it can be sensible to adopt a market-value buy-out method for the first year (or some other set time) with the express provision that another more accurate method will be adopted at the end of that period.

Here's how a market-value buy-out clause works. As of the date the departing partner leaves, the net worth of all partnership assets is calculated; the departing partner receives his or her ownership percentage of this amount, under whatever pay-out terms you agree on (e.g., equal monthly payments over the next twelve years, etc.). The net worth of a business normally includes:

• The current market value of all tangible assets of the business. This includes both the net value of current inventory, plus the present value of other items, from manufacturing machinery to the stained glass lamps in the waiting room.[5]

• All accounts receivable that are reasonably collectable.

• All cash (after subtracting all debts owed).

• All earned but unbilled fees. (This is particularly important in professional partnerships—an architectural firm, for instance—but it can also apply where construction work was done, or anywhere else where money was earned although a bill had not yet been sent out. This, technically, would not be an account receivable.)

Here is an example of what a market-value buy-out clause can look like:

> *The value of a partner's interest in the partnership shall be his or her ownership percentage in the business; the value of the business shall be the sum of the following items, as of the date that value is to be determined.*
>
> *1. The credit balance in the business capital account(s), less all outstanding debts owed by the business;*
>
> *2. All accounts receivable that are reasonably collectable, and all unbilled but earned fees.*
>
> *3. The current market value of all assets.*

In drafting a market-value buy-out clause, you will want to be aware of, and solve, several other potential problems. What happens, for example, if at the time one partner withdraws or dies, there's a conflict over the actual calculations made to determine market value? Who makes those calculations anyway? Again, the solution to this potential problem is up to you. The important thing is to adopt a clear and simple scheme in advance. You can, for example, name an outside accountant to make these calculations. Or, you can provide that the partnership books, and remaining partner's calculations, will be sufficient to determine book value, but should there be any conflict regarding the figure arrived at, it will be resolved by mediation or by arbitration, under the dispute-resolution clause of your agreement.

Okay, so far so good. With the help of an accountant, nothing set out above should be that difficult to determine. But there is a serious drawback with this valuation method which can be summarized under the heading "good will." In many businesses, the intangible asset called "good will" is, in fact, a valuable asset. As you can see, good will won't be calculated at all by adding up the totals of the items set out above.

---

5. You do get to decide how picky to be here. We advise against trying to value every last wastebasket. Worrying about the value of paperclips or stamps reminds us of the divorce we heard about where the departing husband inventoried the food in the ice-box before he left, and claimed one-half its worth as part of his community property.

Good will is traditionally defined as "the well-founded expectation of continued public patronage." The concept is especially applicable in retail businesses (for example, a retail store with a good location and good reputation), but is often less of a factor with businesses that depend primarily on personal service. A plumber, or podiatrist, may have acquired personal good will, but it's often hard to transfer that good will to another person in the partnership. In many businesses, it takes a while to establish good will. That is, there will be little good will built up for several years.

If you feel that you want to make allowances for good will in your valuation, you could simply add good will to the list of items to be valued. However, this is really avoiding the problem. Good will is inherently subjective, and difficult for outsiders to evaluate. In fact, good will is another term for the reality that a prospering business is worth more than the market value of its tangible assets. If you decide this is—or will be—the case for you, we advise you to set up a method for calculating that extra value to the business and not to postpone the problem by simply adding good will to the list of business assets to be valued when the partnership ends. The wisest course is probably to create a valuation method which is based on actual earnings, as we describe next.

The "Capitalization of Earnings" Method

"Capitalization of Earnings" is a fancy concept useful to answer the question of what the business is really worth. That worth depends at least in large measure on its earning capacity. If the business is successful and likely to remain so, the capitalization of earnings method attempts to reflect the fact that there's a real value in the on-going nature of a successful business. For example, if John and Fred each put $25,000 in separate 50/50 partnerships, and the profits of John's partnership are roughly $5,000 a year, while Fred's are near $15,000, it seems clear Fred's partnership interest is more valuable, even if the market value of the assets of both partnerships is identical.

Under the capitalization-of-earnings valuation method, the average yearly (net) earnings of the business for a set period of time are calculated, then multiplied by a set figure (called the multiplier) to determine the current value. Normally, "earnings" here means there's a deduction for wages at current market value for services partners contributed. In other words, if a two-man plumbing partnership had profits of $70,000 *but* the value of the plumbers' work, by current wage standards, was $50,000, the "net earnings" would be $20,000. Here's a very simple example of how it works.

EXAMPLE: Emily and Anne are 50/50 partners in a wine and cheese store that's thrived during the last decade. Net income (in profits) has been roughly between $40,000 and $60,000 a year (each partner initially invested $30,000). Emily and Anne have agreed in their partnership agreement that the average earnings over the past four years will be capitalized by a multiplier of five. Thus, average annual earnings will be multiplied by five to determine the value of the business. Anne decides to move on. The calculations are as follows:

Average Annual Earnings over 4 years:

$60,000 per year x 5 (the multiplier rate) = $300,000.

So, Anne's one-half interest is valued at $150,000.

At first glance, this method may seem arbitrary. Where does that multiplier come from? Thin air? Well, this method does have problems that must be resolved for each distinct business, but as we hope you'll see, it's not really that arbitrary. The first decision to make is whether you want net profits to be the base for valuation of the worth of the business. Other bases have been used, from gross sales to book value. We suggest net profits is the appropriate base, because we believe that it's normally the figure that gives the best gauge of the actual earning capacity of the business. The next decision is how far you want to go back in determining average earnings. If you just use the most recent year, you're greatly increasing the risk that the base won't be representative, because it might have been a particularly good, or bad year. Usually, a three to five year period is selected.

Obviously the most difficult problem is to agree on a multiplier that will produce a fair result. How do you decide if it should be four or six or ten times average annual earnings?[6] One way is to see what works for similar businesses. Most accountants have tables indicating what current prices are being paid for businesses and what multiples of net profits these prices represent. For example, a hairdressing business may sell for, maybe, six times net profits; a pet supply business seven times net profits; etc. The trouble with relying on industry-wide figures is that they don't provide you with a truly reliable indication of how profitable *your* business will be in the future. One way to try and reflect the actual earning capacity of your business is to base the multiplier on your percentage of return on your initial investment. Suppose you calculate this after an allowance for partners' salaries is subtracted, and determine that your profits are 16 percent.[7] In this situation, perhaps a multiplier of one-half the profits, or eight, would be fair.

We say "perhaps" because no outsider can say what a fair multiplier is for you. The best advice we can give you is to try it out. Sit down and go through some projections. Assume you made net yearly profits averaging X or Y or Z percent. What should the multiplier be? Try some different ones out. How do the figures feel? Would you be willing to sell for this price? Or to pay it out in order to continue the business? This method of determining value can be as flexible as you want it to be. For example, depending on your business, you could have two (or even more) multipliers; one for "normal" returns, one for "extra earnings," etc.

EXAMPLE: The A-B printing partnership decides that 15 percent yearly profits on capital investments is a return they can reasonably expect. They also agree that the multiplier for average yearly "reasonable" profits will be ten. However, if there are additional profits, due to the particular skills (or luck) of the partners, these won't be valued (for sale purposes) as highly as reasonable profits because they are not as likely to continue. So the multiplier for them will only be six.

ANOTHER EXAMPLE: If there are non-working partners in the business, calculation of average profits should be adjusted to reflect the efforts of the working partner. Let's say that John and Al are 50/50 partners in a trucking business. John put up the capital to start the business. Al does the work. They split profits 50/50. If John wants out, they determine the "profits" of the business for sale purposes with an allowance for Al's personal efforts; if Al hadn't been a partner, John would have to hire someone to do

---

6. A lot can depend on how hard the partners work in the business to produce the earnings. If two partners work ten hours a day to produce a $100,000 profit, there is little or no business earnings over and above a fair return for their labor Obviously a business which nets $100,000 without much work by the partners is a good deal more valuable.

7. You should make this subtraction whether what the partners took out to compensate them for their labors was called a salary, a draw, profits, or whatever. This money reflects your labor and is not really a return on investment.

his work, thus reducing his profits. To restate this, at least part of Al's "profits" are, in reality (though not in tax terms), a disguised salary. John and Al determine a reasonable salary for Al to be $26,000 a year—and agree to deduct this from the average yearly profits in determining net profits. Since John doesn't work in the business, no similar deduction is made if Al decides to leave and John buys him out.

Here's an example of a capitalization of earnings buy-out clauses:

The value of a partner's interest in the partnership shall be his or her ownership percentage of the value of the partnership on the date of his/her departure from the partnership, which shall be determined as follows:

The net profits of the business shall be determined for the three fiscal years preceding the partner's departure. The average net profit shall then be calculated, then multiplied by a multiple of _____ giving the value of the business.

NOTE: As we've said, many different versions of this approach are possible. For example, the preceding clause could be used as only part of the overall scheme to value the business. The departing partner could receive his or her share of the market value of tangible or specific assets of the partnership (section "b" above), with the "capitalization of earnings" method used only to calculate the value of the business "good will."

Another variation would be to start the period for which profits are averaged from the most recent quarter of the partnership's fiscal year—i.e., a time likely to be closer to the actual departure date of the partner.

WARNING! If your partnership business isn't in existence very long when the departing partner leaves, the "capitalization of earnings" method is obviously hard or perhaps even impossible to apply; there simply isn't time to make a fair determination as to profitability. For that reason, you probably want to adopt another valuation provision for the first year or so to take care of this possibility and then switch over to the "capitalization of earnings" method.

Post "Departure" Appraisal Method

Using this method, you simply agree to have an independent appraiser (usually named) determine the worth of the partnership at the date of the partner's departure considering all factors. This method can be costly, but assuming that you choose a good appraiser, it's fair. If you wish, you can supply the appraiser with some criteria to use in arriving at a conclusion, but if you supply many, you are likely to end up with a result not too different from a combination of the market-value method and capitalization of earnings method. Even without your guidelines, there are fairly set methods an appraiser will use. Some businesses, particularly those whose major assets have a ready market, like real-estate holdings, are quite suited to valuation by appraisal; and appraisal-valuation clauses are conventional in real estate partnership agreements. For most small service businesses, all you're doing is passing the buck. If you have a complicated business and decide to hire a big national appraiser (yes, there are such outfits), the cost can be prohibitive. We've heard of appraisals costing $10,000 or $15,000 on businesses that weren't worth a lot more than that.

Another disadvantage to this method is that it can take some time to get the appraiser's report, unless you name an appraiser who is both experienced and prompt. Also, the appraisal method (unlike the first three we discussed) makes it difficult to determine in advance what a partnership interest can be worth. Needless to say, this sort of information can be extremely desirable.

Here's a sample valuation-by-appraisal clause:

> *The value of a partner's interest in the partnership shall be his or her ownership percentage of the value on the date of his/her departure from the partnership, as determined by an independent appraisal of the worth of the partnership on that date conducted by _____. The appraisal shall be commenced within _____ days of the partner's departure. The partnership and the departing partner shall share the appraisal expenses equally.*

Other Valuation Methods

As we've said, there's an infinite number of (theoretically) possible valuation methods. If you come up with one that suits you, fine. Write it up and put it in your agreement. Don't worry about putting it in legalese, clear English will suffice.

Here are some other possibilities regarding valuation. First, base the valuation on some other simple formula that's practical and agreed upon by all the partners. For instance, the partners could agree that each deceased partner's estate will accept the payment on life insurance policies purchased for each partner as full payment for the partner's interest. Or, you could adopt the method a lawyer friend refers to as "the golden handshake"—if you're buying out a partner, pay him or her a little more than you think it's worth, just for the good vibes and good karma of it. Finally, you can combine and alter the valuation method we've described to suit your needs. For example, you might combine the appraisal method to value all fixed assets with some multiple of net earnings (agreed upon in advance) to cover "good will," etc.

---

6. PAYMENTS TO DEPARTING PARTNERS

Cash Payments

Now let's assume that you have solved the problem of who has the right to buy the share of a departing partner, and you have also decided on how that share will be valued by picking a valuation method. Your next task is to decide how a departing partner is to be paid for his/her partnership interest. It is essential that you do this, because if you fail to the U.P.A. provides in essence, that the departing partner has the right to collect for the full value of his/her interest promptly. This can be a particular problem in the event of a partner's death, since the deceased partner's estate, and inheritors, may well insist on receiving whatever cash they can get as soon as possible rather than receiving payments over time.

The reason that you normally want to avoid the situation where your partnership must pay off a departing or deceased partner's share all at once is obvious. Doing so very often requires selling important partnership assets and may (1) destroy the business; and (2) bring in much less than the full value of the sold assets because you had to resort to a hurried "distress" sale.

We suggest that it's good business to adopt a payment method that puts a premium on the survival of the business. If the payment terms are so severe the business can't afford them, all involved will lose. And even if the terms wouldn't necessarily end the business, if they're too severe, the remaining owners may still decide "the hell with it," and liquidate the partnership business. Also, we believe it's simply bad karma to set up a situation which will wipe out your former partners. In ending a partnership—as in starting and running one—the general rule is that benefits should be shared fairly.

The usual way to deal with buying out a partnership share is to provide for installment payments. This can work well for everyone if the departing partner has faith that those staying on will manage the business competently and money will be available to make the time payments. However, it can cause problems if the person who is pulling out is doing so because he doesn't trust the others. Another method can be to obtain a bank loan to pay off the departing partner. This method requires that the business be able to obtain a substantial loan, and the remaining partner(s) agree to the added obligation of the loan interest.

There's no one formula for installment payments. Once again, you have to create a method that suits your business and your temperaments. In most situations, payments are not extended over more than two or three years.[8] A common provision is to delay the first payment for some set time, such as ninety days, in order to give the remaining partners time to start gathering the money they'll need. Here's a clause providing for equal installment payments:

> *Whenever the partnership is obligated or chooses to purchase a partner's interest, it shall pay for that interest, at its option, in cash or by promissory note of the partnership, or partly in cash and partly by note. Any promissory note shall be dated as of the effective date of the purchase, shall mature in not more than _____ years, shall be payable in equal installments that come due monthly, shall bear interest at the rate of _____ percent per annum [and may, at the partnership's option, be subordinated to existing and future debts to banks and other institutional lenders for money borrowed.]*[9] The first payment shall be made 90 days after the date of the promissory note.

Insurance

Just because there's a contract provision which states that the interest of a departing partner will be paid off on a certain schedule does not mean the business will actually earn sufficient money to make those payments. Or, even if the business can barely make the payments, doing so can impose a serious, even grave, drain on cash necessary for other business purposes. So, many partnerships choose alternative means of paying of the interest of a partner, especially a partner who dies. A conventional method for doing this is to purchase life insurance. You can also purchase disability insurance for much the same purpose.

We'll repeat here—we're not normally great fans of individual life insurance.[10] The business traffics too much in fear and anxiety for our taste, as well as using questionable sales techniques that often result in people buying more insurance than they need, or the wrong kind of insurance. Also, all those tranquilized deer, antique railroad stations, and calvary charges littering our TV screens do get annoying. Nevertheless, for many partnerships, life insurance can be a sensible way of obtaining the money needed to pay off a deceased partner's interest, especially by purchasing "term" insurance, the cheapest form of life insurance.

---

8. This may seem to be a short period of time to raise all the money you will need, but remember that if the business is prospering, you will be able to borrow from a bank or if necessary can find a new partner with capital to contribute.

9. This means that this note may be given a lower priority in debts of the partnership which can be a help for the partnership in borrowing money in the future.

10. Ambrose Bierce defined the business of life insurance as "An ingenious modern game of chance in which the player is permitted to enjoy the comfortable conviction that he is beating the man who keeps the table."

If a partner dies, the partnership-financed insurance policy pays off his or her share, not partnership operating income. If you do decide to go the life insurance route, consider solving two problems at once by providing that the amount of life insurance payment *is* the value of the deceased partner's interest in the business in your valuation clauses. You don't have to do this, of course, and could use the "capitalization of assets" method for valuation and buy enough insurance to (you hope) make the payment. Notice that using life insurance to pay off this interest means that you will know in advance what the payout will be. This means that you will have to make adjustments so that you don't have too much, or more importantly, too little life insurance. Obviously, life insurance isn't useful for paying off living partners who depart or are thrown out. Sometimes a new partner takes the old partner's place, and pays him for his interest. Otherwise, you still have to find some way to raise the necessary cash for those payments.

Here are some useful points about using life insurance policies to finance a buy-out agreement:

● Partners have an "insurable interest" in the life of their partners, so they can buy policies on them directly. You can also purchase additional insurance to cover extra costs to the business, such as hiring a new employee, caused by the death of a partner.

● There are two different methods of buying life insurance policies: either the partners buy policies on each other ("cross-purchase") or the partnership itself buys the policies. For small partnerships, a cross-purchase plan is usually more desirable. This is because if the partnership itself pays for and owns the policies on the partners, it has been held in some circumstances that the proceeds of the policy are partnership assets and are included in the value of the partnership thus artificially increasing the worth of the deceased partner's share. In a cross-purchase agreement, each partner buys policies on the life of each other partner and this problem is avoided. The following is a provision for the cross-purchase of life insurance.

> *Each partner shall purchase and maintain life insurance [and disability insurance] on the life of each other partner in the face value of $ _____.*

In a larger partnership, a cross-purchase scheme can get cumbersome. If there are six partners, for example, each partner must buy five policies (one on each of the other partner's lives) which means a total of thirty policies. To avoid this much complexity and paperwork, it's probably better to have the partnership pay for a policy on each partner's life, despite the problem mentioned above. If you do adopt this type of clause, specify explicitly that (only) the cash surrender value of the life insurance policies before death is a partnership asset, whereas the proceeds themselves are not. Since the cash surrender value is far less than the pay-out at death, this sort of provision works to have the insurance counted as a less valuable asset, if it is counted at all. Here is an example of such a provision:

> *The life insurance policies owned by the partnership on the lives of each partner are assets of the partnership only in so far as they have cash surrender value preceding the death of a partner; any amount paid to the estate of a deceased partner pursuant to any such life insurance policy shall not be included in any valuation of the value of the partnership, or the deceased partner's interest in it.*

There's also the question of what happens to a life insurance policy if a partner quits or resigns. The usual solution is to allow the departing party to purchase the policy, since the partnership no longer needs that protection. Here's a clause that covers this:

> *On the withdrawal or termination of any partner for any reason other than his or her death, any insurance policies on his/her life, for which the partnership paid the premiums, shall be delivered to that partner and become his/her sole and separate property. If the policy has a cash surrender value, that amount shall be paid to the partnership by the withdrawing or terminating partner, or offset against the partnership's obligations to him/her.*

Here are some more facts you should know about life insurance:

● Insurance payments made by a partnership are normally not tax deductible.[11]

● If a partner can't pass a life insurance physical, you have a new problem. But, unless you think this is reasonably likely, there's little reason to worry about it in the original partnership agreement; solve it when (and if) it arises.

● You may want to do some estate planning.[12] This isn't a book about estate planning, but we do want to alert you to the fact that buy-out agreements should be coordinated with the estate planning done by each partner individually. For example, if the proceeds of the insurance are payable to the deceased partner's estate, these proceeds are subject to probate and will increase probate fees. In order to avoid probate, someone other than the estate of the deceased partner should be specified as the beneficiary of each policy. This can often be done by simply naming the people closest to you as the policy beneficiaries. Or, you could create an insurance trust (a separate one for each policy), and make the proceeds payable to the trustee, who both pays the ultimate beneficiary and is responsible for insuring all the other terms of the buy/sell agreement.

---

7. OTHER PROVISIONS CONCERNING CONTINUITY OF THE BUSINESS

There are many other provisions you may want to consider regarding what happens at the death or departure of a partner. Some of these, as set out below, take the place of a buy-out agreement. Others are complimentary.

Substituting for a Deceased Partner

There is a provision that if a partner dies, a person named by the deceased partner takes the partner's place in the partnership. For example, each partner might name a spouse, or lover, or whomever else they want to inherit their property and take their place. Usually, it's agreed that the new partner will have no management powers but will share in the profits

---

11. Treasury Reg. 1.264-1; unless the policy is a condition for a bank loan with the policy assigned to the bank in case of death.

12. See Clifford, *Plan Your Estate with Wills, Probate Avoidance, Trusts & Taxes*. This book comes in two editions—one for Texas and one for California. See the back of this book for order information.

(and losses) of the partnership, in the same share as the deceased partner did. The purpose of this kind of provision is to insure continuity of the business, and to avoid the expenses involved in a buy-out provision. Notice that it makes sense to use this type of provision only if the partnership, in reality, can continue to function well if a partner dies. For many small partnerships, this wouldn't work, either because they're dependent on each partner's ability, or they don't want new partners, even inactive ones, etc. Here is an example of a situation where this sort of agreement does make sense.

EXAMPLE: Samantha, Ben, and Julie start a health spa business. Each is married and all three couples are friendly. Indeed, the spouses, who are all independent business people, have all helped get the business going in many ways, from painting the ceiling to guaranteeing a loan. Until the business gets established, the partnership shares have little value, so it is decided to provide that each partner's spouse will substitute for them if they die during the first three years of the partnership. After three years, the partners agree to examine the situation again and decide if another method makes more sense.

Business Continuation Requirement

A Business Continuation Requirement states that a business must be continued for a certain time after the death of a partner. Whatever eventually happens to a partnership business, it's often undesirable to be required to liquidate the business shortly after a partner's death. In particular, all interested persons, including the inheritors of the deceased partner, may want the business to be continued, at least long enough so that it can be sold in an orderly fashion and not at a fire-sale price. For other reasons too, you may decide that you want the surviving fathers obligated to continue the business for a set period of time. Here's a provision to do that:

> *In the case of a partner's death, permanent disability, retirement, or voluntary withdrawal from the partnership, the partnership shall not dissolve or terminate but its business shall continue without interruption and without any break in continuity. On the death, disability, or withdrawal of any partner, the others shall not liquidate or wind up the affairs of the partnership, but shall continue to conduct a partnership under the terms of this agreement for a period of at least _____ (e.g. one year)*

Joint Tenancy Plans

In some situations, you may want to have all (or some) of your partnership property placed in "joint tenancy" with your partners. If you do this, when any partner dies the surviving partners automatically inherit this share of the business. This sort of plan would only be appropriate if your partner is the person you want to inherit your property. "Joint tenancy" is a legal term of art, i.e., magic legal words that have automatic consequences when used. Owning property in joint tenancy means that there's an automatic "right of survivorship." Upon the death of one joint tenancy owner, the surviving owners automatically inherit his/her interest in the property, even if there is a will to the contrary. The advantage of partners owning property in joint tenancy is that it eliminates problems regarding the transfer of property ownership and continuity of the business. The main drawback, and one that prevents joint tenancy from being used in most instances, is that the person who dies may not want his/her partnership property interest to go to the other partners. However, it can work well for unmarried couples, and longtime friends, or relatives who want their partner to have their share should they die.

ESTATE PLANNING NOTE: There can be other potential problems with joint tenancy ownership. Some states provide for a widow(er)'s "right of election." This means that a surviving spouse can elect to take a certain percentage of the deceased spouse's estate, if he/she is not adequately provided for. If a surviving spouse makes such an election, and the only, or major, asset is the partnership joint tenancy property, he/she can collect the share out of those assets—even forcing a sale of the partnership assets, if need be. Problems can also develop in community-property states if creating the joint tenancy has the effect of giving away more than half of your (and your spouse's) community property.

There can also be gift/estate tax problems if joint tenancy is used. For example, if there wasn't equal contribution by the partners to the joint tenancy property, there will be a gift made by one partner to the other(s) at the time the original transfer to joint tenancy is made. The federal government and state governments (except Nevada) tax gifts in excess of $3,000 per person per year. We don't have space to go into all the ramifications of the gift tax here; but do check your plan out with a tax expert before creating a partnership joint tenancy.

To show you how easy it is to place property in joint tenancy, here are two examples, including a deed:

& & &

JOINT TENANCY OWNERSHIP DOCUMENT

Ownership of the personal property identified below is held by _____(your name)_____ and _____(partner's name)_____ as joint tenants.

Said joint tenancy property is described as: (list and clearly identify the property).

Said joint tenancy property was purchased on _____, 19_____ for a purchase price of $_____, of which _____ contributed $_____ and _____ contributed $_____ of the purchase price.

Dated: _____   _____

                                                  (your name)

Dated: _____   _____

                                                  (partner's name)

RECORDING REQUESTED BY

AND WHEN RECORDED MAIL TO

NAME Alfred Smythe
ADDRESS Easy Street
CITY & STATE El Dorado Hills, Ca.

Title Order No._____ Escrow No._____

——————————————— SPACE ABOVE THIS LINE FOR RECORDER'S USE ———————————————

MAIL TAX STATEMENTS TO

NAME Alfred Smythe
ADDRESS Easy Street
CITY & STATE El Dorado Hills, Ca.

𝕴𝖓𝖉𝖎𝖛𝖎𝖉𝖚𝖆𝖑 𝕲𝖗𝖆𝖓𝖙 𝕯𝖊𝖊𝖉

~~FOR A VALUE RECEIVED~~

Alfred Smythe
GRANT**S** to
(partner's name) And Alfred Smythe, as Joint Tenants
all that real property situate in the   City of El Dorado Hills

County of   Dreams   , State of California, described as follows

(property described and identified)

Said property to be owned in joint tenancy by Alfred Smythe
and (partner's name)

Dated_____

_____   _____

_____   _____

STATE OF CALIFORNIA
_____County of _____ } ss.
On_____, 19_____ before me, the undersigned,
a Notary Public, in and for said State, personally appeared_____

known to me to be the person   whose name _____
subscribed to the within instrument, and acknowledged to me that
__he__ executed the same.

_____
Notary Public

FOR NOTARY SEAL OR STAMP

MAIL TAX STATEMENTS AS DIRECTED ABOVE

107

Disability

Do you want to cover disability in your partnership agreement? Often this is wise. If a partner becomes seriously disabled, it's good to have an established method for the other partner to buy him/her out. Most types of disability/buy-out provisions are the same as any other buy-out provisions. Indeed, the usual way to handle the problem is simply to include the word "disability" in the basic buy-out provision. Or, you can include a separate disability clause if for some special reason you decide you want more detail, such as defining what you mean by disability. For example, we have a friend, an ex-lawyer, who was declared "psychologically unable to work," and collected state disability after freaking out over lawyering.

Non-competition Agreements

If a partner voluntarily leaves the partnership, should he or she be allowed to compete with the former partners? Forbidding a partner from engaging in his/her usual way of earning a living is obviously a drastic solution. However, non-competition agreements can be legal, and if they are, can be enforced by court order if necessary.[13] To be legal in most states, a non-competition agreement must be "reasonably" limited in both time and geographical area, and be otherwise fair (or, realistically, seem okay to a judge). Thus, an agreement which said that a partner who voluntarily withdrew from a partnership which ran a hair-cutting salon couldn't open up a competing business within ten miles for a period of three years would probably be enforceable, but one that said no competing business could be run within 1,000 miles for thirty years would almost certainly be thrown out by a judge. We're generally not in favor of non-competition clauses. It's supposed to be a free country, after all. However, in some cases they may actually be fair. For example, if a partner is taught some unique skill upon admission to the partnership, and the local area can only support one enterprise selling that skill, a non-competition agreement seems fair. Note that since the agreement must be reasonably limited in geographic scope to be legal, the worst that can happen is that the departing partner must move.

Here's a non-competition clause:

> *On the voluntary withdrawal of any partner, the withdrawn partner shall not carry on a business similar to the business of the partnership within the (describe area) for a period of _____ years.*

Control of the Business Name

In some businesses, the right to use a name has great value—a famous rock band's name is one obvious example. At the other extreme, "Joe & Al's TV Repairs" is unlikely to be more valuable than "Joe's TV repairs." If your name does matter, you should decide who gets to keep it. If there are several partners, the usual solution is to let the majority keep it. However, if yours is an equal number partnership, you could obviously face trouble with

---

13. Because the law having to do with non-competition clauses can vary in all of our fifty states, if this sort of clause is important to you, we advise you to see a lawyer in your area or do some of your own legal research (see Elias, *Legal Research: How to Find and Understand the Law*, Nolo Press).

this situation. Also, it may be that one partner really coined the name and wants to be entitled to use it. Or, more seriously, suppose the business uses one person's name (i.e., The Toni Ihara band)? When our friend John H. was thrown out of "John H . . . Furniture," he had to open a new business in the name "John H . . . Studios," because his old business had a partnership contract provision allowing them the sole business rights to the name "John H . . . Furniture." It can also happen when a partnership ends, that one partner doesn't want the name of the former business used at all. When one two-person partnership we know of split up, they agreed—at the insistence of one of them—that neither would use the old partnership name. The other partner then printed up letterhead with a new name but stating boldly "Successor to . . .(the original name)." By this time, the objecting partner had had enough squabbling and shrugged her shoulders. We tell you all this to better equip you to decide on how thorough you want to be.

Retirement Provisions

Do you want to say anything about retirement? Imposing a mandatory retirement age seems foolish to us. It's your business, so why force a partner to quit if he or she wants to work?

But suppose someone does want to retire? How can this be distinguished from simply quitting the partnership? Do you want to allow a partner to "retire" (or partially retire) and still retain an active interest in profits of the business?

Here are two examples of ways to handle retirement problems.

Voluntary Retired—Partner Continues to Receive Full Profits

At the end of the partnership's fiscal year, any partner who has reached his or her _____th birthday during that fiscal year may retire from active participation in the management of the business of the partnership. Such a retirement shall not affect the retiring partner's interest in the partnership, its properties, or its profits and losses.

Mandatory Retirement

After his or her _____th birthday, any partner may be compelled to retire from the partnership by a vote of a majority of the other partners. A retired partner shall receive payment for the value of his/her interest in the partnership on the date of retirement, as provided in section _____ of this agreement.

C. Transfer of a Partner's Interest

1. Assignment of a Partner's Interest

Most partnership agreements contain clauses prohibiting a partner from assigning his/her interest in the partnership to a third party without at least giving the remaining partners the first chance to buy him/her out.[14] We think this is a good idea. Normally you will never have to worry about a partner assigning his/her interest without all partners' consent. But should the personal relationships between partners disintegrate, it's wise to have legal protection against this possibility. Here's a sample clause which limits the assignment of a partner's interest without approval of all the partners:

A partner may transfer all or part of his/her interest in the partnership only as follows:
1. To the partnership or to any other partner, as provided in Section _____ of this agreement
2. On his/her death, by will or other transfer means, as limited by the terms of this agreement.

NOTE: In some rather unusual small businesses, you may want free transferability of partnership shares—a real estate syndication could be one example. If you do you can write a provision expressly allowing for free transferability upon whatever terms, or limits, you decide are appropriate. Before you do this, though, we suggest you evaluate whether you'd be better off with a limited partnership (see chapter 7), a legal structure better suited to transferring interests.

In the absence of anything in the partnership agreement, what happens to the partnership if a partner's interest is assigned to a third party? The answer is that this, in itself, does not dissolve the partnership. The remaining partners can dissolve the partnership if they want to, or they can continue the partnership business "without interference" of their new associate who is not granted the rights of a full-fledged partner.

---

14. The "Right of First Refusal" discussed in section B(1) of this chapter.

The new "associate" has a right to receive the profits to which the transferring partner would have been entitled. But the new associate doesn't have the legal rights of a partner. He/she can't demand an accounting, nor does he/she have a right to see and inspect the partnership books while the partnership business lasts.[15]

2. Sale of a Partner's Interest

In some instances, a partner will (with the other partner's concurrence) sell his/her partnership interest to a new partner. Aside from the question of the debts of the partnership (discussed in chapter 4, section 2), tax problems can arise. If substantial amounts of money are involved, we advise you to see a tax expert. Tax problems are discussed in more detail in chapter 6, Partnership Taxation. Suffice it to say here that the sale or exchange of a partnership interest can result in taxation at ordinary income *or* capital gain (or loss) rates and there is often a lot you can do to control which of these occurs.

The seller of a partnership interest may also want a separate agreement with former partners (and the buyer, if it is someone other than a partner) protecting the seller from future lawsuits by third parties. This is often done by giving the person leaving the partnership the right to be reimbursed by the partnership if he or she is sued. Matters covered in this kind of agreement normally include:

• Assumption by the new partnership of the seller's liability for the debts of the old partnership.

• The express agreement by the continuing partnership to defend any lawsuits for old debts or other liabilities brought against the selling partners, including provisions for indemnification for any judgments and attorneys fees.

• A statement signed by all partners that the old partnership has been terminated as of a specific date.

D. Expulsion of a Partner

Expelling a partner is a drastic decision, one you surely hope you never have to consider, let alone implement. It's often a subject that new partners find very difficult even to consider at a time when they feel optimistic about their new enterprise and each other. However, if yours is a partnership involving more than a few partners, it should be provided for.

We are not sure how common expulsion of a partner is. We know of many partnerships that have dissolved completely, or some where (say) two partners remained and one left, but we can't ever recall hearing of a formal expulsion of a partner. Perhaps this is because many partners in small businesses decide not to cover possible expulsion in a separate provision. Everything we do and decide must be unanimous, they reason, and if we ever reach the stage where we're considering an expulsion, it's time to disband the partnership. This makes some sense where you have a two or three person partnership, but much less in a larger one, where it may mean disbanding the business

---

15. *Section 27 U.P.A.*

111

just to get rid of one malcontent. So, if yours is a partnership with four or more partners and you want to allow yourselves flexibility, here are some suggestions and sample clauses for handling an expulsion:

#1

> *A partner may be expelled from the partnership by a vote of _____ ("¾ of the voting partners" or "the other partners holding at least 60 percent of the capital interest in the partnership," or whatever you choose) if, by this vote, it is determined in the sole discretion of these partners that the partner has significantly breached his/her obligations under their agreement or is unable or unwilling to perform them, or that the continued membership of that partner in the partnership is detrimental to the best interests of the partnership's business. Expulsion shall become effective when written notice of expulsion is served on the expelled partner. When the expulsion becomes effective, the expelled partner's rights to participate in the partnership's profits and his/her other rights, powers, and authority as a partner of the partnership shall terminate. [If, as of the effective date of expulsion, (a) his/her share of the partnership's undistributed profits for the current fiscal year, (b) the credit balance in his capital account, and (c) partnership indebtedness to him/her, reduced by (1) any indebtedness of the expelled partner to the partnership and (2) his/her drawings for the current fiscal year, is a credit balance, that balance shall be a debt due on demand owed to the expelled partner by the partnership. If that balance is a debit balance, it shall be a debt due on demand owed to the partnership by the partner.] Expulsion shall not cause dissolution of the partnership for the remaining partners.*

#2

In the preceding clause, the expelled partner received only the minimum valuation of his partnership interest. We think that it's wise to be more generous. There will very likely be enough bitterness and animosity already without putting a partner out with what might be viewed as less than his or her fair share. If you agree, substitute for the bracketed clauses:

> *[An expelled partner shall be entitled to receive the value of his/her interest in the partnership, as that value is defined by Section _____ of this agreement.][16]*

A Partner's Bankruptcy

Under the U.P.A., a partner's personal bankruptcy, now technically called "becoming subject to an order of relief" from the bankruptcy court, causes dissolution of a partnership, even if the business itself is still viable. In large partnerships, therefore, it can be appropriate to have a provision planning for immediate expulsion of a bankrupt partner, such as:

---

16. Insert the number of the clause which covers valuation should a partner die, become permanently disabled, or otherwise leave the partnership. By doing this, you treat the partner who is expelled the same way you treat a partner who leaves for a neutral reason and by so doing probably lower the level of bitterness that is likely to surround an expulsion.

A partner shall cease to be a partner and shall have no interest in common with the remaining partners or in partnership property when the partner does any of the following:

1. Obtains or becomes subject to an order for relief under Bankruptcy Code;

2. Obtains or becomes subject to an order or decree of insolvency under state law;

3. Makes an assignment for the benefit of creditors;

4. Consents to or suffers the appointment of a receiver or trustee to any substantial part of his/her assets that is not vacated within _____ days;

5. Consents to or suffers an attachment or execution of any substantial part of his assets that is not released within _____ days; or

6. Consents to or suffers a charging order against his/her interest in the partnership that is not released or satisfied within _____ days.

From the date of that event, he/she shall be considered as a seller to the partnership of his/her share of the partnership's assets at a price equal to the credit balance of his capital account at that date [add any additional terms] _____. That amount shall be considered a debt owed by the partnership to that partner or his/her assignee or trustee, and all necessary deeds and other documents shall be executed for the vesting of the partner's share in the partnership.

If a partner is expelled under one of the above provisions, the partnership shall not be dissolved, but shall continue to function without interruption.

LAW NOTE: Provisions regarding expulsion of a partner are strictly construed by the courts. For example, courts are reluctant to expel a partner, or enter a decree of dissolution of a partnership based on the mental or bodily health of a partner. If it's important to you that all partners be healthy and you want them out if they're not, say so clearly and set up some sort of criteria under which a determination can be made. This same sort of definiteness should be the hallmark of any expulsion clause. Can a simple majority expel a partner? Do there have to be "grounds" justifying the expulsion or can a partner be expelled for reasons that appear to be sufficient to the other partners?

2. PARTNERSHIP CONTRACT NOTE

Expulsions are one area where you *don't* want to go to arbitration. You don't want to risk an arbitrator deciding you can't expel a partner, after you said you had. What a mess that would be! So, if you have an arbitration clause in your contract, it's wise to restrict it from applying applying to expulsions. A simple way to do that is to include the phrase "except as otherwise provided in this agreement..." in the arbitration clause, and then add the following to the expulsion clause:

Any decision of expulsion made by the partners pursuant to this section shall be final and shall not be subject to arbitration or other review.

Also, you might want further protection against an expelled partner—protection of your trade secrets, customers lists, etc. If you think you need to be this cautious, perhaps you should question the validity of your partnership itself. But if you decide to go ahead and do want these protections, simply adapt (or graft) the appropriate clause from section B(3) of this chapter onto your expulsion provision. You might also want to show this sort of agreement to a lawyer to be sure that it will accomplish your purpose.

E. Termination of a Partnership

Perhaps you've prospered and decide to sell out and retire to Tahiti, or Tashkent, or Timbuktu like you always dreamed. Or perhaps, contrary to all your hopes, your business just hasn't worked out. You're not making enough money and you're tired of it all and wish to move on and try something else. Or maybe one partner wants to leave and one wants to stay, terminating the partnership but carrying on the business. In all these situations, you face problems caused by termination of the partnership.

By "termination" of a partnership we mean that the business no longer functions as a partnership. The partnership books are closed, and the partners go their separate ways. The former partnership business may be continued in some other form by one of the former partners, or as is probably more common in cases of partnership termination, the business may end as well.

1. WINDING UP THE PARTNERSHIP

Many of the basic matters, such as the share of each partner in partnership assets that will be important in the final termination of a partnership will be covered in the original partnership agreement. But commonly there are matters involved in a termination that weren't foreseen when the partnership agreement was drafted. Here is some information you will find helpful.

Once the decision has been made to end the partnership, existing partnership business should be completed as speedily as possible. Legally, as we've mentioned earlier, the ending of a partnership business involves three states:

● First is the "dissolution" of the partnership—the decision to end it. No *new* partnership business can be undertaken after this time.

● Next is winding up of the existing partnership business. Partners in a "dissolved" partnership do retain the authority to do those things necessary to wind up the existing partnership business. Under the U.P.A. (Section 34), each partner is liable for his/her share of any liability created by partners in the course of winding up partnership business, just as if the partnership had not been dissolved.

● Finally, there is actual termination of the business. This means that the partnership is ended and no partnership business of any kind is legally authorized. If after your partnership is dissolved, you have any doubts at all about the honesty of any of your partners, play it safe. Just because you know that your partnership has been dissolved and your business wound up, doesn't mean your creditors know it. If a creditor, acting in good faith and without knowledge of the dissolution of a partnership, extends credit to a partner—for matters which the partner represents as being partnership business but which in reality have nothing to do with winding up the partnership business—all the partners may be liable for that bill. Likewise, if an unknowing good faith creditor extends credit to what he believes is the partnership, even after termination, you can be stuck for that bill. The U.P.A. (Section 35(b)) effectively requires that *actual delivery* of notice of dissolution be made to all individuals or businesses who have previously extended credit to the partnership to relieve partners of this potential liability. A simple written letter, as given in the example below, is sufficient notice:

To Whom It May Concern, and All Creditors of the _____Partnership:
This is to inform you that the _____partnership was dissolved by a decision of the partners on _____, and no new partnership business is authorized after that date.

Sincerely,

---

2. TERMINATION AGREEMENTS

Commonly when partnerships end—especially when they do so with the partners on reasonably good terms, and when partners have a good partnership agreement—things go easily as far as major matters such as the division of partnership assets. However, even in the best terminations, there are bound to be some things that weren't foreseen when the partnership agreement was drafted. For example, you might want to specify who gets what furniture, who is responsible for which bills, who gets specific assets, or customers, etc. In short, there are always some loose ends to tie up and some things that you didn't think to cover in your original agreement. To handle these you should prepare a separate termination agreement covering, in specific detail, all matters in the break-up of the partnership. Be precise here. This is your final partnership document, and it's safer to pin everything down. (You'll find a sample termination agreement in the Appendix.)

Some notes on termination that may prove helpful:

• The U.P.A. states, regarding contributions after dissolution (i.e., if the partnership is broke and can't pay its bills), that if at least one, but not all, of the partners is personally insolvent, the non-broke partner must contribute additional amounts sufficient to cover all liabilities in the proportion the partners shared in the partnership profits.

• Insurance policies. It's usual to permit the partners to purchase the existing insurance policies on their lives paid for by the partnership for a price equal to the policy's cash surrender value.

3. INTEREST

• Under the Uniform Partnership Act (Section 18), any (or all) of the initial cash contributions returned to partners (i.e., net assets after all bills have been paid) are *not* entitled to interest, except that interest will be paid "after the date when repayment should have been made." So, if you want interest to be paid on contributed capital when it's distributed, include or adapt the following clause:

Each partner shall be entitled to interest on his/her capital contribution at the rate of _____ percent per year from the date the contribution is paid. This interest shall be treated as an expense charged against income on the partnership books, but shall be paid to the partner entitled to it only upon dissolution and actual termination of the partnership.

4. DISSOLUTION OF A PARTNERSHIP BY COURT ACTION

Under the Uniform Partnership Act, the courts have the power to order a dissolution leading to termination of a partnership for any of the following reasons (Section 32 U.P.A.), no matter what the partnership contract provides:

- A partner has been declared a lunatic by any judicial proceedings;
- A partner is incapable of performing his part of the partnership agreement;
- A partner has been guilty of conduct that "prejudicially" affects the carrying on of the business;
- A partner willfully or persistently commits a breach of the partnership agreement (or is generally a bad egg, etc.);
- The business can only be carried on at a continuing loss;
- Any "other equitable reasons."

Here are examples of some of the types of behavior that the courts consider to be misconduct of a partner sufficient to dissolve a partnership:

- failure to contribute capital funds urgently required by the business;
- failure to account for proceeds of sales, etc.;
- appropriation of firm property for personal debts;
- constant quarrels, etc. (irreconcilable differences, intoxication, gambling, etc.)

A lawsuit about any of this will be disastrous (really—take our word for it). First of all, from the would-be remaining partner's point of view, these aren't easy matters to prove. The courts usually require a "strong case" for dissolving a partnership for misconduct of a partner. They greatly dislike dealing with what they feel are "trifling cause or temporary grievances." In any case, as we've urged before, lawsuits are just generally horrendous and in this situation should be unnecessary if you have provided for the expulsion of a partner.

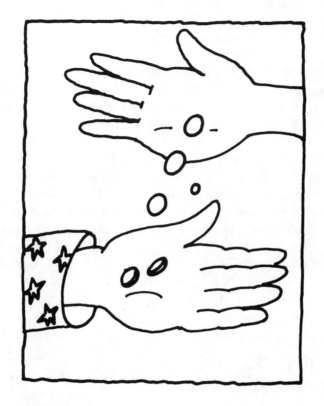

Chapter 6:

Partnership Taxation

A. Introduction

Let us say here at the beginning that neither of us has been trained as a tax specialist. We've had to develop a pretty good peasant knowledge of the subject to survive in business and law, but we've done so out of necessity, not love. Generally, we both have found tax law to be full of frustration, loaded with boring complexities, and liable to be expensive in the end. This is particularly true of partnership tax law, which at its more complicated levels is generally recognized as one of the most difficult areas of the Internal Revenue Code.[1] Nevertheless, understanding the basics of partnership taxation has been critically important to us and will be equally so to you. So please — don't give up; go forward and learn at least the rudiments of partnership taxation. Do it with cheer if you can, or with gritted teeth if you must, but do hang in there or that old I.R.S. bogeyman will get you sooner or later.

In putting this chapter together, we've made a lot of judgment calls as to how deeply we should go into different areas of partnership taxation. We've also had the problem of not being sure how much knowledge we should assume an average reader already has. In resolving the problem, we arrived at two controlling decisions. First, partnership taxation is so complex that we'll stick to the basics.[2] Second, since the focus of this book is on starting a partnership, we will likewise concentrate on the likely tax problems of a new business. In many complicated areas of partnership taxation, all we can safely do is to alert you to warning signals and advise you to see a tax expert.

B. Partnership Business and Personal Income Taxes

Before we review the various tax rules applicable to partnerships, let's ask a larger question. What is the tax reality of being in a business? Are there tax advantages you can receive by being in business, without regard to complex matters of partnership contributions or distributions? Our answer, in general, is a strong YES. The tax structure, as a whole, is sympathetic to business activity and money spent for business purposes. People unfamiliar with the realities of small business occasionally believe that they're passports to tax-free land. Not so. If your business is successful, you'll pay taxes. Still, you'll probably find you're a lot better off than if you remained a salaried employee.

---

1. Reuschlein & Gregory, *Agency & Partnership*, West Publishing Co., 1979. Here's one tax judge's lament about partnership taxation. "The distressingly complex and confusing nature of the provisions of [federal partnership tax laws] present a formidable obstacle to the comprehension of these provisions without the expenditure of a disproportionate amount of time and effort even by one who is sophisticated in tax matters with many years of experience in the tax field." *David A. Foxman*, 41 T.C. 535 (1964); Judge Rauml.

2. In Appendix C, we list treatises covering numerous sophisticated questions on partnership taxation in case you do face an unusual problem, and want to do some research on your own.

This isn't a book on how to beat the tax man, nor an explanation of business tax deductions. As you probably know, business expenses are generally deductible. However the 1986 Tax Reform Act significantly altered and restricted the deductibility of some types of business expenses. For example, that famous three martini-lunch may no longer be tax-subsidized. Meals may be deducted when they are directly related to the active conduct of the business and cannot be "lavish or extravagant." Even then, only 80% of the cost of the meal is deductible. Despite the 1986 Tax Act, the great majority of valid business deductions remain. One thing's for sure. If you're running a small business, it's foolish not to check out the tax laws and deduct every business expense you legitimately can.

• Business entertainment (Yes — that famous three-martini lunch is still deductible, as long as the meeting can be said to have involved, or furthered, your business);

• Automobile expenses (except travel to or from home);

• Classes taken to "improve skills" needed in your business (Thus, a commercial illustrator could deduct the cost of a drawing class, but a dentist couldn't).

One thing's for sure. If you're running a small business, it's foolish not to check out the tax laws, and deduct every business expense you legitimately can. While we do suggest you have a good tax advisor, you might also decide to do research on this yourself. Ask around, and see what other business people do. Also, there are several good books out on business taxation. We refer you to some in the Appendix in case you want to study the subject.

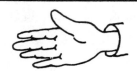

C. Using Tax Experts

Let us emphasize one point before we get down to specifics. Unless your business is very simple, you should work out an arrangement with a knowledgeable tax person (see chapter 2 for a plan to handle this at reasonable cost) to give you the periodic help you will need. In many — if not most — partnerships, this should be done even before the partnership is organized. An uncomplicated partnership might well not need a tax expert's services. For instance, a service business with very little in the way of inventory costs, and where all the partners contributed the same amount of start-up cash, probably won't need expert help at the start. But change a few facts — such as some partners contributing property that's appreciated in price since they bought it, or the necessity for even a modest inventory — and you quickly find yourself in the situation of most partnership businesses, where expert advice will be helpful.

We know this recommendation to use a knowledgeable accountant/ tax expert is somewhat at variance from our usual position, that you can handle most partnership legal and organizational matters yourself. Unfortunately, the tax code is so complicated, especially for partnerships, that unless you want to make understanding it your hobby, you'll be better off allocating money for expert help. This should not be enormously expensive, since many small business partnerships simply don't have tax problems that will cost a great deal in tax accountant fees. Also, remember that you are becoming involved with a tax system that rewards people in business with all sorts of perfectly legal loopholes. Taxation is a great American game. The richer you get, the more plays there are in the game; thus, many millionaires have paid (at least in some years) no income tax at all.[3] We'll see if the 1986 Tax Act changes matters.[4] We do want to remind you that by opening your business, you move from the ranks of the salaried and rigidly taxed to the land of free enterprise and business tax deductions. That's one more reason to hire a tax person. Any tax expert worthy of the name should be able to make suggestions that will save you far more in taxes than you pay in fees.

Just because you are going to get some expert tax help doesn't mean that you shouldn't take the time to understand the basics of the tax laws applicable to your business. If you're going to run a successful business, you will have to develop at least a good generalist's view of how the I.R.S. intrudes on your business. We alert you to the main problem areas in this chapter, and we provide a list of further sources of information in the Appendix.

There are four distinct areas where tax laws may intrude on your partnership:
- Contributions made by partners when starting the business;
- Taxation of partnership operations and partners' income;
- Distribution of partnership profits;
- Transfer of partnership interests.

For any new business, the start-up contribution is most immediately important. Once you have your business going, it will be time to worry about areas No. 2 and No. 3. (We hope you won't have to worry about No. 4 for a long time.)

D. Definitions

Before we go further, let's define a few basic concepts. As your business grows, you'll find these terms to be quite useful. While a lot of this may sound like gobbledygook, it's important gobbledygook, so hang in there:

- *Active Income:* In practical terms, this is income received as the result of your own efforts. Active income and losses are, for federal tax purposes, taxed separately (and often less favorably) than passive income and losses. A partner's income is active if he or she materially participates in partnership business, which means regular, continuous and substantial involvement in partnership business operations.

It is generally desirable to have partnership income treated as active income. Why? Because if it is and the partnership suffers a loss, the loss can be used to offset income earned from other active sources, such as other employment. By comparison, losses that result from passive investments cannot be offset against income actively earned. For most readers of this book who are involved in the day-to-day operations of their

---

3. Michael Harrington some years ago defined the American economic system as one of "socialism for the rich and free enterprise for the poor."

4. Personally, we won't believe it until we do see it.

businesses, there is absolutely no need to worry about these rules. They are active in their businesses, sometimes too active, and should their partnership suffer a loss, there is no question but what it is an active loss.

●*Passive Income:* Income received from businesses in which you do not materially participate. A loss in passive income cannot be used to offset active income.

EXAMPLE: Mr. Smartbuy has invested in a movie deal but has no active involvement in the business, i.e., he is an "investor." He loses $50,000 on the deal. He cannot deduct this $50,000 from his income earned as a corporate lawyer.

●*Rental Real Estate:* Real estate partnerships are an area where income is generally treated as passive income. However, there's a special exception for individual owners, allowing them to offset up to $25,000 of losses from passive real estate income against active income if the owner "actively participates" in the real estate business. "Active participation" is a lesser standard than is "materially participate," which we discuss above. To actively participate, an owner must be involved in management decisions, such as approving new tenants, repairs, capital expenditures, deciding upon rental terms.

● *Basis:* In order to determine your profit on the sale of an asset, you have to know what you paid for it. "Basis" is a tax term that means, essentially, the purchase price.

● *Net Adjusted Basis:* Often your profit on a sale cannot simply be determined by deducting your original purchase price from the sale price. Other factors are involved, such as depreciation, other tax credits, or other costs, like subsequent improvements or additions. "Net adjusted basis" means the figure you or your accountant use as your overall cost for the item at any time you sell it.

● *Depreciation:* Some types of property wear out gradually. A typewriter may last ten years, a building thirty, a car fifteen. Eventually, when the item is completely worn out, it is worthless. Depreciation is a system that the I.R.S. and state tax authorities allow for allocating the loss caused by the decrease in value of your property over a certain time and deducting the amount from your income for tax purposes.[5] A simple example: A car sells for $10,000. Al, who uses his car in his business, depreciates it, for tax purposes, at the rate of $3,333 a year (that is, he depreciated it the same amount each year). In three years, the total cost of the car has been depreciated.

● *Accelerated Depreciation:* Depreciation for tax purposes is a tricky game, or can be. Lots of money can be saved by using the most advantageous method of depreciation. "Accelerated depreciation" means deducting more from your taxes now, and less later. There are various methods of calculating accelerated depreciation.

● *Capital Account:* A partner's "capital account" is, essentially, the dollar amount of net/ownership interest (or equity) the partner has in the business. For example, Merv and Hayden start a 50/50 real estate partnership to purchase rental property. Each contributes $20,000 cash. Thus, at the start of the business each partner's capital account is $20,000. Now suppose the business runs at a net loss of $10,000 for the first year? Each partner's capital account will now be $15,000.

● *Depreciation Recapture:* Suppose a building where accelerated depreciation has been taken for three years is sold? Clearly, it isn't fair that the seller get a better tax break than someone who used straight-line depreciation (that is, depreciated at the same amount each year). Accelerated depreciation assumes you retain the asset for the full term it's depreciated. If you sell it earlier, there are complicated tax provisions "recapturing" (i.e., retroactively disallowing) some of that accelerated depreciation.

E. Tax Consequences of Contributions of Property to a Partnership

The tax area that is probably of most concern to new partners involves contributions made when getting the business started. If all the partners contribute cash, there aren't any tax consequences to worry about. No gain or loss occurs when money is transferred from a partner to the partnership. Similarly, there's no taxable gain or loss if a partner withdraws some or all of the money he has contributed to the partnership.[6] But if one partner contributes property, the tax consequences of these transactions can become complicated. Likewise, there are complexities, although different ones, if a partner receives his or her partnership interest in exchange for a pledge of services (discussed in section F).

---

5. Another way to look at depreciation is that it's a system whereby the I.R.S. requires you to spread out (or deduct) the cost of a "capital" asset over so many years, regardless of whether or when the asset actually wears out.

6. Note that a withdrawal of contributed capital is most definitely not the same as a partner's distributive share of partnership profits, which is taxable income to the partner who receives it.

1. CONTRIBUTIONS OF PROPERTY

Suppose Harry contributes a building he owns to a new partnership in exchange for a one-half partnership share valued at $70,000, and Jennifer, the other partner, contributes $70,000 in cash? If Harry just bought the building for $70,000 there won't be any tax consequences, because the general rule is that contributions of property which have not gone up in value since the partner bought it have no tax consequences.

But suppose now that Harry bought the building years ago for $20,000.[7] As the building's market value is now $70,000, his partnership interest will reflect this market value. Does this mean that Harry has now realized a gain for tax purposes of $50,000? The answer is NO! The tax code provides that when a partner contributes property to a partnership that is worth more than he paid for it, no gain or loss is recognized.[8]

This sounds fine so far, but as you might expect, the tax consequences don't always stay so simple. For example, what are the tax consequences of this transaction to the partnership? What tax basis does the building have as far as the partnership is concerned? Since no taxable gain or loss is recognized on the transfer from Harry to the partnership, it follows that the tax basis of the building to the partnership must be the same amount as Harry's basis for it, i.e., $20,000. Now, let's suppose that the partnership decides to sell the building for its market value, $70,000. As far as the tax man goes, the partners have realized a taxable gain of $50,000. However, for purposes of partnership bookkeeping, there's been no gain or loss because a $70,000 asset has been traded for a like amount of cash.

Now you should begin to see the problem. The taxable gain (i.e., the increase of $50,000 in value from $20,000 to $70,000) is divided equally between the two partners under normal partnership-income distribution rules. This means that Jennifer will have to pay tax on a gain of $25,000 (i.e., one-half of the $50,000 gain) although in fact she hasn't received income (remember the property was valued at $70,000 for partnership purposes). Theoretically (we won't bore you with the calculations), the extra tax burden Jennifer gets stuck with will be equalized when the partnership is eventually terminated, but this may be years away.

Before we deal with how to solve this sort of potentially unfair situation, let's look at another common problem area. This is the similar sort of inequity that can result regarding depreciation attributed to contributed property that has increased in value since the partner bought it.

---

7. The tax basis of a building, to the owner, is normally his acquisition cost, less any depreciation taken. Here we're assuming, for the sake of simplicity, that the original cost alone remained Harry's basis.

8. I.R.C. Section 721. This also applies to a contribution of goods to be given to the contributor over time, called "installment receivables," although normally a gain is recognized when installment receivables are disposed of. [Treasury Regulation 1.453-9(c)(2).]

EXAMPLE: Marty and Fred become 50/50 partners in a donut shop. Marty contributes some donut making machinery with an agreed market value of $20,000. Marty's basis for the machinery was $8,000. Fred contributes $20,000 cash. Now, for the purposes of this example only, let's assume the partnership will depreciate the machinery at the rate of 10 percent a year straight line, for ten years, i.e., depreciation will be (for partnership purposes) $2,000 per year. However, for tax purposes, the machinery is depreciated at 10% from the "basis" of $8,000, i.e., $800 a year. Now assume the partnership's net profits, before depreciation, in the first year are $10,000. What are the consequences to each partner? Here's a chart comparing the tax consequences to the figures in the partnership books.[9]

Partnership Books		*Taxable Income*
Profits	$10,000	$10,000
Less depreciation	2,000	800
Net income	8,000	9,200
Each partner's share	4,000	4,600

The result is that Fred, for tax purposes, has an extra $600 in taxable income, compared to what the partnership books show he earned, because of the low basis of the depreciated machinery.

In inflationary times, it's common that property contributed to a partnership has increased in value since its date of acquisition. Unfortunately, the tax problems this can cause partnerships are often far more complex than the simplified examples we've given. Our point here is simply that in these situations, the partner(s) who don't contribute appreciated property will often suffer a tax detriment either if the property is sold, or when it comes to depreciation calculations. Therefore, you may well want to cover this problem in your partnership agreement.

NOTE: The I.R.S. will issue advance rulings on whether any gain or loss will be recognized on the transfer of contributed property to the partnership. This takes time and paper work, of course, but can be valuable if you (and your tax expert) don't know if it is a taxable transfer or not.

The tax laws do permit the partnership — if the partnership agreement so provides — to allocate to one partner the depreciation, and gain or loss, regarding contributed property; this is in order to take account of any variation between the "basis" of that property to the partnership, and its fair market value at the time of contribution.[10] You are not required to adopt the same approach for all contributed property; you can adapt your agreement to each specific item of contributed property, if you want to. There are several ways you can solve this type of problem. Here are the most common:

1. You could adopt a clause in your partnership agreement which shifts the tax, or depreciation, consequences resulting from contributed property solely to the

---

9. In reality, small partnerships won't really keep two sets of books. If you face this type of problem, do see a tax expert.

10. I.R.C Section 704(c)(2). There's a complex regulation governing the limit of the total loss, gain, or depreciation allowed here. Treasury Regulation 1.704-1-(c)(2)(i). If you're in this area, it is advisable to check with a tax expert.

contributing partner. Usually, the precise dollar amounts of these tax consequences cannot be foreseen in advance. For example, who can predict exactly what a particular piece of property will sell for, if it's sold? Thus, it's best to put in the partnership agreement a general statement that the tax consequences will be borne by the contributing partner and leave the actual calculations to be made, probably with your accountant's assistance, when the need arises. Here's an example of this type of clause:

> *Exhibit* _____ *to this agreement sets forth several items of property contributed to the partnership, the federal income tax basis of each item for the partner(s) who contributed them, and the agreed-upon market value of those items as of the date of contribution. For the purpose of computing each partner's share of the partnership's federal [and state] taxable income, the depreciation expenses as to these listed item(s), and any gain or loss on disposition of these item(s), shall be allocated among the partners so that the tax treatment of the partners who did not contribute that item will, as far as possible, be the same as would have been the case if the partner who contributed that listed item had instead contributed cash equal to the agreed-upon market value of that item.*

2. You could simply estimate (again, most likely with an accountant's help) the present dollar value or the tax detriment suffered by the non-contributing partner, and discount the agreed-upon market value of the contributed property by that amount.

EXAMPLE: In the Harry-Jennifer partnership discussed earlier, we saw that Jennifer has a potential tax liability for a $25,000 gain if the building Harry contributed is immediately sold. Jennifer and Harry see an accountant who computes that Jennifer's actual tax liability would be (say) $6,000. Accordingly, the partnership decides to value the contribution of the building at $5,000 *below* its market value (the tax basis, of course, remains unchanged — Harry's acquisition cost). This means that Harry must now contribute $6,000 in cash, or $6,000 worth of non-appreciated property, if he and Jennifer want to make equal contributions to the partnership.

3. Another solution would be for Harry to contribute $70,000 cash. The Harry-Jennifer partnership would then buy the building for its $70,000 market price. This would result in its tax basis to the partnership being the same as its market value and would mean that Harry (not the partnership) would have to pay tax on the $50,000 gain.[11]

In most situations, the first method of resolving this problem is the wisest. This is because nothing need be done until a problem of depreciation or sale actually arises. When that occurs, you'll have the precise dollar figures necessary so that you and your accountant can calculate exactly how much money is involved, and how it can be distributed fairly among the partners. However, if you do face this type of problem, we suggest you see a tax expert *before* drafting the final version of your partnership agreement, in order to gain at least a rough estimate of what the tax consequences are likely to be.

---

11. Harry might see a tax expert to discuss the best way to handle their income.

2. COMPLEX TAX PROBLEMS INVOLVING CONTRIBUTIONS

We've just begun to cover the tax problems that can arise regarding contributed property. You should know that there are potentially many more complex problems. We don't go into these in depth because we doubt if many people establishing new partnerships will face them. Nevertheless, it makes sense to highlight several areas that may affect you.

Mortgaged Property

What happens if a partner contributes property that's subject to a liability — for instance, a mortgage on real property? Assume the building Harry contributed to the Harry-Jennifer partnership had a $10,000 mortgage outstanding on it (so the net worth or equity of Harry's contribution was $60,000, not $70,000). Since the partnership now owns the building, for tax purposes the mortgage (or any liability on contributed property) is regarded as having been assumed by the partnership, and the contributing partner (Harry) is regarded as having received a cash distribution equal to the percentage of his liability assumed by the other partners. In this situation, since Jennifer has a 50% share in the partnership and the partnership has assumed the liability for the $10,000 mortgage, Harry will be held to have received $5,000 present income.

Here's another example that shows how severe this tax problem can become. Suppose Jennifer contributes her mint condition, lemon-yellow, 1970 Jaguar XKE to the partnership. She bought it for $2,000 (call that her basis). It's now worth $10,000. She has used the car as security for a $9,000 loan. Under the treasury regulations, Jennifer is treated as having received a cash distribution of $4,500, i.e., the one-half of the $9,000 liability assumed by her partner. Since the basis of the car to Jennifer was $2,000, the tax authorities state that she has a net taxable gain on the transaction of $2,500.

What all this means is — watch out if you're contributing property that is subject to a liability. It's only a paper transaction, but you could still get stuck with a hefty tax bill. Play it safe and see a tax expert.

Recapture of Past Taxes

Problems can also arise regarding certain tax breaks previously given to owners or property contributed to a partnership. One question is whether the government will recapture the deducted cost of these tax breaks. The answer is — generally no, but if you're at all in doubt check with your tax expert. For instance, there is no depreciation recapture for property contributed to a partnership,[13] except for contributions of certain farming equipment.[14] Will there be a recapture of any investment credit upon contribution of property to the partnership? In most cases, the answer is no, because tax laws provide that there is no recapture of the investment credit "by reason of mere change in the form of conducting the trade of business,"[15] so long as (1) substantially all the assets will be retained in the business, and (2) the contributing person retains a "substantial interest" in the business.

F. Tax Consequences of Contributions of Service to a Partnership

Okay, so much for property. Now let's look at the tax consequences if a person receives an interest in a partnership in return for the contribution of services. Under the tax laws, services are not regarded as property. So, if the contributing partner receives a capital (equity) interest in the partnerhsip in exchange for (the promise of his/her) services, he/she has received taxable income.

EXAMPLE: Alicia, Rose, and Ruby form a partnership to operate a hair-cutting business. Alicia and Ruby each contribute $7,500 for start-up capital and plan to work part-time in the business. Rose has no cash to contribute, but she receives a one-third interest in the partnership in exchange for promising to work full-time for a year. As far as the tax laws are concerned, Rose's partnership interest is worth $5,000 to her, one-third of the total capital of the partnership. This means that she has received taxable income of $5,000.[16]

Now, suppose the partnership agreement does not give Rose a present ownership (or capital) interest in the partnership, but just the right to receive one-third of the future profits in return for her services. Unfortunately, in this situation Rose's tax liability isn't clear. Until recently, tax experts believed there were no tax consequences where only future profits were involved. However, in the one case *(Sol Diamond)*[17] that involved receipt of future profits in a partnership in exchange for the promise of future services, the tax court held that this amounted to a cash distribution, and the *present* value of this right to receive future profits was taxable income to the services-contributing partner.

Many tax practitioners believe that the *Sol Diamond* case is an aberration — or explainable by, and limited to — its peculiar facts. Among these is the fact that it was admitted that the dollar worth of the present value of the right to receive future profits was readily calculable, and in fact, had actually been determined by a sale of that right.

---

13. I.R.C. Section 1245(b)(3), Section 1250(d)(3)

14. I.R.C. Section 1251(d)(5)(B)

15. I.R.C. Section 47(b)

16. If the interest the contributing partner receives is subject to "a substantial risk of forfeiture" there is no taxable gain. This is an unusual occurrence. A "substantial risk of forfeiture" means that the partnership interest received is in property that is subject to a lien or otherwise subject to foreclosure by creditors.

17. *Sol Diamond*, 56 T.C. 530(1971), att'd 492 F.2d 286 (7th Cir. 1974)

Indeed, it's arguable that this case involved an attempted tax scam of disguising a present cash interest by calling it "the right to receive future profits."

Returning to our example of Alicia, Rose, and Ruby, it's quite possible that Rose will have no tax liability if all she receives is a right to share in future profits. After all, who can tell if there will be any profits? However, if the partnership had existed for a while when Rose was invited to join in exchange for her promise to work full-time, and the partnership has been profitable, Rose would have incurred a tax liability. Why? Because the track record of business profitability establishes a basis for assigning a present value to Rose's present right to receive future income.

In more involved service contribution situations, the tax rules can become extremely complicated. If your partnership will involve this kind of problem, we urge you to see a tax expert. Here are some examples of complicated situations:

● *Appreciated partnership property:* In exchange for services to be rendered, a partner receives an interest in partnership property that has appreciated in value since being acquired by the partnership.

● *Restrictions on Transfers of a Partnership Interest:* There are also special tax rules governing transfers of a partnership interest for promised services which are subject to certain types of restriction. An example of one such restriction that could cause tax problems is a restriction on the time when a service partner can withdraw from the partnership or sell his or her interest in it.

G. Some Other Points Regarding Taxation of Partnerships

● If a contributing partner receives cash or property (called a "boot" in taxland), in addition to a partnership interest, taxable gain will be recognized on the cash value of the boot.

EXAMPLE: Patti, Norman, and Tiiu form a construction partnership. All are to be equal partners. Patti contributes machinery with a market value of $17,000. Norman and Tiiu each contribute $15,000 in cash. To equalize the contributions, the partnership pays Patti $2,000 in addition to the one-third ownership interest she receives. This $2,000 is taxable income to Patti.[18]

● Property must *actually* be contributed to the partnership for the non-recognition of gain or profit rules discussed in section D of this chapter to apply, For example, if property is pledged only for a partnership's limited use — such as security on a loan — but is not owned by the partnership, this does not constitute a non-taxable transfer to the partnership.

● If you give someone an interest in a partnership, the gift tax laws apply to the transaction. There are substantial federal regulations regarding transfers of partnership interests, both to prevent disguised gifts and to prevent the lowering of an individual partner's income by spreading it among several other "alleged partners." For example, merely stating that a partnership interest is transferred in exchange for future services does not automatically mean the transaction is effective for tax purposes. The key is who

---

18. It will normally be "active" income.

actually retains control of the partnership interest which has supposedly been transferred. Thus, under the federal tax laws, the fact that you've executed a legally valid document transferring part ownership to your new partner is only one factor to be taken into account in determining if a bona fide transfer has been accomplished. **Particular scrutiny is given to family partnerships**. Transfers between members of a family are examined not only at the time of the (purported) transfer, but also during times preceding and following it. The questions asked are designed to establish whether the transaction is a true "arms-length" business deal (allowable) or a scheme whose principal purpose is to lower tax liability (forbidden).

If gift tax laws are complied with, gifts of a partnership are normally valid *if* ownership of the business (i.e., the business' capital) itself is a significant income factor. For example, a gift of a partnership interest in an apartment house would, normally, be tax legitimate, because the income the business receives is due largely to its capital asset — i.e., rent from the building which you have partially given away. However, a gift (say to your spouse or lover), of a partnership interest in a service business such as a dental practice or a termite inspection business, would most likely *not* be acceptable, since capital assets are not a significant income-producing factor of this kind of business. In this situation nothing is really given to the family member except the right to receive income from someone else's labor.

There are also numerous special tax rules which govern partner-partnership transactions. Again, the I.R.S. is looking for sham "tax lowering" strategies that have no legitimate business purpose. Watch out for:

● Any transaction where the partner involved owns more than 50% of a partnership and can call all the shots;

● Transactions involving family partnerships because of the I.R.S. rules regarding "constructive" ownership in a partnership.

If you find yourself in either of these situations, see a tax expert.

H. Payment of Taxes

1. The Partnership Tax Return

As we've discussed several times in earlier chapters, a partnership is not itself subject to income tax. Income and profits generated by a partnership business "flow through" the partnership and are taxed to the individual partners. Nevertheless, a partnership *must* file an "informational" federal tax return. I.R.S. Form #1065 (see chapter 2 for a review of tax forms). This return lists the computed partnership income, expenses and other financial items, many of which must be separately identified. Thus, the government has a way of learning all the basic economic facts about your partnership, in addition to the net income reported on each partner's individual return. The Internal Revenue Service publishes aids to completing partnership returns, including Form #1065 instructions, Publication #541, "Tax Information on Partnership," and Publication #334 "Tax Guide for Small Business."[19]

---

19. Available free at any I.R.S. office.

The yearly Federal I.R.S. partnership return must be filed by the 15th day of the fourth month following the close of the partnership tax year. In most cases, this will mean the partnership-tax return has to be filed by April 15. Why? Because an I.R.S. rule requires that the tax year of a partnership be the same as the tax year of principal partners (anyone with over a 5% ownership of the partnership), unless there's a valid business purpose for the partnership to adopt a different tax year. It's rare that such a valid business purpose will exist. As you might guess, trying to defer payment of taxes is most defiinitely not an acceptable reason.

Most states also require an "informational" partnership return be filed. Like the federal government, the states do not tax partnership income per se. In addition, the federal government, and most states, require partners, as self-employed persons, to file quarterly estimates of their income, with the appropriate tax payments (see chapter 2).

2. SOME RULES REGARDING THE PARTNER'S INDIVIDUAL TAX RETURN

Obviously we haven't space to provide a thorough explanation of the many intricacies that can be involved in a partner's tax return. Nevertheless, there are some basic points you will want to be aware of from the start:

• An individual partner's return must report a partner's distributive share of the taxable income or loss of the partnership. This includes certain items of income as well as deductions which must be placed into separate classifications for tax purposes. [20]

• A partner's distributive share of partnership profits is not limited to money actually received by him/her. By distributive share, the I.R.S. means all monies a partner was entitled to receive as profits income, whether he/she actually received them or not. It doesn't make any difference whether profits are actually divided, or left in a partnership bank account; either way they must be reported as part of a partner's distributive share. This means that the partnership business can't retain substantial earnings for the future expansion of the business and thereby avoid taxation to the individual partners. [21] If, for example, your partnership books show $50,000 in income as "retained earnings for business expansion," the I.R.S. will simply claim this sum is disguised profits that must be included in the distributive shares" of partners. [22] Indeed, the rules on distributive shares are so strict, a partner will be taxed on his/her distributive share even though a dispute among the partners prevents any actual distribution of partnership profits.

• A partner's distributive share of partnership profits is determined by the partnership agreement. If the agreement makes no specific mention of the manner of sharing particular income, gains, losses, depreciation, or credits to be allocated, a partner's

---

20. I.R.C. Sections 702(a), 703

21. As we discuss in chapter 1, section c, corporations do have the opportunity to retain earnings for future expansion in the corporation. Income taxes must be paid but the corporate tax rates may be lower than those for individuals. In addition, money left in a corporation will often be taxed in a lower bracket than if it is added to the income of the business owner, which may already be fairly considerable. There are some restrictions as to how much income a corporation can retain, but the point is that some very profitable partnerships will find that there are tax reasons why forming a corporation makes sense.

22. What partners often hope for is to retain earnings and then, somehow, transfer them to their capital accounts, so this income will be taxed as capital gain. This ruse is not legal.

distributive share is determined by the I.R.S. in accordance with the provisions of the partnership agreement for division of general profits or losses. For example, in our discussion — earlier in this chapter — of Harry and Jennifer, and Harry's contribution of appreciated property, we saw that the partners could adopt a clause varying the usual split of partnership profits as far as sale or depreciation expense of that property goes. However, if Harry and Jennifer had adopted no such clause, the basic partnership rules governing splitting of the profits (in this case 50-50) would apply to the sale or depreciation of that item.

• The I.R.S. will disregard special provisions as to distributive shares of partnership profits if it determines that the provision lacks "substantive economic effect," i.e., has been adopted as a tax dodge. In that case, the I.R.S. allocates distributive shares according to the partners' ownership interest in the partnership.

• There are special income tax rules governing allocations of partnership income to individual partners to or with whom one partner sells or exchanges his partnership interest,[23] or where there's a shift of the percentage of ownership interest (or sharing of profits and losses) during the year. If this happens to you, you'll certainly need tax assistance.

• Each partner also takes his or her share of any loss into account each year. It may become part of his/her "carry-back" or "carry-forward" for tax purposes.[24]

• Each partner must pay his or her own individual social security separately as part of his/her tax return.

• If a partner has a "subpartnership" contract, sharing his or her partnership profits with someone not a member of the partnership, the partner is still required to report, as his/her income, the entire amount of the profits he/she was entitled to receive from the partnership, with a subsequent deduction for the share allocated to the subpartner.

• As we've mentioned several times, the 1986 Tax Act provides different tax treatment for "active" and "passive" income. This is a legal distinction, sure to be subject to much scrutiny and "creative" tax planning. If you've any doubts or questions concerning these types of income, see a tax expert. In particular, if you're looking for tax shelters, be wary.

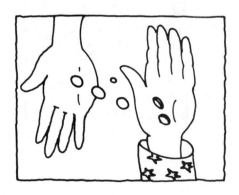

---

23. I.R.C. Section 706(c)
24. I.R.C. Section 172

3. THE PARTNERSHIP AS A SEPARATE TAX ENTITY

We have now established that a partnership is basically a conduit allowing income to pass through to the individual partners for income tax purposes. However, as is so common in the tax field, no sooner do we learn something than we have to deal with qualifications, exceptions, and "but ifs." Or, to be more specific, for certain purposes, a partnership is not treated as a conduit, but is viewed as a distinct entity by the I.R.S. For example:

● For computation of partnership income — profits and losses — a partnership is regarded as a unified enterprise.

● Certain tax elections, such as the choice of the method of accounting, or depreciation, must be made by the partnership as an entity.[25] For instance, there are several different methods of depreciation, such as straight-line depreciation, declining-balance depreciation, the sum-of-the-years-digit depreciation, etc., which can produce very different tax results. The partnership must elect one, and only one, method of depreciation. The different partners can't elect to use different depreciation methods regarding their interest in depreciable property.[26]

● No tax deductions are allowed to a partnership or to any partner for amounts paid anyone to organize the partnership or to sell an interest in the partnership. However, the partnership's other "organizational expenses" may be amortized over a 60-month period.

● In the unusual instance where a partner has a different tax year than the actual partnership, the time for inclusion of an item or distributive share of income or loss in a partner's tax return, will depend on the tax year of the partnership itself.[27]

---

25. I.R.C. Section 703(b)

26. Any partnership that will own valuable real or personal property will have to deal with depreciation. If you aren't familiar with this concept, see Kamoroff *Small Time Operator* which is discussed in the Appendix.

27. I.R.C. Section 706(a)

I. Taxation and the Disposition of a Partnership Interest

The sale of a partnership interest, or the retirement/death of a partner, often has tax consequences that make advance tax planning almost essential. We've discussed some of these consequences in chapter 5. Here we give you a summary of some basic tax points regarding disposition of a partnership interest. Since we imagine most of our readers are starting a business, not selling one, we don't go into great detail.

1. SALE OF A PARTNERSHIP INTEREST

Here are some of the types of tax problems that may arise from the sale of a partnership interest. Some examples:

• The (partnership) tax year for the selling partner (only) closes on the date of the sale. The selling partner's interest in net partnership income for the entire year must be determined on a pro-rata basis for the shorter period (the selling partner's year). The I.R.S. permits the use of "reasonable" estimates by the partners to determine that income. For example, suppose John sells his one-third interest in the Alice-John-Joan partnership on March 1. The partnership is on a January 1 to January 1 fiscal year, and profits are determined quarterly. Under the I.R.S. rules, John's tax year for his partnership interest closes on the date of Sale — March 1. But what is his portion of partnership profits for the two months he was a partner that year? Since they haven't yet been calculated, the partners can make a "reasonable" estimate of the profits John is entitled to.

• The sale or exchange of any partnership interest of 50 percent or more of the total worth of a partnership poses special tax problems, and a tax expert should be consulted. In a two-person, 50/50 partnership, sale by either partner obviously terminates the partnership. However, if one partner essentially buys out the other, the partnership can, if the remaining partner so desires, be regarded as continuing, for tax purposes only. Thus, when payments are made to a retiring partner of a 50/50 partnership, that partner will be regarded as remaining in the partnership until his or her entire interest is liquidated,[28] even though state law specifically provides that the partnership has been

---

28. I.R.C. Section 736

terminated. Otherwise, the partner continuing the business would also be liable for payment of income taxes on his/her interest in the business when the other partner retired — an unfair burden to impose on one who wants to continue an existing business, not cash it out.

● If a partnership interest is transferred (either by sale or because of death or retirement), no adjustment may generally be made by the partnership to the tax basis of the incoming partner's (pro-rata) interest in the partnership property.

EXAMPLE: Suppose John paid $20,000 for a one-third interest in a three-person flower business. One of the main assets of the partnership business is the flower stand, from which the flowers are sold. It has a market value of $30,000, one-half the total worth of the partnership. However, when the original partnership bought the flower stand, it paid only $3,000 for it, and this $3,000 remains its partnership basis. Since no adjustment to this basis of $3,000 is permitted for the new partner, John's tax basis for that stand is one-third of $3,000 or $1,000. This means that if the stand is sold for $30,000, John, who gets one-third of that, or $10,000, has made a profit, for tax purposes, of $9,000. Yet in reality, all John would have done is recoup the $10,000 he paid for his interest in the flower stand.

Obviously, these tax rules can lead to inequitable tax results for incoming partners, such as John, where partnership property has appreciated well over its basis to the partnership. To mitigate this potential unfairness, the tax code permits a partnership to elect to make adjustments to the tax basis of certain assets.[29] These adjustments cover the difference between the new partner's basis of his/her partnership interest, and the partnership's tax basis of his/her proportionate share of all partnership assets. This is called a "Section 754" election. In other words, certain assets can have one tax basis for the partnership itself (and thus the original partners) and a different tax basis for an incoming partner, which reflects his/her actual purchase price.

So, to be equitable, any buyer of an interest in an existing partnership where the value of property has appreciated will want the partnership to make the Section 754 election, and to adjust the basis of his/her share of any appreciated partnership property. There are, of course, some specific requirements and controls imposed regarding this election. These include:

● It must be made in a statement filed with the partnership tax return for the taxable year in which the transfer or distribution occurs;

● The election must cover both transfers and distributions;

● Once made, the election remains in effect for subsequent years. It can only be revoked with the approval of the I.R.S. District Director.

---

29. I.R.C. Section 754

2. RETIREMENT OR DEATH OF A PARTNER(S)

Much of what we discussed in section 1 just above also applies to the tax consequences regarding the death or retirement of a partner. Here are some additional points:

● Any income payments to a retiring partner, which are income to him/her, are deductible business expenses by the partnership.

● However, payments made in exchange for a partner's partnership interest are considered a distribution of partnership profits and therefore are not deductible.

● The valuation placed on a retiring partner's interest in an "arm's length," or bona fide, transaction, will normally be accepted by the I.R.S.

● If a partnership business is to be terminated completely, with all assets sold, and the enterprise liquidated, complex tax rules are involved. Before you take steps to liquidate your business, conduct a careful review with your tax advisor.

J. Tax Aspects of Joint Ventures

As we said in chapter 1, a joint venture is basically a partnership formed for a specific purpose, and operating for a limited duration. Tax treatment of joint ventures is the same as for any other partnership, with a few exceptions. Like other partnerships, joint ventures are not taxed themselves, but are regarded as a conduit through which the participants in the joint venture derive income and deductions. However, like partnerships, the Internal Revenue Code imposes certain obligations on the joint venture itself.

● *Tax Returns:* A joint venture must normally file an "informational" tax return (§ 6031, I.R.C.), except that certain real estate-joint ventures do not have to file informational returns.

● *Elections:* With rare exception, tax elections —such as methods of depreciation, etc. — affecting the computation of a joint venture's taxable income must be made by the venture itself.

● *Taxable Year:* A joint venture adopts its own taxable year, but it may not adopt a taxable year different from that of any principal partner[30] without the consent of the I.R.S.

● *Self-dealing:* Generally, transactions between the joint venture itself, and one member of the joint venture, are treated as if they occurred between the joint venture and an outsider, one *not* involved in the venture (§ 707(a) I.R.C.).

● At the election of *all* it's members, a joint venture can be excluded from all or part of the partnership taxation provision of the Internal Revenue Code (called subchapter K of the Revenue Code) if the joint venture is basically a passive investment, not an active business (see the discussion on §761(a) Tax Code, section G of this chapter).

● *Allocation of Profits:* Income and deductions may be allocated as the joint venturers decide. These decisions can be changed and modified at any time before the due date of the federal informational return for the taxable year.

---

30. One with more than 5% interest in capital or profits.

The Story of the Chocolate Moose

INTERLUDE V

Let's push the fast forward button and let our little movie about Sara and John speed up until two years have past. The two friends are having breakfast in the cooking area of their quite prosperous Chocolate Moose.

"Pass the waffles and a little more of that sour cream please, Sara," John asked, looking tanned, thin, and more than a little pleased with himself.

"You look like a cat who's swallowed a saucer of cream," Sara replied, laughing. "And if you want my opinion, anyone who's both skinny and has cream on his moustache is close to insufferable."

"Well, the vacation in France was nice, even if it was only for two months and not the rest of my life," John replied. "Ah, you should taste those eclairs, crepe suzettes, and especially the profiterolles—ooh, la la!"

"Well, it's my turn now," Sara said. "Doug and I finally decided. We're going to Peru and Guatemala for six weeks. By the time I get back from walking to Machu Picchu, I'll have my seventeen-year old figure back. Of course, I was a little plump when I was seventeen! Anyway, while I'm gone, it's your turn to work your fingers to the bone and see that our moose brings in a lot of cabbage."

"You know, I think I'll actually enjoy being back, at least for a few weeks," John said. "Hey, did you make any progress on our master plan while I was away?" For some time before John left on his vacation they had been discussing and evaluating the possibility of opening a full-scale dessert and coffee restaurant to go with the bakery.

"I'm still all for it," Sara said, "but I think that to really do it right, we have to move closer to the lake. Also, having a deck where people can order simple meals would be a real plus. The bakery and the catering should stay at the heart of the business, but the restaurant would certainly give us another dimension."

"I agree," John replied. I know I said we should keep our old location for the bakery and choose another one for the restaurant, but that doesn't really make sense. If this is going to work, it will be largely because people patronize both businesses at the same time—fill themselves up at the restaurant and then take something out for later."

"It'll work," Sara urged with her perpetual enthusiasm. "And I think it's time to do it. We each made $19,000 last year and maybe we can do a little better where we are, but I want to buy a house, and Doug and I are thinking of having a kid in a year or two, if you can believe that. So I really would like to make more money."

"Me too," John interrupted. "French vacations aren't likely to come down in price. My guess is that we should be able to remodel an existing building and move for about $70,000. We could easily spend three times as much, but if we serve as our

own general contractor, hire friends, supervise the work, and economize where we can, $70,000 should about do it. By scrimping a little, I think we can finance $15,000—maybe $20,000 ourselves—after all, we won't close our existing store until after we move."

"That leaves somewhere around $50,000 to raise some other way. Sarah continued, with a tone of efficiency she'd developed over the past few years. "Why not say $60,000 and make sure we have enough to do a good job. Can we borrow it from a bank?"

"I think we can get at least half of that from a bank," John replied, "but I don't think they will give us the whole amount—anyway these interest rates are killers. My idea is to get $35,000 by selling seven limited partnership shares. If we can put up $20,000 in addition to the equipment we already have, we should be able to get the rest from a bank easily."

"A limited partnership means that we're selling people a share in the business, is that it?" Sara asked.

"Sort of, but not completely. We can work out the details later, but in outline it could work like this. We sell seven limited partnerships for $5,000 each. We still run the business—we're the only full partners. The others all get some return on their investment. Maybe we give them 2 percent of the profits, say."

"Forever?" Sara asked in a horror-stricken voice.

"No, no," John tried to calm her down. "We decide what's a fair return over some set time, then we give them back their money and the limited partnership's over."

"You mean this is really a private loan?"

"Well, sort of. If we were a corporation instead of a partnership, we'd say they're shareholders. If it works right, everybody wins. We can raise the money we need and they'll get a good return."

"Sounds good to me," Sara said. "You'll take care of the details, right?"

"Alright," John sighed. "Back to Clifford and Warner. I'll draft something up and show it to you in a few days. Oh, one problem—just who are we going to sell these limited partnerships to?"

"John," Sarah pronounced, "we are a highly successful business! We're making money, and for lots of people it would be fun to be a part owner of all this. I can just hear them talking to their friends now. 'Why don't we go down to my restaurant for lunch?' No, I definitely don't think we'll have any trouble raising the money. It's paying it back that worries me."

"And keeping our sanity." John added.

"Forward!" Sarah cried. "Better truffles! More profits! Longer vacations!"

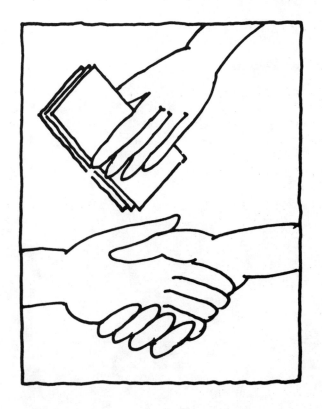

Chapter 7:
Limited
Partnerships

A. Introduction

We briefly discussed limited partnerships in chapter 1 as one possible legal way to organize your small business. You may want to reread this material before proceeding if you are unsure how a limited partnership differs from a small corporation or a partnership. Here we cover limited partnerships in more depth, and we include sample clauses, agreements, and other forms that you will need if you decide that a limited partnership is for you.

Limited partnerships are, essentially, a money-raising or investment device. They allow investors a safe, legal way to put money into a business, without incurring the responsibilities and risk inherent in a full partnership. (However, income or losses to limited partners is "passive" income.) Viewed from the other side of the window, people operating or forming a business can often raise additional capital for their venture by forming a limited partnership and selling limited partnership shares to investors. This is commonly less burdensome than having to sell shares in a corporation or borrow money from a bank.

A limited partnership must be attached to an enterprise managed by at least one general partner, who has all the duties and responsibilities of a partner, including personal liability for all partnership debts.[1] "Limited" partners, however, do not have this larger personal liability; they can only lose the amount they invest, no matter how great the debts of the business. In other words, limited partners are in much the same basic position as shareholders/investors in a corporation. However, just as shareholders in small corporations can lose their limited liability protection under some circumstances, limited partners are also in danger of jeopardizing their limited liability partnership status if they don't follow the rules. First and most important, limited partners are basically restricted to the role of passive investors; in general, if a limited partner becomes actively involved in the management and operation of the business, he or she will lose their limited liability status. Second, the limited partnership must be on the level—attempts at manipulation, chicanery, and other nefarious practices (often involving a "dummy" as a general partner, perhaps a sole general partner who has no assets, while the limited partners have substantial wealth) can also result in a court deciding that so-called limited partners are in fact general partners before the law.

Limited partnerships are very common in the small business world because they are such a good way to raise cash, either to open, or to grow and expand. We personally know a number of owners of small businesses, including several restaurants, a house renovation company, and a retail store, who've raised the cash they needed to open, or expand, their business by selling limited partnership investments, mostly to friends and acquaintances who knew and trusted both the business and the general partners. Obviously, in this type of limited partnership, it's particularly important that the limited partners trust, and have a good working relationship with, the general partner(s). Especially where the limited partners' return is geared to the profits of the

---

1. Most states do permit a corporation — which itself creates limited liability for its owners — to be the general partner of a limited partnership. The corporate general partner of a limited partnership must be a bona fine corporation, which mostly means it must have sufficient cash (called "adequate capitalization" in legalese) to operate the business. If the corporation is a dummy — a shell, merely a legal entity created without sufficient cash in order to protect the limited partners — these limited partners will lose the basic legal protection normally granted them — limited liability.

business, they'll want to be secure that the recorded figures reflect the actual operation of the business, particularly in the kinds of enterprises, such as a bar or restaurant, where "skimming" of cash has been known to occur.

There are some technical requirements and paper work involved in establishing a limited partnership over and above the sort of partnership agreement we have discussed for general partners. In particular, a "Registration Statement," is needed. This is not difficult and most small business people should be able to complete it without a lawyer. However, if you are considering a more sophisticated deal — such as investing in a manufacturing business which will generate substantial tax write-offs in the initial research and development stage — we do suggest you confer with an attorney before signing the final agreement.[2] Also, limited partnerships are legally regarded as investments, or "securities," and are thus regulated by state and sometimes federal securities laws in an attempt to curtail investment fraud. Check the materials on securities law in section D of this chapter carefully. In garden-variety, small business limited partnerships, you'll probably discover there is no serious risk you'll run afoul of the securities laws. However, if you have any doubt whether your deal does comply with the requirements of the securities laws, have it reviewed by a knowledgeable lawyer. Mistakes can be very costly. In this area, an ounce of prevention *is* worth a pound of cure.

Limited partnerships were first used in Pisa and Florence in the twelfth century as a method for owners of capital — mostly clergy and nobles — to invest their money without being known or named. Although anonymity didn't remain a feature of limited partnerships, the form itself proved useful. The limited partnership form spread to France, and was then brought to America by French explorers and settlers in Louisiana and Florida.

A limited partnership requires the existence of at least one general partner, but not necessarily a partnership. Sound odd? Not really, once you realize that a sole proprietor of a business can create a limited partnership with himself as the only general partner. This allows him to retain complete managerial control over the business at the same time that he raises money for expansion or whatever. In this situation, the one general partner will need to have a written agreement defining his rights and duties vis-a-vis the limited partners.

However, it is also both legal and common to have a general partnership (with two or more partners) running a business, which also has limited partners. In this situation, it's important to realize that the limited partnership attached to the partnership business requires a separate (if overlapping) agreement. Thus, there's one partnership agreement for the general partnership and another for the limited partnership. We present sample limited partnership agreements in section F of this chapter.

---

2. Note also that there can be serious conflicts inherent in the relationship between the limited partners and the general partners; in some deals, this means each group hires their own attorney.

EXAMPLE: John and Clem form a 50/50 partnership to produce honey. After several years of small-scale success, they decide to triple the number of their hives. To do this they need capital and decide to sell four limited partnerships in their enterprise for $5,000 each. They do this and have several very good years. John and Clem, as general partners, share in this prosperity equally, after they pay the limited partners their rate of return as defined in the limited partnership agreement.

The return received by limited partners on their investment is determined by the terms of the limited partnership agreement. These terms can vary widely — from a flat percentage return on the investment, which is the equivalent of interest, to a percentage of the profits, or both. Likewise, the time span of the investment is determined by the agreement. Sometimes, limited partners get a share of business profits for a set period of time, while in others their return continues until a certain dollar figure is reached. We know of some limited partnerships where the limited partners get a share of the business in perpetuity, in return for their investment, but we don't normally recommend this sort of arrangement.

After reading this chapter and thoroughly familiarizing yourself with all alternative ways of organizing a limited partnership, we think you should have a meeting with all your potential investors who will likely be friends and family. Consider the choices regarding return and the duration of the agreement and try to arrive at mutually acceptable terms. In a larger limited partnership, the terms are usually fixed at the start and the deal is offered, take-it-or-leave-it, to potential investors; but in our experience, this sort of procedure doesn't work well for most small businesses.

EXAMPLE: When John and Clem began to consider selling limited partnerships in their honey business, they had to decide what return their investors would receive. Rather than try to resolve this in the abstract, they came up with a couple of proposals acceptable to them (either 15% interest payments for two years, and the original money returned at the end of the term, or a flat 10% of the net profits for some set time — perhaps four or five years). Then they had a meeting with several friends who liked them, liked honey, and thought the business looked promising. Most of the people they discussed selling the limited partnerships to said they preferred fixed payments, so they selected the fixed-interest method for payment to the limited partners.

& & &

SUMMARY — LEGAL REQUIREMENTS TO FORM A VALID LIMITED PARTNERSHIP

- There must be at least one general partner.
- If there is more than one general partner, then you need two agreements; one defining the general partners' liabilities vis-a-vis each other and one setting out the general partners' rights and duties vis-a-vis the limited partners.
- The limited partners cannot normally have any day-to-day management or control over the business.
- A Certificate of Limited Partnership (or Registration Statement) regarding the limited partnership must be filed, as defined by state law.

B. How a Limited Partnership Works

Limited partnerships are governed by the "Uniform Limited Partnership Act" or the "Revised Uniform Limited Partnership Act"[3] Also, the Uniform Partnership Act applies to limited partnerships, except where it is inconsistent with the Uniform Limited Partnership Act, or state law. Unlike general partnerships, limited partnerships cannot always dispense with or alter the legal provisions applicable to them, even if everyone involved—all general and limited partners—wish to. Certain legal duties, especially the registration of the limited partnership (see section C, below) *must* be complied with, or the entity will not be held to be a valid limited partnership, and the limited partners will lose their limited liability status.

Under the U.L.P.A., the general partner(s) in a limited partnership have all the powers of any partner in any regular partnership (Section 9, U.L.P.A.). However, in addition, the general partners also have fiduciary duties to the limited partners which are similar to the duty of a member of the board of directors of a corporation to stockholders. This means that the general partners are held to a special duty of trust to the limited partners and must protect their interests.

In general, a limited partner loses her protected "passive investor" status if she becomes involved in the management and control of the business. However, in states which have adopted the Revised Uniform Limited Partnership Act, there are excep-

---

3. Some form of one of these Acts has been adopted, often with slight variations, in all states except Louisiana. For many purposes, especially for small business limited partnerships, the Revised Uniform Limited Partnership Act and the (original) Uniform Limited Partnership Act function the same. In the text, when we refer *simply* and *solely* to the Uniform Limited Partnership Act (or U.L.P.A.), that means the Revised U.L.P.A. is basically the same.

tions to this rule. These involve ailing businesses, where a limited partner can assume a management role, partnership position, and partnership salvage efforts generally. Also, under the Revised U.L.P.A., limited partners can be given such rights as the right to vote on the election or removal of general partners, without losing their passive investor status. Essentially, under the Revised U.L.P.A., limited partners have rights similar to the minimum rights of voting shareholders in a corporation.

The extent of business involvement which is permitted for a limited partnership depends on state law. In most limited partnerships, this isn't a problem, because all the limited partner wants to be is a pure investor, getting a return on an investment, and not bothering with the details of management. Sometimes, however, a limited partner wants some involvement in the business itself, perhaps as a way to impose controls that will protect the investment, or because the partnership is obviously in financial trouble. If this happens to a limited partnership you're involved in, it's best to see a lawyer and review your state's law regarding the extent of activities, or involvement in a business, permitted a limited partner who still retains limited liability status.[4]

WARNING! When a business starts to go bad, limited partners often panic and try to intervene to save an investment that looks to be disappearing behind the horizon. This is often a mistake without a detailed understanding of what state law allows a limited partner to do and still retain limited partner status. Again, if a limited partner gets too involved with the details of the business, she may well be subjecting herself to unlimited liability for business debts if the business fails altogether, at precisely the moment when it's in jeopardy. Or, in other words, proceeding without knowing your rights and responsibilities in detail is a little like booking a ticket on a ship after it has hit an iceberg to try to protect an item of cargo.

Unless prohibited in the limited partnership agreement or Registration Certificate, a limited partner, unlike a general partner, can legally engage in competition with the partnership business — and, in fact, this frequently happens, especially in real estate. Also, a limited partner normally and legally can do business with the partnership, such as loaning it money or purchasing its product or services. However, there are certain activities that are prohibited for limited partners. Under the U.L.P.A. (Section 13), a limited partner *cannot:*

● Receive or hold as collateral or security any property of the partnership.

● Receive from a general partner, or the partnership, any money payment, or release of liability, if at that time the partnership assets are insufficient to pay partnership debts (to outsiders, other than general or limited partners).

The U.L.P.A. (Section 9) provides that the interest of a limited partner *is* assignable or transferable to third parties. However, this can be (and often is) restricted by the terms of the limited partnership agreement or Registration Certificate. This is because many owners of small businesses want to be sure they'll know who they'll be dealing with, and thus restrict the transfer of limited partnership interest to the extent possible. **A flat**

4.. For example, a few states — such as Nevada, Oregon, Washington — permit the limited partners to have the power to vote to remove the general partners in certain circumstances; most states generally don't allow this. Also, the *revised* Uniform Limited Partnership Act does permit the limited partners to participate in certain specified ways in management of the partnership business. As a practical matter, no small business owners we know of would become involved in limited partnerships where they could wind up expelled from their own business, even if that were legal.

prohibition against any transfer of limited partnership interest is not permitted under the U.L.P.A., which instead provides:

1. If all the members of the partnership agree, or if the limited partnership agreement (or Certificate of Registration) so provides, the limited partnership interest is transferable. In this situation, the person who receives the (former) limited partner's interest is called a "substituted" limited partner, and acquires all the rights of any other limited partner.

2. If the members of a partnership don't want or allow free transferability, a third party can nevertheless receive a (former) limited partner's interest. In this situation, however, he or she does *not* become a substituted limited partner. He/she acquires an interest in the partnership business, and is entitled to receive the return or profits the former limited partner was entitled to, but is not entitled to an accounting, or any of the other inspection rights of full-fledged limited partners (Section 9, U.L.P.A.).

1. DETERMINING THE RETURN TO LIMITED PARTNERS

In a small business context, the most important decision involved in creating limited partnerships is to decide what return the limited partners will receive. This should, of course, be set forth explicitly in the limited partnership agreement. As we outlined in the introduction to this chapter, there's no one method of defining the return to limited partners. You can come up with any method that seems fair to you and the limited partners.

There are, however, two general principles regarding the return to limited partners that we almost always recommend to friends. First, be sure that the limited partners get a fair return on their investment. If in doubt, err on the side of generosity. You don't want to lose your friends or suffer the headaches involved in dealing with frustrated limited partners who feel that they have been cheated. Second, be sure that once the limited partners have received a good return on their investment (however you define that) they're either automatically bought out, or have their money returned, or are somehow foreclosed from future participation in the business. This is particularly important in case your business becomes very successful. In one real-life situation we know of, four friends started a restaurant in San Francisco. They were all equal general partners. To raise some of the capital they needed to start, they sold nine limited partnerships to friends, for $2,500 each. At that point, the limited partners were worried about the consequences of possible failure; so the limited partners demanded that the general partners would be personally liable to them if their investments were lost. Everyone was so nervous about the new venture that nobody thought much about what happened if the restaurant was a smashing success. The only provision as to profits was to give each limited partner a 10% yearly return on his or her investment, and 1% of the profits. There was no buy-out or other provision limiting the term of the limited partner's investment. Perhaps you can guess the rest of the story. The restaurant almost instantly became (and still is) one of the most popular and successful in the city. People make reservations months in advance and brag about the wonderful food. Profitability was never in doubt from the day the doors opened. Very quickly, the limited partners recovered their investment, made a good profit, and had the prospect of a bonanza. The general partners realized that they had made a terrible mistake. They had given away almost 10% of their total profits, forever, and for a relatively small investment. Fortunately, this story has a happy ending. The limited partners — who were friends, after all — agreed it wasn't fair that they gain a lifetime interest in the business for their small investment, and the general partners were able to negotiate a buy-out, even though they had no legal basis to compel one.

NOTE: Under the U.L.P.A., a limited partner has the right to demand full return of his contribution, in cash, on the date specified in the Registration Certificate (see Section C) or, if none is, six months after giving written notice of this demand to the other members of the limited partnership. So, for certainty's sake, it's almost always advisable to specify a specific date for return of limited partners' contributions.

2. A FEW OTHER POINTS ABOUT LIMITED PARTNERSHIPS

● The surname of a limited partner(s) should not be used in the partnership name, "unless it is also the name of a general partner, or unless the business had been carried on under a name in which the limited partner's surname appeared, prior to the time when the limited partner became involved." [Section 5(b),(c) U.L.P.A.]

EXAMPLE: If Herbert Crumb becomes a limited partner in the partnership of Cookie and Cake, it would be improper (as well as ridiculous) to change the partnership name to Cookie, Cake, and Crumb. However, if this was already the name of the partnership, because Herbert's uncle Philip Crumb was already a general partner, it would be proper for Herbert to join as a limited partner.

● In any limited partnership, it's wise to have at least two general partners, or make other provisions for continuity of the business in case the one general partner dies, withdraws, etc.

● Limited partnerships doing business in more than one state have to register in each state in which they do business.

● The U.L.P.A. does not contain a section on dissolution of limited partnerships. Limited partnerships can end:

1. By expiration of the terms set forth in the Certificate of Registration, and limited partnership agreement. This method of ending a limited partnership is the wisest, because everyone is clear as to what it involves from the start.

2. By the unanimous agreement of all the members of the limited partnership.

3. By changing any of the matters set forth in the registration statement (i.e., any change in the partnership requires a new Registration Statement).

4. By judicial decree.

Normally, limited partners do not become involved in lawsuits brought by, or against, the partnership (other than suits brought by the limited partners themselves against the partnership).

● The partnership business is not dissolved if a limited partner withdraws, or dies, or goes bankrupt, etc., but, unless the agreement provides otherwise, it is dissolved if a general partner withdraws, or dies, or goes bankrupt.

C. The Registration Certificate

Under the U.L.P.A., a limited partnership must complete and file a Registration Statement containing detailed information about the composition of the partnership with a government agency. Some states, such as California, have a specific registration form you must use.* In other states, there is no set governmental form for the Certificate. In several states, this statement must be filed with the Secretary of State. However, that's not always true. Under Section 2 of the U.L.P.A., each state decides where the Registration Certificate must be filed. In some states, the Certificate must be filed in more than one place. For example, in Connecticut, the Certificate must be filed both with the corporate division of the Secretary of State and the local town clerk. The Certificate must also be published in a local legal paper in some states. To determine where you have to file in your state, contact your Secretary of State, or Corporations Commissioner.[5] This agency will always have an office at your state capital and may have regional offices in major cities.

The primary purpose of the Registration Statement is to protect creditors of the partnership by giving them information that allows them to better assess the risks involved in the partnership business. It also protects investors, because it reveals to them the composition of the business and allows state authorities to examine the situation to see if fraud seems likely. The U.L.P.A. provides that a valid limited partnership has been formed "if there has been substantial compliance in good faith" with the registration requirements of the act.

> The first American statute authorizing limited partnership was adopted in New York in 1822. The judges then didn't like limited partnerships (we're not sure why) so the statutes were "strictly construed," and limited partnership status denied for trivial technical flaws, especially in registration statements. Eventually, this judicial hostility passed, especially after the promulgation of the Uniform Limited Partnership Act, which was first proposed in 1916. The U.L.P.A. was based on the traditional capitalistic notion that a willing investor should be able to put his/her money in a limited partnership and depend upon others for "investment skills" without incurring personal liability in the process. In recent years limited partnerships have become extremely popular.

Here's what's required to be covered in a Limited Partnership Registration Certificate:

- The name of the partnership business;**
- A brief description of the character, or purpose, of the business;
- The location of the principal place of business;***
- The names and residence addresses of all general and limited partners;

---

5. Names vary somewhat from state to state. If you have any trouble finding the correct agency, find out where incorporation papers are filed. Limited partnership certificates are normally filed at the same location. If this is not the case, they will be able to direct you to the correct agency office.

* Forms can be obtained by writing California Secretary of State, Limited Partnership Division, Box 704, Sacramento, CA 95803.

** California requires that the name of the limited partnership end with " . . . a California Limited Partnership." This requirement is fairly typical.

*** Many states, such as California, require that an office be maintained within the state where an agent for the service of process resides.

- The term or duration of the limited partnership;
- The amount of cash and a summary description and the agreed value of any other property contributed by each limited partner;
- Any additional contributions which must be made by limited partners, including the time of contribution, and any contingencies on it;
- The details of any agreements to return limited partners' investments;
- Arrangements for profit-sharing, compensation, or other means of return to the limited partners;
- How (and if) limited partners can "substitute" others in their place (i.e., transfer provisions);
- The rights, if any, of general partners to admit new limited partners;
- Any priorities in receipt of profits between limited partners;
- The right, if any, of a general partner(s) to continue the partnership business upon the death, retirement, etc. of another general partner;
- The date(s) of the expected dissolution of the general partnership (if planned) or expiration of any limited partnership interest;
- The right, if any, of any limited partner to demand and receive back his/her initial contribution.

To comply with the registration requirements, you have two options in those states which do not have a mandatory Certificate form.

1. You can create and file a separate document, containing all the information required (see the examples below).

2. You can have the limited partnership agreement also function as the Registration Statement. In that case, be sure that the Agreement contains all of the information required, such as the name *and residence addresses* of all general and limited partners. Also, it's standard to start the agreement with a clause such as:

> *This document shall constitute both the limited partnership agreement and the certificate of limited partnership. The general partners shall cause this document to be recorded as required by the law of the State of _____ "*

Here's a form of a Registration Certificate, which you can use or adapt if you decide to file a separate document after you have checked with your state agency to see if they have any special requirements.

REGISTRATION CERTIFICATE

1. The name of the partnership is _____ .

2. The character of the partnership business is _____
_____ (a very brief description — e.g., "retail shoe store,"
"bar and grill," "real estate development," etc.).

3. The location of the principal place of business of the partnership is

_____ .

4. The names and places of residence of the members of the partnership are:
General Partners   *Addresses*

_____   _____

_____   _____

_____   _____

Limited Partners   *Addresses*

_____   _____

_____   _____

                       _____

etc.   *etc.*

     5. The partnership shall begin on _____, *19____ and continues* _____ (whatever you decide, e.g., "continue indefinitely," or "continue for three years," or "continue until the limited partners have received..." etc.)

     6. The limited partners have contributed the following cash, and property of the specified agreed upon value, to the partnership:

Name	*Cash*	*Property (identifed)*	*Agreed-upon Value*	*Total Contribution*
_____	_____	_____	_____	_____
_____	_____	_____	_____	_____
_____	_____	_____	_____	_____

etc.

7. (Provisions regarding additional contributions by limited partners; put in whatever you've decided, e.g.:)

     No additional contributions are to be made by any of the limited partners.

                       or

     Additional contributions are to be made [or, may be made] by limited partners under the following terms: (state what they are) _____
_____ .

8. (Provisions for return of limited partners' contributions; put in whatever you've decided, e.g.:)

     No time has been set when the contribution of any limited partner is to be returned.

                       or

     The contributions of the limited partners shall [or may] be returned as follows: (specify the terms agreed on) _____
_____ .

     9. The return provided the limited partners is as follows:
Name

_____   _____

_____   _____

_____   _____

(state return agreed upon, e.g., 10% of the profits for three years, then return of contribution, etc.)

10. (Provisions regarding assignment of limited partners' interest. If you want to restrict assignability as far as you can, use the first option; if you want free assignability, use the second.)

A limited partner has no right to substitute another person or organization a. a contributor in his place.

or

A limited partner does have the right to substitute another person or organization as a contributor in his place.

11. (Provision regarding admission of new limited partners; include whatever is decided, e.g.:)

The partners have no right to admit additional limited partners.

or

The partners may admit additional limited partners, under the following terms (specify what's been agreed on) _____
_____ .

12. (Provision regarding any priority between limited partners in distribution/ payment of return. Usually there will be no distinctions made in this regard, so use the following; if you do make this type of distinction, simply state what it is — who has what priority.)

No limited partner has any priority over any other limited partner as to compensation or return, or as to return of initial contribution.

13. (Provisions regarding continuity on death, etc. of a general partner. If the business will terminate in that event, say so. Usually it will continue, so use or adapt a clause like one of the following:)

If a general partner dies, retires, becomes incompetent, _____
_____ (add any other contingency covered, such as "withdraws" or "is expelled," etc.) *the business may be continued by the remaining general partner or partners* (if appropriate, add, "as defined in the general partnership agreement").

14. (Provisions regarding limited partners' right to receive specific contributed property back. If, as is usual, there are no such provisions, use the first option; if there are some, use the second.)

No right is given a limited partner to demand and receive property other than cash in return for his contribution.

or

__(Name of limited partner)__ *may demand and receive back* _____ (describe the contributed property) *originally contributed by him, under the following terms:* (state them).

15. (Provisions regarding voting control rights of limited partners. Unless they have no such rights, see a lawyer.)

No right is given a limited partner to vote on, or take any active part in, management of any of the business affairs of the partnership.

16. (Signature clause. Most states require notarization as a condition of filing.)

_____ _____
_____ _____
_____ _____

AMENDMENTS OF THE REGISTRATION CERTIFICATE

You must keep your registration certificate up-to-date. Any amendment must state where the original certificate was recorded, what change is made in that certificate, and it must be personally signed by all partners.[6]

Amendments to a Registration Certificate are required under the U.L.P.A. if _any_ of the following changes occur:

- The partnership name is changed;
- The amount or character of any of the limited partners' contribution changes;
- A new limited partner is admitted, or substituted;
- A general partner retires, dies, becomes insane, or withdraws and the partnership business is continued;
- The character of the partnership business is changed;
- The time for dissolution of the partnership, or return of a partnership contribution, is changed;
- The limited partners receive voting rights over management of the partnership business.

D. The "Security" Aspects of Limited Partnerships

As we've learned, a limited partnership is primarily a money-raising method, a way of investing in a business without forming a corporation and issuing stock. As such, a limited partnership interest is legally a "security." A security is conventionally defined as an investment in a common business enterprise managed by others, where the investor's expectation of return depends primarily on the efforts of others. The most common form of a "security" is shares of stock issued by a corporation. However, there are numerous other types of securities, and most are subject to federal and state laws which regulate the sale of any "security."

---

6. Except the limited partners can authorize the general partners to sign for them by duly executing a legally valid Power of Attorney for this purpose.

1. FEDERAL REGULATION

The sale of securities has, historically, been an area with much fraud and chicanery. Swindlers and con men have sold the securities in all sorts of worthless, or non-existent, businesses to the gullible and greedy. As a result, the sale of securities has come under strict regulations. A series of federal laws, e.g., the Securities Act of 1933, the Securities and Exchange Act of 1934, the "Investment Advisors Act" of 1940 and others, put the sale of securities under supervision of the Securities and Exchange Commission (S.E.C.) and other federal regulatory agencies. In addition, the states have passed their own securities laws, usually referred to as "blue-sky" laws, which also control the sale of securities.

The federal securities laws are a real hassle. They require considerable paperwork from securities' sellers; indeed, the drafting of S.E.C. "security prospectuses" has become a major, and quite lucrative, legal industry. Also, those involved in selling securities covered under federal law usually have to register with the S.E.C. as "broker-dealers." Certainly any small business forming a limited partnership wants to avoid having to comply with these laws. Happily, this can normally be accomplished without difficulty if you keep things small. The federal securities laws are designed to apply to the big guys, and the big deals. These laws provide two exceptions from their coverage which apply to almost all small business limited partnerships. As you read on, you will probably conclude that you're exempt from the federal securities laws.

WARNING! If you believe federal securities laws could apply to what you're planning, you'd better hire a securities lawyer and get ready to spend some money.

2. LIMITED PARTNERSHIP EXEMPTIONS FROM FEDERAL SECURITIES REGULATION

If you qualify under *either* of these exemptions, you're not subject to federal securities laws.[7]

Intrastate offerings are not subject to the federal securities law. This means that all interests in the limited partnership are offered and sold in one state, the state where the limited partnership was formed and the Registration Certificate filed. If you're relying on this exception, be sure you know the actual source of the funds used to buy each limited partnership. If Frank gets the money he uses to buy a limited partnership from his uncle Jason living in another state, this could be sufficient to make it an *inter*state transaction — thus subject to federal securities laws.

Private offerings are likewise not subject to federal securities laws. A "private offering" is more restricted than the sale of securities to the general public, which is called a "public offering." There's no one simple test for determining what's a private offering.[8] Several factors are involved:[9]

a. The people offered the security ("offerees" in legalese) must be kept to a minimum. State law, not federal law, defines the precise number of offerees or sales

---

7. Note that neither exception applies if there is any fraud involved.

8. There's a new S.E.C. rule — rule 146 — that supposedly makes the test "more objective" — but not a whole lot more.

9. *S.E.C. v. Ralston Purina Co.*, 346 U.S. 119 (1953).

allowed in a private offering. You must be able to identify each offeree. If you're dealing with 10 or fewer buyers, you're safe in any state. Beyond that, you should check the rules in your state. They vary widely. Also, if you are raising money from more than ten investors, you should realize you are about to get involved in a fairly complicated transaction; *be sure* you want to do it.

The other factors involved in determining whether a sale of a security is exempt from federal securities regulation are all subjective; their purpose is simple, though — to prevent unsophisticated buyers from being taken advantage of by sharp sellers. These factors include:

b. The relation of the offerees to each other and the seller;

c. The number of units offered and the size of the offering;

d. The manner of the offering;

e. The sophistication of the offerees;

f. The offerees' access to financial and other information about the partnership and its business.

All of this can seem rather vague, surely. What does it mean to you? If you are offering limited partnerships to prospective buyers in one state, you don't have to worry about it. However, if your prospective limited partners reside out of your state, you must qualify under each state's private offering rules to be exempt from the federal securities laws. Check the law of your home state and each of the other states involved regarding the maximum number of people a "private" offering can be offered to, or sold to. If you plan to exceed that number, hire a securities lawyer or cut back on your plans and keep within state law requirements. Regarding the subjective elements of a private offering, the only safe course is honesty. There should be full, complete disclosure of all significant facts about the business — and the risks — to all prospective purchasers of limited partnerships. In big money private offerings, this often means a bulky document, prepared by securities lawyers, full of disclaimers, figures, and legalese. Frankly, for two partners to raise money from their friends, we don't believe such expensive, formal disclosure is necessary. However, if you think there are *any* risks, however slight, that any limited partner could become angry if things go wrong, put your disclosures in writing — send all prospective buyers a letter in which you state the facts and risks about the business in plain, common sense terms. If you're engaged in a rather complicated and expensive transaction, you may need to prepare (or have prepared) a full disclosure memorandum, which usually is not too different from what is required for full S.E.C. registration.

EXAMPLE: Let's return to John and Clem and their limited partnership honey business. They might write the four limited partners a letter such as the following before finalizing the deal:

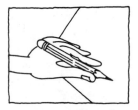

Dear

We are pleased that you are planning to invest $5,000 in Fatbee, our partnership honey business, in exchange for a limited partnership interest.

In this connection we thought that it would be appropriate to review the prospects for our business in writing. We have operated Fatbee as a general partnership for four years and have made a substantial profit on a relatively small investment. We believe that expansion and equipment modernization will produce greater profits.

However, we do want to emphasize that there is risk involved in the honey business. Bad weather and disease can affect our little flying workers, and our prices are dependent on national and international factors beyond our control.

As attachments to this letter, we enclose the general partnership agreement between ourselves, the proposed limited partnership agreement (which will also function as our registration certificate and will be filed with the Secretary of State's Office), and our partnership tax returns for the last 3 years.

If you have any questions, please give either of us a call. We're looking forward to pleasant (and hopefully profitable) business relations.

Sincerely,
John Sweet
Clem Clover

3. STATE REGULATIONS

State laws governing the sale of securities in one state (i.e., sales exempt from federal securities laws) are usually almost as detailed and burdensome as federal laws. In other words, even if you only have to comply with state securities laws, you'll still need a lawyer. Fortunately, state securities laws also exempt private offerings from their requirements.

As we've said, state blue sky laws vary considerably with regards to private limited partnership offerings. In many states the offer and sale to not more than a specified number of persons during a specified period is exempt. In some states, the exemption is based on the number of offers made within a 12-month period. In other states, the limitation is based on the number of sales, not offerees. In some other states, the numerical test is not applied to all offers, but only to offers to residents of that state and so on. Also, different requirements may apply to different types of securities. For example, in New York, a syndication of real estate interests (through limited partnerships) is subject to special registration rules. Again, offerings to 10 or less people are safe anywhere. Beyond that, contact the relevent officials in your state for details. Generally, if you're offering limited partnership shares to ten or less people in your state and don't do it often you will have little to worry about.

E. Tax Aspects of Limited Partnerships

A limited partnership is not subject to federal income tax. The partnership entity must file an "informational" partnership tax return.[10]

Limited partnership income received by general or limited partners must be reported on their individual return. Income or losses to the general partner(s) is active income. Income (or losses received by limited partners) is passive income. As previously explained, passive income (see Chapter 6, Section D, Partnership Taxation) must, for I.R.S. purposes, be treated separately from all active income received by the limited partners.

Income or losses from limited partnership investments made before October 22, 1986 may be partially used to offset regular, active income until 1990. Under federal law, the following % of a loss from such a limited partnership investment can be deducted from active income.

% Deductible	Tax Year
65%	1987
40%	1988
20%	1989
10%	1990
0	After 1990

1. JOINT VENTURES

Certain real estate limited partnerships are exempted from the requirement of filing an informational partnership tax return. If the business of the real estate limited partnership qualifies as a "joint venture" — which means it is a specific enterprise of limited scope and duration — no partnership tax return need be filed. Often, the transaction is inherently limited in time or duration — a single house or unit is to be built, renovated, or managed. The active partners need to raise cash for the business, but don't want to spread management power to other owners. So a joint venture is created, limited partnership interests sold, and the only tax requirement is reporting of income on individual returns.

2. CORPORATION LOOK-ALIKES

Limited partnerships are inherently similar to corporations in the sense that investors gain limited liability status. However, there is a real danger that if a limited partnership becomes *too much* like a corporation, the I.R.S. will determine that the entity really is a corporation, and it will be taxed accordingly. This is not normally desirable because it means that investors in the so-called limited partnership will find that the venture's corporate profits are taxed twice — both at the corporation and personal level — not "passed through" as a partnership's would be. This is not something you have to worry about if you're a typical small business — a relatively simple enterprise with just a couple (or a few) general partners, raising operating money by selling limited partnership

---

10. Only one return is required, not one for the partnership and one for the limited partnership.

interests in the business. However, in a more complicated limited partnership transaction, the question of whether the business is really a corporation for tax purposes can become troublesome.

EXAMPLE: Suppose several partners have created a very successful leather purse manufacturing business. Eventually there are four factories, over thirty partners, a management committee, and complicated partnership provisions designed to ensure that the business continues, no matter what happens to any individual partner, or partners. To raise money, limited partnership interests are sold to twenty-five investors. Is this really a corporate transaction? It might be.

The I.R.S. will examine limited partnerships to see if the traditional attributes of a corporation are present. One telling factor that will very likely result in an entity being treated as a corporation for tax purposes is if, in reality, there are no general partners who will be personally liable for the debts of the business. How can this be possible, you ask, since all limited partnerships must, by definition, proclaim that have at least one general partner? Well, one way it can happen is if the general partner is, in reality, a dummy — a person or corporation with no substantial assets — selected for that very reason to be the fall guy in case things go bad.

Like so many legal aspects of partnerships, the taxation of limited partnerships as corporations can become exceedingly complex. However, these complexities will apply to so few of our readers that it doesn't make sense to give you more detail here. You should know, however, that the I.R.S. will issue advance rulings on whether a limited partnership will be recognized for income tax purposes. If your limited partnership becomes a complicated business matter, it would be wise to be sure, in advance, that there will be no trouble with the I.R.S. Discuss this matter with your accountant in detail.

F. Limited Partnership Agreements

1. INTRODUCTION

In this section we present two limited partnership agreements. The first one is a general purpose sample agreement. It assumes there is a separate general partnership agreement between the general partners. We do recommend that two separate agreements be prepared, one for the general partners, and one for the limited partners; otherwise, the one consolidated agreement can get very bulky and confusing. There must be full disclosure of all terms of the general partnership agreement to all limited partners. This sample agreement covers just the basics. If you want to consider more sophisticated problems, we provide additional sample clauses and list resources for further research in the Appendix.

The second sample is one that was prepared for a friend of ours who recently opened an excellent restaurant in Benicia, California (we have changed the names). We include this Agreement for several reasons. First, it is an agreement with only one general partner —so you can see how that alternative can work. Secondly, it is much more detailed, and will give you a good idea of some complexities that sensible folks have found to make good sense. And finally, it's drafted in lawyer language, so you'll get a chance to see if you think that type of wording suits you.

2. SAMPLE LIMITED PARTNERSHIP AGREEMENT

AGREEMENT OF LIMITED PARTNERSHIP OF___[Partnership Business Name]___

By this agreement the signers form a limited partnership under the laws of the State of _____, as of _____, 1981, and agree to the following terms and conditions:

1. Members

The general partners are _____, _____, (etc.)

The limited partners are _____, _____, _____, (etc.)

(You might want to list the limited partners in an attached exhibit "A," for they may change frequently.)

2. Place of Business

The partnership's principal place of business shall be at _____.

(If you want to be cautious, add "or such other place as the general partners determine in the future").

3. Purpose

The purpose and character of the business of this limited partnership are

_____

(give a summary description).

4. Term (Coordinate with 7(b) on return of contribution)

This partnership begins on the date of this agreement and shall continue until _____, 19_____, at which time it shall dissolve, as under the terms provided here, and the contributions of the limited partners be returned.

(As we discussed in section B, it's normally wise to limit the duration of a limited partnership to a set time; if you do adopt another approach, you can substitute for the above "shall continue indefinitely," or "shall continue indefinitely, subject to the buy-out provisions of this agreement," etc. If you do so, be sure to specify a date for return of limited partners' contributions.)

5. Formalities

a. The general partners shall do what is needed to

1. Record a Certificate of Limited Partnership;

2. Record a Fictitious Business Name Statement;

3. Deliver to each limited partner within _____ days of the close of the fiscal year the financial report of the partnership's activities for that year prepared under Section 6(C).

(You can add as many specific provisions here as you want; our preference is to keep them to a minimum.)

b. Power of Attorney

Each limited partner appoints each general partner as his/her attorney-in-fact, with the power to execute, acknowledge, and file any of the following documents in his or her name:

(1) The original and any amendment to the certificate of limited partnership, and any other instrument that may be required to be recorded or filed by the partnership;

(2) All documents that may be required to effectuate the dissolution and termination of the partnership; and

(3) A fictitious business name statement.

(This noticeably simplifies some of the bureaucratic hassling involved in forming and running a limited partnership business.)

6. Accounting and Records

(a) The partnership shall use the _____(cash, or accrual)[11]_____ method of accounting.

(b) At all times during the terms of this partnership, the general partners shall keep (or cause to be kept) books of accounts in which each partnership transaction shall be fully and accurately entered. These books of account shall be kept at the partnership's principal office and shall be available during reasonable business hours for inspection and examination by any limited partner or his/her representative, who shall have the right to make copies of any of those books at his/her own expense.

(c) At the close of each fiscal year, the general partners shall hire an accountant to prepare a financial statement, including net profit or loss, for that year, which shall be delivered to each limited partner.

7. Contributions, and Return of Limited Partners' Capital

(a) Contributions

Each partner shall initially contribute to the partnership as capital cash or property with agreed-upon value as follows:

_____*(Name)*_____ : _____*(Cash/$)*_____
_____*(describe other contribution)*_____
_____*with an agreed value of $*_____ _____*Total $*_____

_____*(Name)*_____ : _____*(Cash/$)*_____
_____*(describe other contribution)*_____
_____*with an agreed value of $*_____ _____*Total $*_____

Limited partners
_____*(Name)*_____ : _____*(Cash/$)*_____
_____*(describe other contribution)*_____
_____*with an agreed value of $*_____ _____*Total $*_____

_____*(Name)*_____ : _____*(Cash/$)*_____
_____*(describe other contribution)*_____
_____*with an agreed value of $*_____ _____*Total $*_____

(This is one of the most important clauses of any limited partnership agreement, and

---

11. Unless the business uses an inventory, where the accrual accounting method is required by the I.R.S.

subject to much variation. For example, the general partners could contribute services, as well as — or in addition to — cash. Or, there can be provisions for additional contributions in the future — either optional or mandatory. Another common clause covers the consequences of a would-be limited partner failing to make a contribution. We present additional clauses involving these and other contribution problems in the Appendix A. Remember, however, that the most important thing to do is to decide what you want. Don't just tack on clauses and hope they'll help, somehow.)

(b) The capital contributed by each limited partner shall be returned to __[him/her]__ *on* __[date of partnership dissolution]__ .

(In most states, if the limited partnership agreement and certificate do not specify a time for the return of a limited partner's contribution, he may demand its return six months after written notice is given to all partners. This is normally undesirable, so you will want to be specific. By using the "date of partnership dissolution" you are in effect saying that the limited partner isn't entitled to the return of his/her capital until the partnership is dissolved under the terms of the limited partnership agreement. If the limited partner doesn't get a fixed return, but a share of profits or losses, his/her contribution may have diminished by the return date, so you can substitute *"The capital account of the limited partners shall be returned to them on* (dissolution date). Further, in case property has been contributed, you may want to state that only the cash value of that property, or its current worth in the capital account, will be returned.)

(c) With respect to capital contributions of property, the limited partner contributing that property is to assume the income tax consequences of any difference between the agreed-upon value thereof and its adjusted tax basis.

(This clause can be used if a limited partner contributes property that has substantially increased in value since he/she purchased it. We discussed this problem in some detail in chapter 6, section E.)

8. Capital Account and Return to Limited Partners
 (a) Capital Accounts
 An individual capital account shall be maintained for each partner. Each partner's capital account shall consist of his/her original capital contribution increased by any additional capital contributions, and decreased by distributions in reduction of partnership capital and his/her share of partnership losses, and other gains or losses attributed to the capital account.

(This is for a situation where the limited partners' returns are geared to the profits — or losses — of the business. If the limited partners are to receive a fixed return, their capital account (see chapter 6, Partnership Taxation, section C for a definition) will stay the same — unless the business goes broke, or runs in the red for quite a while.)

(b) Returns to Limited Partners
 During the term of the partnership, the partnership's annual net profits and losses (you may want to define these two concepts with more specificity) *as determined by an accountant using the accounting procedures used on the tax return filed, shall be credited and charged to the limited partners as follows:*

_____ [name] _____   _____ %
_____   _____ %
_____   _____ %
_____   _____ %

_If the limited partners are due a return of the yearly profits, that payment shall be made within _____ days of the close of the fiscal year._

(This is another crucial provision, and as you'd expect, can be arranged in innumerable ways. There could be quarterly payments, for example. Or the return could be fixed at 15% yearly interest on the capital contributions. Again, it's not really the drafting here that can be hard — it's working out between all the general and limited partners a mutually acceptable method and rate of return. And for that, you're on your own.)

9. Management

(a) The partnership business shall be managed by the general partners. Each general partner shall have an equal voice in the management of the partnership. (If that's what they've agreed upon.) _Limited partners shall have no right to take part in the management of the partnership or to transact any business on its behalf._

(b) General partners are not required to devote all their business time to the partnership, but each of them shall devote the time to the partnership that he/she deems appropriate.

(c) The general and limited partners, either individually or collectively, may participate in other business ventures of every kind, whether or not those other business ventures compete with the partnership. Neither the partnership nor any other partner shall have any right to any income or profit derived from any such other business venture of any partner or partners.

(Clause (b) and (c) reflect a partnership where competition by partners will be allowed. If you want the business to be the exclusive concern of the general partners, say so — by putting "not", or deleting the clause, where appropriate. And, to be repetitive, once again you can insert any particular management provision you desire. In particular, if the general partners are to receive salaries, you might want to cover that.)

(d) The general partners will receive salaries [or guaranteed payments] of _____, _____ (specify the amounts, etc.; include this clause if the general partners are to receive salaries, or guaranteed payments, in addition to whatever profits they're entitled to).

10. Assignments

(As we discussed earlier, you can't totally prohibit transfer or assignment of a limited partner's interest. You can restrict that right, though, so that the person buying that interest does not have the full rights of regular limited partners. We present sample clauses covering this below.)

Option A

A limited partner's partnership interest is freely assignable, and the assignee (i.e., the buyer) _shall become a substituted limited partner, effective when the appropriate amendment to the Certificate of Limited Partnership is recorded._
(If you want free transferability, this does it.)

Option B

A limited partner's partnership interest shall not be assignable without the written consent of _____

(e.g., all general partners, all general and limited partners, etc.)

If any limited partner shall assign his/her interest without receiving the consent of the general partners, his/her assignee shall have no right to an accounting of partnership transactions or to inspect the partnership books. On giving notice of the assignment to the general partners, the assignee shall be entitled to receive only a return of the assignor's contribution to capital and the share of profits to which the assignor would have been entitled, diminished by the assignor's share of losses, if any.

11. Withdrawals of Partners, Dissolution and Termination

(There are three different methods for coping with the withdrawal of a general or limited partner without the substitution of a new partner. These apply whether death, retirement, or expulsion is involved. Before getting into them, let us remind you that the problems of the withdrawal of a general partner were discussed in detail in chapter 5 and won't be repeated here except to emphasize that provisions for withdrawal in the limited partnership agreement must be coordinated with those in the general partnership agreement. Now as to the three methods. First, either the withdrawing general or limited partner's interest can be bought out by the remaining partners: if you decide to do this, adopt what you need from the clauses presented in chapter 5, section B. Second, you can have the partnership terminate, which is normally undesirable. Thirdly, you can have the business continue. Voluntary withdrawal by general partners is not allowed, or is highly discouraged. If a general partner dies, his/her estate or inheritors become limited partners, entitled to the same return as before.)

(a) Events Not Causing Dissolution

Dissolution shall not be caused by the (a) death or disability of a partner, (b) withdrawal or expulsion of a partner, (c) admission of a new partner, or (d) insanity of a general partner.

(b)(i) Withdrawal of a General Partner

Upon the death, retirement, disability, withdrawal, or expulsion of a general partner, that partner's interest shall be purchased by the partnership as provided in the general partnership agreement and the partnership business shall be continued by the remaining general partners.

or

(ii) Upon the death or insanity or disability of a general partner, the partnership business shall be continued by the remaining general partners. The executor, guardian or successor to that general partner's interest shall become a limited partner.

(If Clause (b)(ii) is used or adapted, the same information must also be stated in the Registration Certificate. Corp. Code Sections 15509(1)(9), 15520, 15520.5.)

(c) Death or Disability of a Limited Partner

Upon the death or disability of a limited partner, his/her executor or administrator or guardian shall have all the rights of a limited partner for the purpose of settling his/her estate, or, if his/her limited partnership interest is held in joint tenancy, the rights and liabilities of the deceased joint tenant shall pass to the surviving joint tenant.

12. Arbitration Clause

(Include arbitration clause from chapter 3, section D.)

IN WITNESS WHEREOF, the parties to this limited partnership agreement have executed it effective as of the day and year first above written.

(Signatures of general partners, typed names below)

(Residence addresses of partners)

———————————————————
———————————————————
———————————————————

———————————————————
———————————————————
———————————————————

(Signatures of limited partners, typed names below)

(Residence addresses of partners)

———————————————————
———————————————————
———————————————————

———————————————————
———————————————————
———————————————————

3. SAMPLE LAWYER'S LIMITED PARTNERSHIP AGREEMENT

Limited Partnership Agreement of Patricia's Restaurant
This limited partnership agreement is entered into as of ——————————— *,*
1981 by the following partners:
Patricia Donahue, General Partner

——————————————————————— *, Limited Partner*
——————————————————————— *, Limited Partner*
——————————————————————— *, Limited Partner*

By this agreement the parties form a limited partnership agreement under the laws of the state of California and agree to the following terms and conditions.

1. NAME AND PLACE OF BUSINESS:

The partnership name shall be Patricia's Restaurant. The partnership's principal place of business shall be in the City of Benicia, County of Solano, State of California.

2. CHARACTER OF BUSINESS:

The purpose of the partnership is to operate a restaurant and other activities incidental thereto.

3. TERM:

The partnership shall begin as of the date of this agreement and shall continue until terminated as provided in this agreement.

4. DOCUMENTATION AND POWER OF ATTORNEY:

a. The partners shall execute, acknowledge, and record a certificate of limited partnership as required by the California Corporations Code.

b. Each limited partner irrevocably constitutes, and appoints the general partner as his or her attorney-in-fact, in his or her name, place, and stead to make, execute, acknowledge, and file any of the following:

1. A fictitious business name statement

2. Any modification or amendment to the certificate of limited partnership admitting or substituting new limited partners.

c. An amendment to the certificate of limited partnership may be signed personally or by an attorney-in-fact by:

1. A general partner and the new partner if the amendment is caused by the additon of a new partner;

2. A general partner, the substituted limited partner, and the assigning limited partner if the amendment is caused by the substitution of a limited partner.

5. INITIAL CAPITAL:

a. Each limited partner shall initially contribute to the partnership as capital cash with agreed value as follows:

Name	Address	Amount
_____	_____	_____
_____	_____	_____
_____	_____	_____

b. The general partner shall not contribute cash or other property to the partnership capital. Her contribution shall consist of services to the partnership as general partner with an agreed value of $_____ (equals total of cash contributed by limited partners).

c. If for any reason the limited partner's initial contributions to the partnership do not total at least $_____ by _____, 19_____, and if for any reason no lease for the premises in which the partnership will operate is signed by _____, 19_____, the contributions shall be returned to the limited partners within _____ days after that date. In this case the general partner agrees to indemnify and hold harmless the limited partners from any and all liability and expense of every nature incurred in connection *with the formation of the limited partnership and its activities.*

When the repayments have been made (a) this limited partnership shall dissolve and terminate, (b) the general partner shall have authority to execute on behalf of all the limited partners and to record a cancellation of the certificate of limited partnership and all other documents necessary to effectuate termination and dissolution of this limited partnership, (c) all partnership obligations shall be taken over and become the general partner's obligations, and (d) except as stated in this section, none of the parties shall have any further obligation to the others arising out of this partnership.

6. ADDITIONAL CAPITAL CONTRIBUTIONS:

a. If the general partner decides that additional capital must be contributed for the partnership's best interests, she shall notify each partner in writing of the total amount to be contributed. Within _____ days after notice is given, each partner may make an additional capital contribution in an amount bearing the same ratio to that total amount that her capital account balance bears to the total capital account balances of all the partners. Additional capital contributions shall be made only as specified in this agreement.

b. If, within the time provided, any partner or partners fail to make an additional capital contribution under section _____, the interest of each partner in profits and losses shall be adjusted under section _____. The general partner shall notify each partner in writing of the total amount of contributions not made, and within _____ days each other partner who wishes to do so may elect, by giving written notice of election to the partnership within _____ days after the general partner gives notice of the amount of contributions in default, to make an additional contribution of a specified amount. If the total of the amounts specified is less than or equal to the total contributions in default, each electing partner shall make the specified contributions within _____ days after the general partner gives notice of the amount of contributions in default. If the total of the amounts specified by the electing partners exceeds the amount of the total contributions in default, each electing partner shall within that time make a contribution of an amount that bears the same ratio to the total amount of contributions not made as the amount specified in his notice of election bears to the total of the amounts specified in all the notices of election timely made. If any partner makes such an additional capital contribution, each partner's interest in profits and losses shall be adjusted under section _____

c. If one or more partners make an additional capital contribution, each partner's share of the net profits and net losses shall be adjusted to reflect the ratio that his/her capital account bears to the total accounts of the partners after any such contribution.

d. The general partner may permit partners to withdraw capital at any time when, in her judgment, funds in excess of reasonable business needs are available. Any such withdrawal by limited partners shall be in the ratio of their respective capital account.

e. An individual capital account shall be maintained for each partner. Each partner's capital account shall consist of his/her original capital contribution increased by any additional capital contributions and his/her share of partnership profits, and decreased by distributions in reduction of partnership capital and his/her share of partnership losses.

f. If any limited partner shall, with the general partner's prior consent, make any loan to the partnership or advance money on its behalf, the loan or advance shall not increase the lending partner's capital account, entitle the lending partner to any greater share of partnership distributions, or subject him/her to any greater proportion of partnership losses. The amount of the loan or advance shall be a debt owed by the partnership to the lending partner, repayable on the terms and conditions, and bearing interest at the rate agreed on by the lending partner and the general partner.

7. PROFIT AND LOSS:

a. The partnership's net profit or net loss shall be determined by the certified public accountant who regularly audits the partnership books,[12] in accordance with generally accepted accounting principles, as soon as practicable after the close of the calendar year.

b. The partnership's profits and losses shall originally be shared by the partners in the same proportion as their initial capital accounts bear to each other. If this proportion changes as a result of additional contributions under Paragraph 6b or as a result of changes in membership under Paragraph 10 of this agreement, then profits and losses shall be shared in this new proportion.

No additional share of profits or losses shall inure to any partner because of other fluctuations in the partners' capital accounts.

c. Distributions of partnership profits shall be limited to those amounts that the general partner shall from time to time determine. Any such distribution shall, however, be in proportion to the partners' shares in the partnership's net profits.

d. The liability of each limited partner for partnership losses shall in no event exceed the aggregate amount of that limited partner's capital contributions required by this agreement.

8. ACCOUNTING AND RECORDS:

a. The fiscal year of the partnership shall be the calendar year.

b. The partnership books shall be kept in the cash basis.

c. At all times during the term of the partnership, and beyond that term if the general partner deems it necessary, the general partner shall keep or cause to be kept books of account in which each partnership transaction shall be entered fully and accurately. All partnership books of account, together with executed copies of the certificate of limited partnership, the fictitious business name statement, this limited partnership agreement, and the amendments to any of these documents, shall be kept at the partnership's principal office and shall be available during reasonable business hours for inspection and examination by the partners or their representatives, who shall have the right to make copies of any of those books and documents at their own expense.

---

12. This will be costly. A better method would be to state "as determined by the accountant who prepares the partnership tax return."

d. The general partner shall deliver to each limited partner, as soon as possible after the tax return is prepared and approved by the general partner, a statement of affairs that shall include:

(1) A balance sheet and profit and loss statement of the partnership as of the close of the taxable year;

(2) A statement showing the capital account of each partner as of the close of the taxable year and the distributions, if any, made to each partner during the year; and

(3) The amount of partnership income reportable by each partner, or the amount of partnership loss deductible by each partner, for federal and California income tax purposes for the taxable year. The general partner shall employ at partnership expense an accountant to prepare items 1-3 above.

9. MANAGEMENT

a. The partnership shall be managed by the general partner who shall devote all her business time to the partnership. Limited partners are not required to devote any time to the partnership.

b. The managing partner shall be entitled to a monthly salary of $1,000.00. She shall be entitled to annual adjustments on the anniversary date of this agreement in an amount equal to the product of her current salary multiplied by the change in the Bay Area Consumer Price Index. Her salary and employment benefits may be changed by the written agreement or consent of partners owning an aggregate interest of _____ percent or more in the capital of the partnership. Her salary shall be treated as a partnership expense in determining its profits and losses.

c. Any of the following actions shall require approval of partners possessing an aggregate interest of _____ percent or more in the capital of the partnership: (1) admission of a new general partner, (2) termination of the partnership, (3) amendment of this agreement, and (4) sale by the partnership of all or substantially all its assests.

10. CHANGES IN MEMBERSHIP:

a. On the death, insanity, or withdrawal of the general partner, the partnership shall dissolve. It shall thereafter conduct only the activities necessary to wind up its affairs.

b. On the death of a limited partner, his executor or administrator shall have all the rights of a limited partner for the purpose of settling his estate or, if his limited partnership interest is held in joint tenancy, the rights and liabilities of the deceased joint tenant shall pass to the surviving joint tenant.

c. The value of a partner's interest in the partnership for purposes of this agreement shall be the fair market value of the partnership multiplied by the ratio that the partner's capital account bears to the total capital account of all the partners.

d. No general partner shall assign, pledge, encumber, sell, or otherwise dispose of all or any part of his interest as a general partner in the partnership.

e. A limited partner may sell, assign, or transfer only his or her entire partnership interest. Should a limited partner desire to sell or exchange his or her partnership intereset, he or she shall give written notice to the partnership and each of the partners. The notice shall set forth the purchaser's name, the terms on which the interest is to be sold or exchanged, and the price. If the interest is to be exchanged for property other than cash, the partner shall place a dollar value on that property. For ten (10) days after the notice is given, the general partner shall have the right to purchase the partner's entire interest for the price or the specified dollar value of the property and in the terms stated in the notice.

If the general partner does not exercise her right to purchase the interest, that right shall be given to the partnership for an additional seven (7) day period, beginning on the day that the general partners' right-to-purchase expires.

If the partnership does not exercise its right-to-purchase the interest, that right shall be given to the other partners for an additional seven (7) day period, beginning on the day that the partnership's right-to-purchase expires. Each of the other partners shall have the right-to-purchase, on the same terms, a part of the interest of the offering partner in the proportion that the other partner's capital account bears to the total capital accounts of all the partners who wish to participate in the purchase, provided, however, that the participating partners may not, in the aggregate, purchase less than the entire interest of the offering partner.

If neither the general partner, the partnership, nor the other partners exercise their rights to purchase the interest, the offering partner may, within seven (7) days from the date the notice is given and on the terms and conditions stated in the notice, sell or exchange his partnership interest to the purchaser named in the notice.

The purchaser of a limited partner's interest under this section shall become a substituted limited partner if he/she is so designated by the selling limited partner. The substitution shall become effective when the appropriate amendment to the certificate of limited partnership is recorded. In the absence of such a designation, he/she shall be entitled to receive only the share of profits or other compensation by way of income and the return of capital contribution to which his/her assignor would have been entitled.

If any partner or the partnership exercises the right to purchase, each partner's interest in profits and losses shall be adjusted under paragraph 7b.

11. MISCELLANEOUS:

a. This agreement may be amended at any time, but any amendment must be in writing and signed by each person who is then a partner.

b. All notices provided for in this agreement shall be deemed to have been duly given if served personally or by first class mail addressed as set forth in paragraph 5a of this agreement or at such other address as the partnership has been notified in writing. Notices to the partnership shall be similarly given, and addressed to it at its principal place of business.

c. This agreement is executed and intended to be performed in the State of California, and the laws of that state shall govern its interpretation and effect.

d. This agreement shall be binding on and inure to the benefit of the respective successors, assigns, and personal representatives of the parties, except to the extent of any contrary provision in this agreement.

e. If any term, provision, covenant, or condition of this agreement is held by a court of competent jurisdiction to be invalid, void, or unenforceable, the rest of the agreement shall remain in full force and effect and shall in no way be affected, impaired, or invalidated.

f. This instrument contains the entire agreement of the parties relating to the rights granted and obligations assumed in this instrument. Any oral representations or modifications concerning this instrument shall be of no force or effect unless contained in a subsequent written modification signed by the party to be charged.

IN WITNESS WHEREOF, the partners have executed this agreement as of the date first shown above.

(Partner name)   *(Address)*

_____   _____

_____   _____

_____   _____

_____   _____

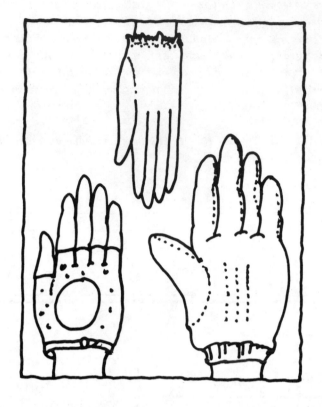

Chapter 8:

Some
Styles of
Partnership
Agreements

A. Introduction

In the first seven chapters we analyzed different issues involved in preparing a sound partnership agreement and running a partnership business. In chapter 9, we show you how to pull your agreement together, step-by-step. Here we take a different approach by setting out several contracts that have been prepared for real businesses we know. These agreements will give you an idea of the great variety of possible methods of preparing a partnership agreement, and confirm that there's no one method—not even the one set out in this book—that is *the* correct one. As you'll see, all these agreements cover basics, like buy-outs or contributions, in some fashion, but otherwise there's little uniformity of approach. Indeed, each is a personal document, reflecting the spirit of the partners and the needs of their joint endeavor.

We've collected a sizeable number of partnership agreements, a number of which could have been included here. Obviously some self-restraint was necessary to avoid creating an encyclopedia. Somewhat reluctantly, we limited ourselves to four agreements—a creative partnership, a real estate venture, a consulting business, and a small manufacturer—with the hope that one or more would have some elements that would speak to your needs. For space reasons, we had to exclude other possibilities, including agreements for professional partnerships (law offices, doctors, architects, accountants), family businesses, communal businesses, etc. In the Appendix we do present some sample clauses for these, and other, specialized partnerships, and list resources for further research in these areas.

B. A "New Age" Partnership Contract Between Two Authors

The two authors (Moira and Phil) involved in this contract were writing a cookbook called *Good Food*, containing recipes which were both nutritional and sophisticated—sort of health-food haute cuisine. They neither believed in nor wanted a traditionally phrased legal agreement. Indeed, for a while they thought they would have no written agreement at all. As the book progressed though, they realized there were some real problems that were not merely lawyer's inventions that they needed to talk about. What happened, for example, if one of them didn't want to do a publicity tour, or how would they handle revisions for subsequent editions? Also, suppose they had some conflict about whether to use bordelaise or tartar sauce with a fish dish and just couldn't resolve it? More importantly, suppose one of them died, or wanted to sell out? What was his or her interest worth?

In discussing these problems, Moira and Phil decided that it would be better to write up an agreement. In case conflict, or the need for a buy-out arose, they wanted ready proof that they'd agreed upon a method for handling that matter. As you'll see, their partnership agreement is quite simple and straightforward; at the same time, it covers many major issues, from distribution of profits to death rights, and includes some more personal matters as well. Here it is:

      & & &

PARTNERSHIP AGREEMENT

between
MOIRA MCGOWEN AND PHIL ANDOVER

This partnership shall be called Rochin Dove Publishing.

Moira and Phil are writing the book Good Food *together, as they enjoy collaborating on cooking meals and writing. They have worked together happily in the past, including work on plays, street fairs, and two unsold movie scripts. They love each other and have fun together; they've been friends for over seven years.*

Moira and Phil are splitting the work, responsibility, and royalties/profits on their book, Good Food, *equally.*

Part of their responsibility includes any revisions and up-dates of future editions, if any. They expect a significant responsibility will be publicity for, and marketing of, the book, including giving interviews, necessary travel, and correspondence.

Upon completion of the book, Moira and Phil plan to meet at least twice a month to review work and responsibility pertaining to the book, and to avoid one person becoming responsible for it. If at any point after the first printing of the book is sold, one person feels he or she is assuming substantially more than 50 percent of the responsibility for the book, Moira and Phil will meet and attempt to divide the work equitably. If they cannot, and one partner becomes essentially passive regarding continued responsibilities for the book, the percentage of the partnership income in subsequent reprints shall reflect that fact and shall be changed, with 75 percent going to the person now responsible and 25 percent going to the inactive partner.

Should Moira and Phil disagree regarding their partnership agreement, they will attempt to mediate their disagreement, with Melinda Terrell serving as mediator. If they cannot resolve their disagreement by mediation, Ms. Terrell shall become arbitrator of the disagreement, with the authority to issue a binding arbitration decision. If Ms. Terrell cannot serve as mediator/arbitrator, those functions shall be served by, in descending order:

> *John Quan;*
>
> *Tony Malbuzzi;*
>
> *Stephanie Harolde*

Either partner shall be able to buy the other's share for a price equal to or less than the previous two years' total of that person's royalty times three.

Death rights shall go to the estate of each partner.

dated _____

dated _____

C. A Real Estate Partnership

This three-man partnership was formed to buy a warehouse in San Francisco. Two of the partners (Robert and Victor) were co-partners in a separate business, a trucking company, which had leased the warehouse. The third partner (Ellen) was an independent accountant who had worked closely with the two trucking company owners. All three saw that buying the warehouse would be an excellent investment. The two trucking company owners decided to include the accountant (1) because they liked her, and (2) because their cash was tight and they could use her contribution. However, the two truckers wanted to make sure they retained effective control over the warehouse, and any trade secrets or customers' lists the trucking business had built up.

This agreement was drafted by one of the authors of this book. When the three prospective partners consulted him, they said only that they wanted to buy the building together and that they wanted him to draw up the partnership agreement. The author's response was to ask them what they wanted in the agreement. They weren't sure, they said, and the author asked them to think about it and discuss the issues they were really worried about, and then to come back after they had outlined their own agreement. The partners did this and all sorts of issues surfaced, from who could sign checks to whether the accountant would still be paid for doing the books of the trucking company. Buy-out provisions posed some problems. Finally, an appraisal method was agreed on for determining the building's market value. Appraisal usually works well with real estate—there is a market, appraisals are common, and competent appraisers are easy to locate and are not exorbitantly expensive. At first there was no agreement on payment terms in case one partner left. After discussion and bargaining back and forth, all agreed that they wanted the right to get all their cash out at once if they left the partnership, etc.

The technical drafting of the agreement was not difficult once the partners decided on what they wanted. Here it is:

& & &

PARTNERSHIP AGREEMENT

This Agreement of Partnership is entered into this _____ day of _____ 198 ____ , between _____ , _____ , and _____ , who hereby form a partnership upon the terms and conditions set forth below.

1) The name of the partnership is _____ , _____ , and

_____ .

2) The partners named are all the partners.

3) The business to be carried on by the partnership is that of ownership, and property management of real property and structures thereon, including, but not limited to, ownership and management of the land and premises at _____ , San Francisco, California.

4) The principal place of business of the partnership is the City and County of San Francisco, California.

5) This partnership shall continue until dissolved by mutual agreement.

6) All capital contribution to the partnership business shall be made equally by the three partners. Each partner shall initially contribute the sum of nine thousand dollars ($9,000.00) to the partnership, to be used for the purchase and necessary expenses of the real property at San Francisco, California.

7) All net income and/or profits or net losses from the partnership business are to be divided equally between the three partners.

8) The partnership shall open a bank account in the partnership name. No funds may be removed or disbursed from that bank account without the written signatures of at least two of the partners.

9) All decisions regarding management of the partnership assets, or other decisions affecting the partnership, shall be concurred in by at least two of the partners.

(a) No asset of the partnership may be sold, transferred, uncumbered, pledged, or otherwise disposed of without the specific written consent of at least two of the partners.

(b) In the event of serious disagreement or dispute between any of the partners regarding any aspect of the partnership business, that disagreement or dispute shall be resolved by submitting the matter to arbitration. The arbitrators of any such disagreement or dispute shall be _____ , Attorney at Law, of _____ . The decision of the arbitrators shall be final and binding.

10) (a) Books of account shall be kept by the partners, and proper entries made therein of all the sales, purchases, receipts, payments, engagements, transactions, and property of the partnership, and the said books of account, and all securities, papers, and writings of the partnership shall be kept at the principal place of business in the City of San Francisco, California, and each partner shall have free access at all times to examine and copy the same.

(b) The partnership's tax returns and financial statements shall be prepared by _____, who is to be compensated at her prevailing rate for such work, at the time such work is completed.

(c) The fiscal year of the partnership shall commence on January 1st of each year and end on December 31st of that year.

11) (a) In the event any partner shall desire to withdraw from the partnership, he or she shall give two months written notice by registered mail to the last known address of the other partners.

(b) Upon the dissolution of the partnership by reason of the death, withdrawal, or other act of any partner, the remaining partners may, if they so desire, continue the business, and they shall have the right to purchase the interest of the other partner in the businss by paying to such partner the value of his/her interest, determined as follows: (1) by mutual agreement as to the net worth of the business; or, if that proves impossible, (2) the partners desiring to continue the business shall select one individual as an appraiser and the retiring partner or his or her representatives shall select one individual as an appraiser. Said appraisers shall determine the net worth of the business and the partners desiring to continue the business shall pay to the other partner one-third (1/3) of the amount so determined; the retiring partner shall execute such documents as may be necessary to convey his/her interest in the business to the other partners.

In the event said appraisers are unable to mutually agree on a net worth for the assets of said business within thirty days after their appointment, they shall select and designate one additional appraiser for this purpose whose appraisement shall be binding on all parties.

12) Upon dissolution of the partnership, the remaining income/losses and assets/liabilities shall be distributed equally between the partners.

13) No partner shall, during the continuance of the partnership nor for five (5) years after its determination, by any means, without the consent in writing of the others of them, or of their heirs, executors, administrators, or assigns, divulge to any person not a member of the firm any trade secret or special information employed in or conductive to the partnership business and which may come to his knowledge in the course of, or by reason of, this partnership.

Executed on _____, 1981 _____, at San Francisco, California.

_____
(signature)

_____
(signature)

_____
(signature)

D. A Quasi-Professional Consulting Business

Now let's look at a different sort of partnership, a consulting business involved in research and planning in the criminal justice/administration and related fields. Originally, there were three partners, one lawyer-criminology professor, one criminal defense lawyer, and a planner-administrator. They opened the business with very little capital and less overhead, operating out of one partner's house, keeping their day jobs, and hoping for the best. They didn't bother with a written partnership agreement.

Their business prospered. Soon they needed an office and employees. A year later, one of the partners left, amicably, to pursue another career. The process of trying to decide what her interest was worth, and how to pay for it, high-lighted what they'd already learned: they'd grown too big and successful to operate as informally as they had. They needed a definite agreement regarding their partnership. They managed, after some difficulties, to resolve everything with the departing partner, but they didn't want to risk the danger inherent in vagueness again. What would happen if one of the two remaining partners wanted to leave? They knew they needed to set up a valuation formula and buy-out terms. Now that they were successful, could they engage in their own private business that might conflict with the partnerships? No, they decided. What would happen if one partner died? Again, there would be a buy-out according to their agreement. Shouldn't they adopt a dispute-resolution method? They did—arbitration.

There weren't any serious problems preparing the actual agreement. Both partners were cooperative, and readily agreed to a buy-out clause which provided that they would meet yearly and agree on a valuation of the business. If they didn't do that, the valuation was the greater of (1) their business insurance on the decedent's life or (2) the balance in the decedent's capital account (which was to be paid off in installment payments). Both parties agreed to name their lawyer as arbitrator of disputes under the agreement.

A couple of years after their agreement was signed, and after the business had grown tremendously, the partnership broke up because of personal conflicts between the partners. Their written agreement proved to be an essential aid in enabling them to agree on a final termination agreement (included in the Appendix) that was, if not always cordial, at least effective.

Here is their partnership agreement.

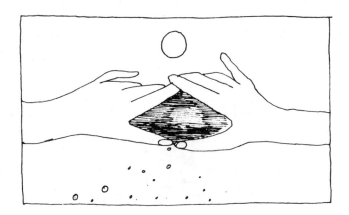

AMENDED AND RESTATED PARTNERSHIP AGREEMENT

This Amended and Restated Partnership Agreement (this "Agreement") dated _____, 19 _____ is between _____ and _____, collectively called the "Partners."

ARTICLE I
ORGANIZATIONAL MATTERS

1.1 _____ and _____ *have been associated as Partners under the firm name _____ . They now desire to amend and restate the terms and conditions of their partnership agreement.*

1.2 *The principal place of business of the Partnership will be _____ , Oakland, California, or such other address as may be agreed upon by the Partners from time to time.*

1.3 *This Agreement is effective on the date hereof and shall continue (i) untill the date specified in a written notice of termination by any Parnter to the other which date shall be at least sixty (60) days after the giving of such notice, or (ii) until otherwise terminated by the terms of this Agreement or by law. Upon any Partnership termination, the Partners shall cooperate in arranging the fulfillment of all Partnership obligations and the collection of Partnership credits under existing contracts.*

1.4 *The purpose of the Partnership shall be to provide consulting and planning, both public and private, in criminal justice and other fields, and to engage in such other businesses as the Partners shall determine.*

1.5 *The Partners or any one of them shall file and publish all notices, statements, or other instruments, including any amendments thereto required by law for the operation of a general partnership in California and in any other jurisdiction where the Partnership may elect to do business.*

ARTICLE II
CAPITAL

2.1 *The Partnership's initial capital shall consist of (1) the net assets of its predecessor partnership as of November 30, 1977, as reflected in the balance sheet attached as Exhibit A and (2) the assets acquired plus the liabilities discharged, less the liabilities incurred but not discharged, and less the assets distributed or otherwise disposed of by the predecessor partnership, through the date of this agreement. Each Partner's capital contribution shall consist of a one-half (1/2) interest in the equity of the predecessor partnership and has been assigned a book value of $12,135.75 accordingly.*

ARTICLE III
ACCOUNTING AND DISTRIBUTION

3.1 *A capital account shall be maintained for each Partner. The original capital contribution of each Partner shall conclusively be presumed to be the amount*

177

shown as the value of the capital account of each Partner as of the date of this Agreement when the Partnership accountant completes such November 30 financial statement.

3.2 The capital accounts of the Partners shall be credited with all contributions and profits, and charged with all distributions and losses, in proportion to their respective capital contributions.

3.3 Until and unless the Partnership agreement is amended, or other partners are admitted, the two Partners shall be equal, and shall share everything equally (that is, participate in profits and distributions, bear all losses and calls, and make any required additional contributions equally).

3.4 Neither Partner shall be entitled to a guaranteed payment of any kind, except salary as provided in Section 4.2. When cash is available for distribution, from time to time, it will be distributed to Partners in proportion to original capital contributions.

ARTICLE IV
ADMINISTRATIVE PROVISIONS

4.1 Each Partner shall have an equal voice in the management of the Partnership business.

4.2 Each Partner agrees to refrain from conducting outside the Partnership any activities that are competitive with the activities of the Partnership as herein described.

4.3 One or more Partnership bank accounts shall be established and checks on the accounts may be signed by either Partner.

4.4 The fiscal year of the Partnership shall be the calendar year.

4.5 No Partner without the consent of the other, shall (a) make, execute, or deliver any assignment of the Partnership's assets for the benefit of creditors or any confession of judgment; (b) pledge or hypothecate or in any manner transfer his/her interest in the Partnership; or (c) cause the Partnership to become a surety, a guarantor, or accommodation party to any obligation other than in the ordinary course of the Partnership business.

4.6 Each of the Partners shall be entitled to monthly reimbursement, upon the submission of an itemized account, of such sums as shall have been reasonably expended for the benefit of the business of the Partnership, but such expenditures shall not exceed during each year of the Partnership, for each Partner, unless otherwise agreed.

4.7 Reasonable salaries shall be paid to each Partner for his/her services to the Partnership, as mutually agreed from time to time.

ARTICLE V
SALE OF A PARTNERSHIP INTEREST

5.1 Each Partner agrees that he/she may not, and shall never attempt to, assign, pledge, give away, or otherwise alienate his/her interest in the Partnership or any part thereof, except that either Partner may pledge or encumber his/her interest in the profits and capital of the Partnership to a lender with the consent of the other which shall not be unreasonably withheld.

5.2 Upon the death of a Partner, the surviving Partner shall purchase the decedent's interest in the Partnership for, and the decedent's personal representative shall sell the same for, a price as determined in accordance with Section 5.3 hereof.

5.3 The Partners agree that the price for purchase and sale of a deceased Partner's interest shall be determined as follows:

(a) Each year, either before March 15 or as soon thereafter as they choose, the Partners hope to meet and agree in writing to the price that will prevail for the ensuing twelve (12) months.

(b) The actual price to be paid for the decedent's interest will be the greater of (1) the aggregate insurance received because of the decedent's death by the partnership as an entity or by the surviving Partner(s), or (2) either (i) the price that shall have been agreed to within twelve (12) months prior to the decedent's death, or (ii) if no price shall have been so agreed to within such period, the decedent's capital account at the calendar month end date next preceding his/her death (excluding insurance proceeds on his/her death).

To the extent of insurance received on the decedent's death, the price shall be paid in cash not later than ninety (90) days following the date of death. If the price exceeds the insurance, the excess shall be paid in no more than sixty (60) equal consecutive monthly installments beginning on the first day of the fifth month following the date of death, with nine percent (9%) interest on unpaid principal.

ARTICLE VI
TERMINATION

6.1 The Partnership shall not be dissolved by the admission of a new general partner. Each of the Partners waives any and all rights to seek a court decree of dissolution. Except as so provided, the Partnership shall be dissolved by any event requiring dissolution under the Uniform Partnership Act of California.

6.2 Upon dissolution of the Partnership, the Partnership affairs shall be wound up, the Partnership assets shall be liquidated, and the Partnership shall be terminated. The proceeds from liquidation of Partnership assets shall be applied as follows: First to payment of debts of the Partnership other than to Partners. Second, any balance to payment of debts of the Partners. Last, any balance to Partners in proportion to their capital contributions.

6.3 Any gain or loss on disposition of Partnership properties in the process of liquidation shall be credited or charged to Partners in proportion to their capital coontributions.

ARTICLE VII
SUNDRY TERMS

7.1 If any controversy or claim arising out of this Partnership Agreement cannot be settled by the Partners or their legal representatives, such controversy or claim shall be settled by submission to _____ as single arbitrator with full power to set all procedural rules for the arbitration, or (if he is unavailable or unwilling to act) settled by arbitration in accordance with the then current rules of the American Arbitration Association.

7.2 This Agreement with respect to the subject matter hereof contains the complete and integrated understanding of the parties.
IN WITNESS WHEREOF, the Partners have signed this Agreement of Partnership.

   & & &

E. A Small Production Business

Finally, let's look at a partnership formed to produce and sell t-shirts. An artist acquaintance of ours (call her Janice) had silk-screened a few t-shirts for presents to some of her friends. Her designs were inventive and colorful. One of her friends, Danielle, thought the shirts could be sold commercially. Janice was intrigued, but also, right from the start, made it clear she didn't want to devote full time to the t-shirt business. "I'm an artist, not a t-shirt tycoon," she explained. So Danielle agreed to do the bulk of the business details. At first she considered actually manufacturing the t-shirts, but quickly abandoned that idea as prohibitively complicated, requiring far too much initial investment. So she located sources where they could buy quality cotton t-shirts for a decent price. Next, she investigated machinery that could be purchased for silk screening the t-shirts. This proved feasible, although it would still require more capital than she and Janice had. So they looked for a third party and, after some searching, met Marilyn, a lawyer. Marilyn agreed to put up most of the cash the business needed, and also do the books. She suggested that her participation made her entitled to a 50 percent interest in the partnership. Janice and Danielle disagreed. Danielle pointed out that she would really be doing most of the work—actually preparing the t-shirts, and then trying to sell them to stores. Janice, who was to be responsible for the artistic ends of the business— from design of the t-shirts to purchase of the inks and dyes to screen them—agreed. It took a while, but eventually the three women decided 50 percent interest for Danielle, and 25 percent for each of the others was fair.

In discussing their proposed partnership agreement, several other problems came up. For example, Marilyn was concerned about possible losses, since she was the one partner with substantial savings. She didn't want to be stuck for losses unless there was no other way out. So the other partners agreed that losses (1) would be paid first from whatever capital they'd contributed; and (2) would be repaid, if necessary, from their future profits. Then they worried about a partner leaving. How would they determine what that interest was worth? They found they all agreed that they wanted to place primary emphasis on survival and continuation of the business. Marilyn suggested various ways to do this and after discussion they decided, basically, to give a departing partner the market value of her interest, without any value for "good will," or the future earnings potential of the business.

Here's the contract they signed.

CLEAR VISION T-SHIRT COMPANY
PARTNERSHIP AGREEMENT

This agreement is executed this _____ day of _____ , 1980, by and among Janice _____ , Danielle _____ , and Marilyn _____ .

ARTICLE I
Name and Place of Business

1. The name of the partnership shall be the Clear Vision T-Shirt Company.

2. The principal place of business of the partnership shall be at _____ Street, _____ , California.

ARTICLE II
Purposes of the Business

1. The partnership shall engage in the business of printing, selling, and dealing generally in t-shirts of all kinds and in such other businesses of a similar nature or related as may be agreed upon by the partners.

ARTICLE III
Capital and Service Contributions, Accounts and Withdrawals

1. The initial capital of the partnership shall consist of $23,000, contributed by Marilyn _____ , $4,000 contributed by Danielle _____ , and $50 contributed by Janice _____ .

2. Marilyn _____ shall also contribute all accounting and bookkeeping services needed.

3. Danielle shall contribute her managerial services, and shall be responsible for production and sales of the business.

* 4. Janice should contribute her artistic services, and shall be responsible for design of the t-shirts, and selection of inks, dyes, and other materials for imprinting or silkscreening the t-shirts.

5. An individual capital account shall be maintained for each partner.

6. Except by unanimous agreement of the partners, or upon dissolution, the capital contributions of the partners shall not be subject to withdrawal.

ARTICLE IV
Profits and Losses

1. The net profits or net losses of the partnership shall be distributable or chargeable, as the case may be, to each of the partners as follows:

Marilyn _____	25 percent
Danielle _____	50 percent
Janice _____	25 percent

2. An individual income account shall be maintained for each partner. Profits and losses shall be credited or debited to the individual income accounts as soon as practicable after the close of each fiscal year.

3. If there be no balance in the individual income accounts, net losses shall be debited to the individual capital accounts. If the capital account of a partner shall have been depleted by the debiting of losses under this paragraph, future profits of that partner shall not be credited to her income account until the depletion shall have been made good, but shall be credited to her capital account. After the depletion in her capital account shall have been made good, her share of the profit thereafter shall be credited to her income account.

ARTICLE V
Management; Salaries

1. Danielle shall conduct the day-to-day management of the business. However, each of the partners shall have an equal voice in overall management of the business. All major management decisions shall be made by majority vote, and each partner is entitled to one vote.

2. Danielle shall receive a salary for weeks she works more than 30 hours on the business. The amount of her salary shall be agreed upon by the partners, but the payment of her salary shall be an obligation of the partnership only to the extent that there are partnership assets available for it, and shall not be an obligation of the partners individually. Her salary shall be treated as expenses of the partnership in determining net profits or net losses.

ARTICLE VI
Dissolution Because of the Retirement, Death, or Insanity of a Partner

1. Any partner may retire from the partnership upon sixty (60) days' prior notice to the other partners.

2. Retirement, death, or insanity of a partner shall work an immediate dissolution of the partnership.

3. In the event of the dissolution of the partnership by the retirement, death, or insanity of a partner, a proper accounting shall be made of the capital and income accounts of each partner and of the net profit or net loss of the partnership from the date of the last previous accounting to the date of dissolution.

4. In the event of the retirement, death, or insanity of a partner, the remaining partners shall have the right to continue the business of the partnership under its present name by themselves, or in conjunction with any other person or persons they may select, but they shall pay to the retiring partner, or to the legal representatives of the deceased or insane partner, as the case may be, the value of her interest in the partnership as provided in the following paragraphs of this Article. If the remaining partners both desire to continue business, but not together, the partnership shall be liquidated in accordance with the provisions of Paragraph 1 of Article VII.

5. The value of the interest of a retiring, deceased, or insane partner, as of the date of dissolution, shall be the sum of:

(a) Her capital account;

(b) Her income account;

(c) Any earned and unpaid salary due her; and

(d) Her proportionate share of accrued net profits.

If a net loss has been incurred to the date of dissolution, her share of such loss shall be deducted.

Inventory for purposes of this Article shall be valued at cost or market value, whichever is lower. Other assets shall be valued at book value.

No value for good will or firm name shall be included in any computations of a partner's interest under this Article.

ARTICLE VII
Voluntary Dissolution

1. Unless dissolved by the retirement, death, or insanity of a partner, the partnership shall continue until dissolved by agreement of the partners. Upon any such voluntary dissolution by agreement, the affairs of the partnership shall be liquidated forthwith. The assets of the partnership shall first be used to pay or provide for all debts of the partnership. Thereafter, all moneys in the income accounts of the partners, and all amounts due for earned or unpaid salaries of the partners, shall be paid to the partners respectively entitled thereto. Then the remaining assets shall be divided according to the proportionate interests of the partners on the basis of their respective capital accounts as they stood upon the date of such dissolution, after crediting or debiting to them the net profit or net loss accrued or incurred, as the case may be, from the date of the last accounting to the date of dissolution.

2. Upon termination of the partnership by agreement of the partners, any two partners shall have the right, in lieu of the liquidation provided for in the preceding paragraph of this Article, to continue the business of the partnership under its present name, by themselves or in conjunction with any person or persons they may select, upon paying in cash forthwith to the withdrawing partner the amounts to which she would be entitled under Paragraph 5 of Article VI, in case of a dissolution under Article VI. If more than one of the partners desires to take advantage of this paragraph, but they do not desire to continue the business of the partnership together, then the affairs of the partnership shall be liquidated in accordance with the preceding paragragh of this Article.

ARTICLE VIII
Partners' Powers and Limitations

1. Checks may be drawn on the partnership bank account for partnership purposes only and may be signed by any one partner.

2. No partner may without the consent of the other partner:

(a) Borrow money in the firm name for firm purposes or utilize collateral owned by the partnership as security for such loans;

(b) Assign, transfer, pledge, compromise, or release any of the claims of or debts due the partnership except upon payment in full, or arbitrate or consent to the arbitration of any of the disputes or controversies of the partnership;

(c) Make, execute, or deliver any assignment for the benefit of creditors, or any bond, confession of judgment, chattel mortgage, deed, guarantee, indemnity bond, surety bond, or contract to sell or contract of sale of all or substantially all of the property of the partnership;

(d) Lease or mortgage any partnership real estate or any interest therein or enter into any contract for any such purpose;

(e) Pledge or hypothecate or in any manner transfer her interest in the partnership, except to another party to this agreement;

(f) Become a surety, guarantor, or accommodation party to any obligation.

ARTICLE IX
Miscellaneous

1. The partnership shall maintain a bank account or bank accounts in such bank or banks as may be agreed upon by the partners.

2. Proper and complete books of account shall be kept at all times and shall be open to inspection by any partner at any reasonable time during business hours. The books of account may, at any partner's request, be examined and reviewed as of the close of each fiscal year by an independent certified public accountant agreeable to the partners, who shall make a report thereon.

4. The parties hereto covenant and agree that they will execute any further instruments and that they will perform any acts which are or may become necessary to effectuate and to carry on the partnership created by this agreement.

IN WITNESS WHEREOF, the parties hereto have hereunto set their hands and seals the day and year first above written.

Witnessed:

. . . . *(Seal)*

. . . . *(Seal)*

. . . . *(Seal)*

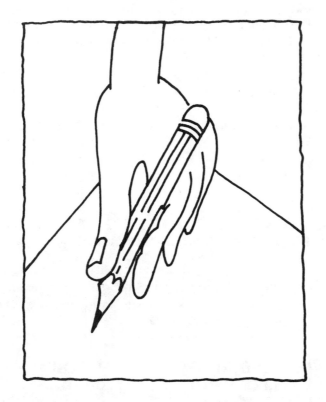

Chapter 9:

Drafting Your Actual Partnership Agreement

Finally the big moment has arrived. It's time to prepare your own general partnership agreement (limited partnerships are discussed in chapter 7). Perhaps it's taken a little longer to get to the typewriter stage than you would have wished, but take heart. You should have more than enough information to carefully draft a document which expresses your specific desires and needs. We could have given you a standardized "form" partnership agreement on page two that would have short-circuited the process, but you would have ended up with a far less useful agreement. Here we take you step-by-step through the basics that should be covered in any partnership agreement. We've included some sample clauses in case they assist you, but *not* to insist you use one of them.

NOTE: In chapter 8, we give you four sample partnership agreements to illustrate what the finished product can look like. You may find elements of these which fit your situation. Fine. As you go through the steps in this chapter, adopt, or adapt, the relevant clauses from the sample agreements that meet your needs. Okay, let's start.

STEP ONE: DISCUSSING WHAT YOU EXPECT AND NEED FROM YOUR PARTNERSHIP BUSINESS

By this time, you should have already done this. You should know at the very least what your business will be about, who will be the partners, who will contribute what, how you hope to make money, how your personal goals and goals of your business can be merged, etc., and you're quite ready to focus on specifics.

STEP TWO: REVIEW AND RESOLVE THE MAJOR PROBLEM AREAS THAT SHOULD BE COVERED IN ANY PARTNERSHIP AGREEMENT

This is, of course, the heart of the matter. Throughout this book, we've discussed specific problems that should be anticipated in your partnership agreement. We assume that by now you have done this and have made some notes on how you'll handle them. Actually putting your agreement together will give you a chance to review problems and notes once more. Nevertheless, we suggest that before you actually start filling in blanks you read through all the "Steps" of this chapter. If any seem confusing, go back and reread the applicable section of the book.

Here we want to remind you yet once again that the final decisions of what subjects you want to cover in your agreement are personal and that only you can resolve them finally. One basic issue involves how detailed you want your agreement to be. In each step of this chapter, we include sample clauses showing different ways of handling the basic partnership problems. We also provide cross references to the text discussions on all major contract points as we go along. These may be sufficient for your needs. But in case they are not, we refer you to Appendix A, where we provide many additional (often more sophisticated) partnership clauses, with explanations of their meaning and possible use where necessary.

STEP THREE: ACTUALLY PREPARING YOUR AGREEMENT

The physical preparation of your partnership agreement is easy. Start by creating a rough draft. You may want to cut sample clauses from this book, draft some of your own, etc. Don't try to arrive at a finished product the first time through. For example, we rewrote this book five times and we do this for a living. Once you have a good first draft, have a clean copy typed. Your next step is to have it reviewed by all the partners. There will almost surely be some changes. Then re-type the agreement (plain bond paper is fine). Have each partner date and sign it. A partnership agreement doesn't have to be notarized unless it has to do with the ownership of real property and you want to record it at your local land title recording office. Notarization has nothing to do with making a contract more binding, but does serve to establish that the signatures are legitimate. Each partner should be given a photocopy of the agreement. Keep the original in some safe place.,

STEP FOUR: THE HEADING

Simply type *PARTNERSHIP AGREEMENT*.

STEP FIVE: PARTNER IDENTIFICATION AND DATE OF FORMATION CLAUSE

Your next job is to identify the partners and the date the partnership is formed, as follows:

This partnership agreement is entered into and effective as of _____, *19* ____ , *by* _____ *(name)* _____ , _____ *(name)* _____ _____ *(name)* _____ , *etc., the partners.*

STEP SIX: STATE IDENTIFICATION CLAUSE

Here you identify the state under whose laws your partnership is governed, as follows:

The partners desire to form a general partnership under the laws of the state of _____ *(your state)*[1] _____ *for the purposes and on the terms and conditions stated in this agreement.*

STEP SEVEN: NAME CLAUSE

Here you simply identify the name of the partnership business, as follows:

The name of the partnership (or business) shall be _____ .

---

1. If you plan to operate in more than one state, you'd usually select the state where you have your principal place of business.

STEP EIGHT: PRINCIPAL PLACE OF BUSINESS CLAUSE

Here you simply state the principal place from which your partnership business will be operating, as follows:

The partnership's principal place of business shall be at _____ in _____, _____ The principal place of business may be changed from time to time and other places of business may be established by actions taken in accordance with the provisions of this agreement that govern management of the partnership's business and affairs.

STEP NINE: THE PURPOSE CLAUSE

Include a concise statement of the business the partnership will engage in. This is usually broadly drafted. Here are three samples to give you an idea of what is commonly included.

#1. "The purpose of the partnership is to operate and maintain a retail health food store, and such other businesses as the partners may agree on."

#2. "The purpose of the partnership is to engage in the practice of architecture and related activities."

#3. "The purpose of the partnership is to produce stage plays, including all activities necessary for or useful to such productions."

(For further information, see chapter 4, section B; Appendix A; and Interlude Two.)

STEP TEN: TERM OF PARTNERSHIP CLAUSE

Here are two alternatives; one with a set term and the other indefinite.

#1. The partnership shall continue for a period of _____ years, at which time it shall be dissolved and its affairs wound up.

#2. The partnership shall continue indefinitely until dissolved by mutual agreement of the partners.

(For further information, see chapter 3, section B; and Appendix A.)

STEP ELEVEN: CONTRIBUTION CLAUSE

Here you deal with the partners' contributions of money or property to begin the partnership. We include four simple alternatives:

A. Equal Shares Contributed

The initial capital of the partnership shall be a total of $ _____. Each partner shall contribute an equal share amounting to $ _____, no later than _____, 198 ____.

B. Unequal Shares Contributed

The partnership's initial capital shall consist of cash to be contributed by the partners in the following amounts:

Name	Amount
_____	_____
_____	_____
_____	_____

Each partner's contribution shall be paid in full by _____, 198 ____.

C. Contributions of Property

_____ shall contribute property valued at $ _____ , consisting of _____ (if the property is complex, you can add "more particularly described in Exhibit A, attached to this agreement.")

(If more than one partner contributes property, repeat this clause for each partner.)

D. Contribution of Service

_____ shall make no cash or property contribution at the commencement of the partnership. _____ shall donate (his/her) full work time and energies to the partnership for a period of _____, [and for those services (he/she) shall be entitled to ____% of the profits of the partnership, as specified in Paragraph ____.]

(For further information, see chapter 3, section C, types of clauses and discussion; chapter 6, sections E, F, tax consequences of contributions; and Appendix A, for more complicated clauses.)

STEP TWELVE: MANAGEMENT POWER AND DUTIES CLAUSE

If you do not want all partners to be materially involved in running the business, do not use this provision. Instead, see a good lawyer and tax man.

All partners shall materially participate in the partnership, which means regular, continuous and substantial involvements in partnership business operations.

Generally, you can put in whatever else you want regarding management decisions, in whatever detail you decide is necessary. Here are several sample cases regarding how your partnership will be managed.

#1. Each partner shall have equal voice in the management and control of the partnership; decisions shall be by majority vote.

or

#2. Each partner shall participate in the management of the business; in

exercising the powers of management, each partner's vote shall be in proportion to his or her interest in the partnership's capital.

or

#3. All partnership decisions must be made by unanimous decision of all partners.

or

#4. Checks drawn on the partnership bank account must be signed by at least two of the partners.

or

#5. The addition of any new partner, or partners, to this partnership may be done only by unanimous agreement of all existing partners, on such terms and conditions as they agree on.

(For further information, see chapter 3, section B on management power and duties; chapter 4, section C on the addition of new partners; and Appendix A for more sample clauses.)

STEP THIRTEEN: DISTRIBUTION OF PROFITS AND LOSSES CLAUSES

Here are two samples:

#1. The partnership's profits and losses shall be shared equally by all partners.

#2. The partnership's profits and losses shall be shared as follows:

Partner	% of Profits	% of Losses
_____	_____	_____
_____	_____	_____
_____	_____	_____

(For further information see chapter 3, section C(2); Appendix A.)

STEP FOURTEEN: BUY-OUT CLAUSE

Now it's time to prepare your buy-out clause. These are most important, and usually complicated, because they involve at least three distinct elements: the right to buy (or right of first refusal); valuation; and method of payment. Here are several samples of each. Be sure that the buy-out clauses you prepare all fit together to form a sensible whole.

A. Right to Buy and Right of First Refusal

If any partner leaves the partnership, for whatever reason, whether he/she quits, withdraws, is expelled, retires, or dies, he/she shall be obligated to sell his/her interest in the partnership, and the remaining partners obligated to buy that interest, under the terms and conditions set forth below.

Right to Buy

If any partner leaves the partnership, for whatever reason, whether he/she quits, withdraws, is expelled, retires, or dies, he/she shall be obligated to sell his/her interest in the partnership, and the remaining partners obligated to buy that interest, under the terms and conditions set forth below.

Right of First Refusal

If any partner receives an offer, whether or not solicited by him/her, from a person not a partner to purchase all (or any portion) of his/her interest in the partnership, and if the partner receiving the offer is willing to accept it, he/she shall give written notice of the amount and terms of the offer, the identity of the proposed buyer and his/her willingness to accept the offer to each of the other partners. The other partners shall have the option, within _____ days after that notice is given, to purchase that partner's interest (or designated portion of the interest) on the same terms as those contained in the offer. (The other partners may exercise this option jointly or individually. If more than one partner exercises the option individually, the partner giving notice may choose whose exercise of the option he/she shall accept.)

B. Valuation Methods

Set Dollar Amount

The value of a partner's interest in the partnership shall be determined as follows:

(1) Within _____ (i.e., ninety) days after the end of each fiscal year of the partnership, the partners shall detrmine the partnership's value by unanimous written agreement, and that value shall remain in effect from the date of that written determination until the next such written determination.

(2) Should the partners be unable to agree on a value or otherwise fail to make any such determination, the partnership's value shall be the greater of (a) the value last established under this section, or (b) the net worth of the partnership.

Market Value

The value of a partner's interest in the partnership shall be his/her ownership percentage in the business; the value of the business shall be the sum of the following items, as of the date that value is to be determined.

1. The credit balance in the business capital account(s), less all outstanding debts owed by the business.

2. All accounts receivable that are reasonably collectable, and all unbilled but earned fees.

3. The current market value of all assets.

Capitalization of Earnings Clause

The value of a partner's interest in the partnership shall be his/her ownership percentage of the value of the partnership on the date of his/her departure from the partnership, which shall be determined as follows:

The net profits of the business shall be determined for the three fiscal years preceding the partner's departure. The average net profit shall then be calculated, then multiplied by a multiplier of _____ giving the value of the business.

Post Departure Appraisal Clause

The value of a partner's interest in the partnership shall be his/her ownership percentage of the value of the partnership on the date of his/her departure from the partnership, as determined by an independent appraisal of the worth of the partnership on that date conducted by _____ . The appraisal shall be commenced within _____ days of the partner's departure. The partnership and the departing partner shall share the appraisal expenses equally.

C. Payment Methods

Equal Installments

Whenever the partnership is obligated or chooses to purchase a partner's interest, it shall pay for that interest, at its option, in cash or by promissory note of the partnership, or partly in cash and partly by note. Any promissory note shall be dated as of the effective date of the purchase, shall mature in not more than _____ years, shall be payable in equal installments that come due monthly, shall bear interest at the rate of ___ percent per annum (and may, at the partnership's option, be subordinated to existing and future debts to banks and other institutional lenders for money borrowed.) The first payment shall be made 90 days after the date of the promissory note.

Life Insurance

Each partner shall purchase and maintain life insurance (and disability insurance) on the life of each other partner(s) in the face value of $ _____ .

(For more information, read chapter 5, sections A,B; Appendix A; and Interludes 3 and 4.)

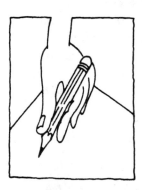

STEP FIFTEEN: DISSOLUTION AND/OR CONTINUATION OF BUSINESS CLAUSE

Here are two sample clauses to cover other problems arising from the departure or withdrawal of a partner. Many others are possible as well.

#1. Continuity of Business
In the event of the departure of a partner, for whatever reason, the partnership shall not be dissolved, but the partnership business may be continued uninterrupted by the remaining partners.

#2. Non-Transfer Clause
A partner may transfer all or part of his/her interest in the partnership only as follows:
1. To the partnership or to any other partner, as provided in Section _____ of this agreement
2. On his/her death, by will or other transfer means, as limited by the terms of this agreement.

(Other continuity provisions are contained in chapter 5, section B(5); and Appendix A.)

STEP SIXTEEN: DISPUTE RESOLUTION CLAUSE

A. Arbitration

1. Any dispute arising out of this agreement shall be arbitrated under the terms of this clause. The arbitration shall be carried out by a single arbitrator, who shall be _____ _____[or who shall be agreed upon by the parties to the dispute]. If the parties cannot agree on the arbitrator, the arbitrator shall be selected by _____ _____ (include any method you wish, such as naming a person all agree, now, is fair, to be the arbitrator, or to select the arbitrator[2]). Any arbitration shall be held as follows.

2. The person(s) initiating the arbitration procedure shall inform the other partner(s) in writing of the nature of the dispute at the same time that he or she notifies the arbitrator.

3. Within _____ days from receipt of this notice, the other persons shall reply in writing.

4. An arbitration meeting shall be held within seven days after the other person's reply. Each partner shall be entitled to present whatever oral or written statements he or she wishes and may present witnesses. No person may be represented by a lawyer or any third party.[3]

5. The arbitrator shall make his or her decision in writing within five days after the arbitration hearing.

6. If the person(s) to whom the demand for arbitration is directed fails to respond within the proper time limit, the person(s) initiating the arbitration must give the other an additional five days' written notice of "intention to proceed to arbitration." If there is still

---

2. If there are more than two sides to the conflict, the appointment of arbitrators becomes difficult. If you can't get at least two of the sides to agree on one arbitrator, you'll probably wind up in court.

3. If you want to allow lawyers in the arbitration, you're free to do so by changing the clause.

no response, the person(s) initiating the arbitration may proceed with the arbitration before the arbitrator, and his or her award shall be binding.

7. The cost of arbitration shall be borne by the parties as the arbitrators shall direct.

8. The arbitration award shall be conclusive on the parties and shall be set in such a way that a formal judgment can be entered thereon in the court having jurisdiction over the dispute if either party so desires.

Dated: _____   *Signature:* _____

Dated: _____   *Signature:* _____

Note on Using Three Arbitrators: If despite our preference you decide you want to use three arbitrators, adopt the three arbitration clause in Chapter 3, Sec. D(1).

B. Mediation

1. _____ , _____ , _____ ,
(etc.,) the partners, agree that any dispute arising out of this agreement or the partnership business shall be resolved by mediation. The partners are aware that mediation is a voluntary process, and pledge to cooperate fully and fairly with the mediator in an attempt to reach a mutually satisfactory compromise of any dispute.
2. The mediator shall be _____ .
3. If any party to a dispute feels it cannot be resolved by the partners themselves, he/she shall so notify the other partners, and the mediator, in writing.
4. Mediation shall commence within _____ *days of this notice of request for mediation.*

(The details of the mediation process could be provided in greater detail, but we don't feel this is either necessary or advisable; if you disagree, add whatever details you decide you want spelled out.)

5. Any decision reached by mediation shall be reduced to writing, signed by all parties, and will be binding on them.

C. Mediation/Arbitration

(Making the mediator the arbitrator if mediation fails. Add to the above mediation clause.)

If the parties cannot reach a decision by mediation, the dispute shall be arbitrated by _____ (the mediator/arbitrator), whose decision will be binding.

(For further information, see chapter 3, section D; Appendix A.)

STEP SEVENTEEN: ADD ANY ADDITIONAL CLAUSES YOU DESIRE

As we've said throughout this book, there's no magic formula for writing a partnership agreement. We've just taken you through the basics that we're sure you should cover in your agreement. But there are many other subjects you might want to cover. Review that possibility here. Check over the notes you made while reading the text. Review the list of subjects often covered in partnership agreements contained in chapter 3, section A. And examine Appendix A to see if there's anything in it you'll need. Don't get too frazzled in all this. Remember, brevity is usually the soul of common sense, as well as of wit.

STEP EIGHTEEN: SIGNATURE AND DATE CLAUSE

(Simply type lines for your signatures and dates, and sign the agreement.)

(partner's name) _____   _____ *date* _____

(partner's name) _____   *date* _____

(partner's name) _____   _____ *date* _____

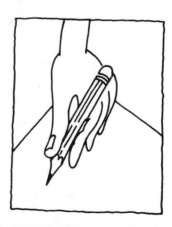

STEP NINETEEN: CHECK YOUR WORK CAREFULLY

Now, that wasn't terribly complicated was it? Many partnership agreements contain only three or four pages. Still, it's extremely important that all of your clauses fit together to make a coherent whole. If you have any substantial doubts that you have achieved this, you may want to have your work checked by a lawyer and/or a tax accountant (see chapter 1, section F). This should be relatively inexpensive.

STEP TWENTY: THE "WE'RE ALL DONE AND WE DID IT OURSELVES AND IT DIDN'T COST TOO MUCH" CELEBRATION PARTY

Parties of course are very personal things, but let us make a few suggestions:

#1. Yeats said it well:

For the good are always the merry,
  Save by an evil chance,
And the merry love the fiddle
  And the merry love to dance.

The Fiddler of Dooney

#2. If you can adopt a two-tier system of accounting (see chapter 2), how about a two-tier system of parties? First, a small private (elegant is our preference) celebration, just for the partners and spouses/lovers; second, a good old-fashioned party to commemorate the actual opening of the partnership business. (We've followed this method, and its been wonderful.)

#3. There are some excellent, relatively inexpensive, California champagnes.

STEP TWENTY-ONE: GOOD LUCK AND OUR BEST WISHES IN YOUR NEW ADVENTURE

May you approach your partnership business with a sense of wonder and excitement and take from it not only material possessions, but personal fulfillment and the centeredness that comes with having actualized your dream.

Appendix

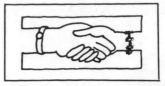

A. Additional Clauses for Partnership Agreements

This section contains numerous clauses you might want to use, or adapt, in your partnership agreement. Many of these clauses are, as you'll see, either limited to certain specific situations, or very detailed. As we've urged before, be cautious and selective regarding the detailing you include in your partnership agreement. You do need to cover the basics and you do get to decide what those basics are. However, it's rarely possible to cover every conceivable contingency in your agreement—not that some lawyers don't try, presenting their client with a 50-page agreement, and a bill for thousands of dollars. You won't need that type of complexity, surely, but you might want more detail and precision in one area than the clauses in the text provide. All these clauses can, of course, be varied in any way you desire. We usually haven't bothered to spell out variations, which are theoretically endless.

INTRODUCTORY CLAUSES/RECITALS

• A recital is a statement about the partners or the partnership; often it explains how and why the partnership came into being. A recital normally has no particular legal effect; its purpose is simply to state in writing facts that the partners want to stress. The possibilities are limitless.

EXAMPLE: The partners have previously been engaged in clothes-making as individuals; they've decided to combine their skills, and energies, and form a women's clothing store . . .

• Use of the phrase, *"intending to be legally boud thereby"* after the initial agreement clause can eliminate certain technical problems possible in some states, such as Pennsylvania, which have adopted the "Uniform Written Obligations Act."

EXAMPLE: ". . . It is mutually agreed by and between the partners, intending to be legally bound thereby, as follows."

• If the partnership will operate in more than one state, you may want to define which state's laws govern construction of the agreement. You do this simply by stating, in the agreement, which state's laws to control.

EXAMPLE: "This agreement has been made and entered into in accordance with the laws of the state of _____, and said agreement shall be construed and applied in all respects in accordance with the laws of that state."

& &

TERM

Many alternatives are possible to the usual open-ended term of partnership agreements.

> *EXAMPLE: "The partnership shall begin as of the date of this agreement and continue until _____ . After that time, the partnership shall continue from year to year unless _____ percent of the partners vote to dissolve it." (e.g., 75 percent.)*

& & &

CONTRIBUTIONS

Contributions are one area of partnership agreements that can get very complex. Clauses for certain different types of complexities are set out below.

● DEFERRED CONTRIBUTIONS:
monthly installments

> *"_____ shall be a partner, but shall not make any contribution of cash or property to the initial capital of the partnership. He/she shall subsequently contribute to the partnership capital, and his/her capital account shall be credited, the amount of $ _____ per month, beginning _____, 19 ____ , until he/she has contributed the sum of _____ ."*

contribution out of profit

> *"_____ shall be a partner, but shall not make any contribution of cash or property to the initial capital of the partnership. He/she shall subsequently contribute to the partnership capital, and his/her capital account shall be credited _____ percent of his/her distributive share of the partnership's profits for each fiscal year beginning _____, 19 ____ until he/she has contributed the total amount of $ _____ ."*

where partnership is successor to an earlier partnership

> *"The partnership's initial capital shall consist of (1) the net assets of its predecessor partnership called '_____', as of _____ , 19 ____ , as reflected in Exhibit (A) (the balance sheet as of that date), and (2) the assets acquired plus the liabilities discharged, less the liabilities incurred but not discharged and less the assets distributed or otherwise disposed of by the predecessor partnership after the date of the balance sheet. Each partner's capital contribution shall consist of his/her interest in the equity of the predecessor partnership and shall be assigned a value equal to his/her proportionate interest*

in the predecessor partnership's net assets as shown in exhibit A, as follows:

Name   *Percentage*

_____   %

_____   %

_____   %

The partners shall make their capital contributions within _____ days after the date of this agreement by executing and delivering the bills of sale and other instruments of conveyance described in Exhibit (B) to this agreement, and the partnership shall execute and deliver to the partners the instrument or instruments set forth in Exhibit (C) to this agreement, assuming the liabilities and obligations of the predecessor partnership."

where loans of property are made to the partnership

"In addition to capital contributions described in this agreement, some partners have transferred or will transfer to the partnership additional items of property on loan to the partnership as set forth in Exhibit _____ to this agreement. Each item of property so lent to the partnership shall remain the separate property of the lending partner and shall be returned to him . . ."

(insert whatever terms you've agreed on, e.g., *"upon dissolution of the partnership,"* or *"upon demand,"* etc.).

contributions of special items of property, such as a patent—ownership retained by individual partner

"   (Name)   is the owner of patent # _____ for   (describe patented subject)   and hereby contributes to the partnership the use of that patent, with the understanding that he/she shall retain sole ownership of the patent and it shall not become a partnership asset.   (Name)   further agrees that until the termination of the partnership, or until his/her death or retirement from it, he/she will not, without the consent of all other partners, sell, assign, or grant licenses under this patent. Any money accruing from a sale or assignment of, or the grant of licenses under such patent, which are so authorized, shall be the sole property of   (name) . For the purpose of profit sharing only, and not for participation in the distribution upon the winding up of the partnership, the partnership will credit   (name)   with a contribution in the amount of $_____.

ownership transferred to partnership

"   (Name)   is the owner of patent # _____ for   (describe patented subject)   and hereby agrees to transfer all his/her interest in this patent to the partnership with the understanding that all his/her interest in the patent shall vest in the partnership and shall not be his separate property. In exchange for this transfer, it is agreed that   (name)   shall be credited with a contribution of $_____ to the partnership. No sale or assignment of, or grant of license

under the patent shall be made without the consent of all the partners. Any moneys resulting from any such sale, assignment, or grant of license shall be divided equally among the partners."

●**ADDITIONAL CONTRIBUTIONS:**

(**NOTE:** Another way to handle the problem of the need for additional cash is to have a partner, or partners, make loans to the partnership, on whatever terms the partners agree on.)

required yearly

"Each partner shall contribute annually _____ percent of his/her share of each year's profits (or $ _____) (choose the lesser amount) to the partnership's capital for a period of _____ years by not withdrawing that portion of his/her share in partnership profits."

can't be made voluntarily

"No partner may make any voluntary contribution of capital to the partnership without the consent of all the partners."

(This is for a situation where distributions of profits or control is geared to the balances in partners' capital accounts, and it is felt that the agree-ment should prevent possible "over-reaching" by one partner.)

if additional money is needed

"If, at any future time, more money is required to carry on the partnership business, and a majority of the partners vote to increase the capital contributions required by partners, the additional capital shall be paid in by the partners . . . ("in equal shares" or "in the proportions as they have respectively contri-buted originally," etc.)

(you can add more detail here, providing how notice of the need for increased capital is to be given, how much time the partners have to make the contributions, etc.)

● **FAILURE TO MAKE CONTRIBUTIONS:**

partnership dissolves

"If any partner fails to pay his/her initial contribution to the partnership as required by this agreement, the partnership shall immediately dissolve and each partner who has paid all or any portion of his/her initial contribution to the partnership's capital shall be entitled to a return of the funds and properties he/she contributed, unless the partners shall have entered into a written agreement requiring an alternative procedure for continuing the partnership, which shall be followed."

partnership continues, no additional contribution required

"If any person fails to pay his/her initial contribution to the partnership's capital as required by this agreement, the partner-ship shall not dissolve or

terminate, but it shall continue as a partnership of only the partners who have made their initial capital contributions as required and without any person who has failed to do so. In that case, the share in the partnership's profits and losses allocated under this agreement to any partner who has failed to make his/her initial contribution shall be reallocated under this agreement to any partner who has failed to make his/her initial contribution shall be reallocated to the remaining partners in proportion to their respective shares of partnership profits and losses as specified in this agreement."

partnership continues—additional contributions *are* required

"If (a) any person or persons fail to pay their initial contri-butions to the partnership's capital as required by this agreement, the partnership shall not dissolve or terminate, but it shall continue as a partnership of the partners who shall have made their initial capital contributions and without any person who shall have failed to do so, but only if the remaining partners pay the initial capital contribution that was to have been made by the noncontributing partner or partners. The partnership shall promptly give written notice of the failure to all partners who have made their initial capital contributions. The notice shall specify the amount not paid. Within _____ days after the notice is given, the remaining partners shall pay the amount of the defaulted contribution in proportion to the respective amounts they are required to pay to the partnership's capital under this agreement. The noncontributing partners' share in the partnership's profits shall then be reallocated to the remaining partners in proportion to their respective shares of partnership profits and losses under this agreement."

PAYMENT OF INTEREST ON CONTRIBUTED CAPITAL

no interest paid

"No partner shall be entitled to receive any interest on his/her capital contri-bution, except that, if he/she is entitled to repayment of his/her contribution, he/she shall also be entitled to interest on it at the rate of _____ percent per year from the date when repayment should have been made."

interest to be paid

"Each partner shall be entitled to interest on his/her capital contribution accruing at the rate of _____ percent per year from the date the contribution is paid. This interest shall be treated as an expense to be charged against income on the partnership's books and shall be paid to the partner entitled to it (specify terms, e.g., "quarterly" or "only upn termination of the partnership.")

(Many variations are possible with interest. For example, you might specify that partners only receive interest in years where net profits exceed _____ percent, or that interest is optional, and shall be decided upon yearly by the partners, etc.)

& & &
—————————————————————————————

MONEY, AND DISTRIBUTION OF PROFITS AND LOSSES

no withdrawal of contributed capital

"No partner may withdraw capital from the partnership without the consent of all the partners."

DISTRIBUTION OF PROFIT:

based on initial capital accounts *only*

"The partnership's profits and losses shall be shared by the partners in the same proportions as their initial capital accounts have to each other. No changes in distribution of profits or losses shall be caused by any fluctuation in the net amounts in partner's capital accounts."

specification of time for distribution of profits

"Within _____ (e.g. 30) days after the end of each fiscal year of the partnership there shall be distributed in cash to the partners, in proportion to their respective shares in the partnership's profits, amounts equal to the partnership's net profit for that fiscal year computed under this agreement."

general limitation on distribution to retain cash business needs

"The total amount distributed to the partners from the partnership's profits shall not exceed the amount of cash available for distribution, taking into account the partnership's reasonable working capital needs as determined by a majority of the partners."

specific limitation on distribution to retain cash business needs

"The aggregate amounts distributed to the partners from the partnership profits shall not exceed _____ percent of any net income above $ _____."

distributions based on *cash flow,* not accounting net profits

"Within (e.g. 30) days after the end of each fiscal year of the partnership there shall be distributed in cash to the partners, in proportion to their respective shares in the partnrship's profits, an amount equal to the sum of the partnership's net profit for that fiscal year but increased by the amounts deducted as depreciation, or amortization on the partnership's federal income tax return, and increased by any payments received and reduced by any payments made, by the partnership during that fiscal year on account of the principal of all debt obligations, other than obligations for which provision was made in computing net profit."

PARTNER'S DRAWING ACCOUNTS (AMOUNTS A PARTNER IS ENTITLED TO WITHDRAW FROM THE THE BUSINESS):

to be decided by partners in the future

"Each partner shall be entitled to draw against profits the amounts agreed on by a majority in interest of the partners. These amounts shall be charged to the partners' drawing accounts as they are drawn."

fixed draws

"Each partner shall be entitled to draw against the profits of the partnership as follows:

_____ $ __   per ____

_____ $ __   per ____

_____ $ __   per ____

        (partner's names)   *(amount)*   *(time of payment, e.g.,*

_____ $ _____ per _____

_____ $ _____ per _____

_____ $ _____ per _____

      (partner's names)   *(amount)*   *(time of payment, e.g., weekly, monthly, etc.)*

draws exceeding actual profits to become loans to a partner

"Notwithstanding the provisions of this agreement governing drawing accounts of partners, to the extent any partner's withdrawals under those provisions during any fiscal year of the partnership exceed his/her distributable share in the partnership's profits, the excess shall be regarded as a loan from the partnership to him/her that he/she is obligated to repay within _____ days after the end of that fiscal year, with interest on the unpaid balance at the rate of _____ percent per year from the end of that fiscal year to the date of repayment."

& &

SALARIES

none

"No salary shall be paid to any partner."

specified

"Each partner shall be entitled to a monthly salary as follows:

Name   *Amount*

_____ $ _____ per _____

_____ $ _____ per _____

_____ $ _____ per _____

or such other amounts that may be determined by the unanimous written agreement of all the partners. These salaries shall be treated as partnership expenses in determining its profits or losses."

INDEMNIFICATION

"Each partner shall indemnify and hold harmless the partnership and each of the other partners from any and all expense and liability resulting from or arising out of any negligence or misconduct on his/her part to the extent that the amount exceeds the applicable insurance carried by the partnership."

MANAGEMENT PROVISIONS

CONTROL OF THE BUSINESS (ACTS REQUIRING MAJORITY CONSENT):

"The following acts may be done only with the consent of a majority in capital interest of the partners:

(a) Borrowing money in the partnership's name, other than in the ordinary course of the partnership's business or to finance any part of the purchase price of the partnership's properties.

(b) Transferring, hypothecating, compromising, or releasing any partnership claim except on payment in full.

(c) Selling, leasing, or hypothecating any partnership property or entering into any contract for any such purpose, other than in the ordinary course of the partnership's business and other than any hypothecation of partnership property to secure a debt resulting from any transaction permitted under (a).

(d) Knowingly suffering or causing anything to be done whereby partnership property may be seized or attached or taken in execution, or its ownership or possession otherwise endangered."

PROVISIONS FOR A MANAGING PARTNER (AUTHORITY OF MANAGING PARTNER):

"The managing partner shall be _____ He/she shall have control over the business of the partnership and assume direction of its business operations. He/she shall consult and confer as far as practicable with the non-managing partners, but the power of decision shall be vested in him/her. His/her powers and duties shall include control over the partnership's books and records and hiring any independent certified pbulic accountants he deems necessary for this purpose. On the managing partner's death, resignation, or other

disability a successor managing partner shall be selected by a majority in capital interest of the partners."

salary to managing partner

"The managing partner shall be paid a monthly salary of $ _____ or such other amount that may be determined by the unanimous written agreement of the partners. This salary shall be treated as a partnership expense in determining its profits or losses.

Any assignment by a partner of his/her interest in the partnership shall terminate his/her rights to receive a salary from the partnership."

managing partner handles *all* money of the partnership

"All partnership funds shall be deposited in the partnership's name and shall be subject to withdrawal only on the signature of the managing partner."

managing partner handles operating funds only

"All partnership funds shall be deposited in the partnership's name and shall be subject to withdrawal only on the signatures of at least _____ partners, except that a separate account may be maintained with a balance never to exceed $ _____. The amounts in that separate account shall be subject to withdrawal on the signature of the managing partner."

OUTSIDE ACTIVITIES

restricted

"As long as any person is a member of the partnership, he/she shall devote his/her full work time and energies to the conduct of partnership business, and shall not be actively engaged in the conduct of any other business for compensation or a share in profits as an employee, officer, agent, proprietor, partner, or stockholder. This prohibition shall not prevent him/her from being a passive investor in any enterprise, however, if he/she is not actively engaged in its business and does not exercise control over it. Neither the partnership nor any other partner shall have any right to any income or profit derived from any such passive investment."

permitted, except for direct competition

"Any partner may be engaged in one or more businesses, other than the business of the partnership, but only to the extent that this activity does not materially interfere with the business of the partnership and does not conflict with the obligations of that partner under this agreement. Neither the partnership nor any other partner shall have any right to any income or profit derived by a partner from any business activity permitted under this section."

permitted

"It is understood and agreed that each partner may engage in other enterprises, including enterprises in competition with the partnership, and that the partners need not offer business opportunities to the partnership but may take advantage of those opportunities for their own accounts or for the accounts of other partnerships or enterprises with which they are associated. Neither the partnership nor any other partner shall have any right to any income or profit derived by a partner from any enterprise or opportunity permitted by this section."

OPERATING PROCEDURES

EXPENSE ACCOUNTS:

authorized

"An expense account, not to exceed $ _____ per month, shall be set up for each partner for his/her actual, reasonable, and necessary expenses during the course of the business. Each partner shall keep an itemized record of these expenses and be paid once monthly for them upon submission of the record."

unauthorized

"The partners individually and personally shall assume and pay:
1. All expenses for the entertainment of persons having relations with the firm, and
2. Generally, the expenses associated with usual business activities."

ACCOUNTANT TO DETERMINE PROFITS AND LOSSES

"The partnership's net profit or net loss for each fiscal year shall be determined as soon as practicable after the close of that fiscal year by a certified public accountant in accordance with the accounting principles employed in the preparation of the federal income tax return filed by the partnership for that year, but without any special provisions for tax-exempt or partially tax-exempt income."

SIGNATURES REQUIRED ON PARTNERSHIP CHECKS

"All partnership funds shall be deposited in the partnership's name and shall be subject to withdrawal only on the signatures of at least _____ partners."

PROHIBITION AGAINST COMMINGLING

"All trust and other similar funds shall be deposited in a trust account established in the partnership's name at _____ bank, and shall be kept separate and not mingled with any other funds of the partnership."

MEETINGS

"For the purpose of discussing matters of general interest to the partnership, together with the conduct of its business, partners shall meet (describe time and days) or at such other time agreed upon by a majority of the partners.

MAINTENANCE OF RECORDS

"Proper and complete books of account of the partnership business shall be kept at the partnership's principal place of business and shall be open to inspection by any of the partners or their accredited representatives at any reasonable time during business hours."

VACATION

"Each partner shall be entitled to _____ weeks paid (or unpaid) vacation per year."

OWNERSHIP OF BUSINESS ASSETS

trade secrets

"All 'trade secrets' used or developed by the partnership, including customer lists and sources of supplies, will be owned and controlled by the partnership."

patents

"Any ideas developed by any of the partners pertaining to partnership business that are the subject of an application for a patent shall be partnership property."

BUY-OUTS

immediate payment of amounts in capital accounts

"On a partner's death, permanent physical or mental disability, or retirement from the partnership, the partnership shall not dissolve or terminate. The

partner, or in the event of death, his/her personal representative or the person legally entitled to payment, shall be paid the following terms and conditions the following amounts as full compensation for that partner's interest in the partnership:

(1) Within _____ days after the last day of the month of the death, disability, or retirement:

(a) The balance of the partner's capital account as of the last day of the month of death, disability, or retirement;

(b) The partner's share of profits for the current calendar year not yet reflected in his/her capital account as of the last day of the month of death, disability, or retirement.

The above payments shall be reduced by the amount of the partner's share of any losses for the current calendar year."

standards of appraisal—some examples

"In arriving at a valuation figure, the appraisers shall use the going-concern concept and observe the following bases for valuation, but not be limited to them in computing the partnership's value:

(a) Inventory shall be valued at fair market value;

(b) Buildings and land shall be valued at fair market value;

(c) Machinery and equipment shall be valued at replacement cost;

(d) In determining fair market value, the existence of a willing purchaser shall be assumed;

(e) A valuation shall be placed on items of substantial value not carried on the partnership's books

(f) Corporate securities owned by the partnership for which there is an established trading market shall be valued at the market price on the effective date of valuation. For this purpose, market price means (i) for securities listed on any national securities exchange, the last reported sales price on that date (or, if no sales on that date are reported, on the next preceding day for which sales were reported), and (ii) for securities traded in any over-the-counter market, the mean between the highest bid and lowest asked prices reported for these securities on that date (or, if no such prices are reported on that date, on the next preceding day for which such prices were reported);

(g) Corporate securities owned by the partnership for which there is no established trading market shall be valued at the amounts at which they are carried on the partnership's books in accordance with generally accepted accounting principles;

(h) Contingent items shall not be specifically deducted from the valuation figure, but they shall be considered in assessing the value of the partnership's goodwill;

(i) Goodwill, including trademarks, trade names, and other intangibles of commercial value such as patents, shall be considered in arriving at a valuation figure;

(j) Past, present, and prospective earnings, including the existing and prospective economic condition in the industry, shall be considered in arriving at a valuation figure; and

(k) Consideration shall be given to the federal and state income tax contingent liabilities on the differences between recorded book values and the market values used by the appraisers."

& & &

BOILERPLATE (STANDARD CLAUSES OFTEN INCLUDED IN PARTNERSHIP AGREEMENTS)

written agreement is all inclusive

"This agreement contains the entire understanding of the partners regarding their rights and duties in the partnership. Any alleged oral representations or modifications concerning this agreement shall be of no force or effect unless contained in a subsequent written modification signed by the partner to be charged."

binding on all successors, heirs, etc.

"This agreement shall be binding on and issue to the benefit of the respective successors, assigns, and personal representatives of the parties, except to the extent of any contrary provision in the agreement."

amendments

"This agreement may be amended at any time but any amendment must be in writing and signed by each person who is then a partner."

severability

"If any term, provision, or condition of this agreement is held by a court of competent jurisdiction to be invalid, void, or unenforceable, the rest of the agreement shall remain in full force and effect and shall in no way be affected, impaired, or invalidated."

B. Additional Clauses for Limited Partnership Agreements

Limited Partnership agreements can be every bit as complex as general partnership agreements. And clauses used for general partnership agreements can, of course, be used or adapted to limited partnership agreements as well. Aside from those clauses presented in the text and Appendix A, we've included some additional clauses here, specifically geared to limited partnership situations.

COMPOSITION OF THE PARTNERSHIP

GENERAL PARTNERS:

departure causes dissolution

"On the death, insanity, or withdrawal of a general partner, the partnership shall dissolve. It shall thereafter conduct only the actions necessary to wind up its affairs."

departure does *not* cause dissolution—if so, this also must be stated in the Registration Certificate

"On the death or insanity of a general partner, the partnership business shall be continued by the remaining general partners. The executive guardian, or other successor to the partnership interest of the general partner, shall be a limited partner."

transfers prohibited

"The general partner shall not assign, pledge, encumber, sell, or otherwise dispose of all or any part of his/her interest as a general partner in the partnership."

TRANSFERS BY LIMITED PARTNERS

written transfer required

"A limited partner may sell, assign, or transfer only his/her entire partnership interest and only by a written document acceptable in form to the general partners; a copy of that document shall be delivered at the partnership's principal place of business before the transfer can become effective."

RIGHT OF FIRST REFUSAL

"If a limited partner desires to sell or exchange his/her partnership interest, he/she shall give written notice to the partnership. The notice shall set forth the purchaser's name, the terms on which the interest is to be sold or exchanged, and the price. For _____ days after the notice is given, the partnership shall have the right to purchase the partner's entire interest for the price and on the terms stated in the notice."

"SUBSTITUTED" LIMITED PARTNERS

"The purchaser of a limited partner's interest shall become a substituted limited partner. The substitution shall become effective when the appropriate amendment to the certificate of limited partnership is recorded. In the absence of such a designation, he/she shall be entitled to receive only the share of profits or other compensation by way of income and the return of capital contribution to which his/her assignor would have been entitled."

Contributions, and Profits/Losses

FAILURE TO MAKE CONTRIBUTIONS:

partnership can purchase limited partner's interest

"If, within the time provided, any limited partner fails to make a required additional capital contribution under section _____ , the partnership may, within a period of _____ days after the contribution was due, purchase the defaulting partner's partnership interest at a price equal to the balance in the partner's capital account as of the end of the time the additional capital contribution was due."

partnership elects not to purchase interest

"If the defaulting partner's interest is not purchased by the partnership or other partners, the defaulting partner shall not withdraw, but shall retain his/her partnership interest. The interests of all the partners in the partnership's profits and losses shall be adjusted to reflect the changes in capital contributed by all partners."

other partners can make up contribution

"If, within the time provided, any partner or partners fail to make a required additional capital contribution, the interest of each partner in profits and losses shall be adjusted accordingly. The general partners shall notify each partner in writing of the total amount of contributions not made, and within _____ days each other partner who wishes to do so may make an additional capital contribution in an amount determined by the general partners."

LOANS

"If any limited partner shall, with the general partners' prior consent, make any loan to the partnership or advance money on its behalf, the loan or advance shall not increase the lending partner's capital account, nor entitle the lending partner to any greater share of partnership distributions, nor subject him/her to any greater proportion of partnership losses. The amount of the loan or advance shall be a debt owed by the partnership to the lending partner, repayable on the terms and conditions and bearing interest at the rate agreed on by the lending partner and the general partners."

WITHDRAWAL OF CAPITAL

"The general partners may permit limited partners to withdraw capital at any time when, in their judgment, funds in excess of reasonable business needs are available. Any such withdrawal by limited partners shall be in the ratio of their respective capital accounts."

RETURN

varied percentages, based on profits

"As return for their investment, the limited partners shall receive an aggregate of 40 percent of net partnership profits, up to total profits of $ _____, the 30 percent of net profits up to total profits of $ _____, then 10 percent of net profits up to total profits of $ _____. Beyond total net profits of $ _____, the limited partners shall receive no further return, but shall be entitled a return of their initial capital contribution."

priority to certain limited partners

"   (Names of limited partners)   shall be entitled to the first $_____ of net profits, if any, each year. Any yearly net profit in excess of $_____ shall be distributed according to the partner's shares in partnership profits.   (Names)   shall be credited with any amounts distributed to them under this priority."

MANAGEMENT FEES

based on net profits

"If the net profits of the partnership total at least $ _____ during any partnership fiscal year, the general partners shall be entitled to a management fee of _____percent of those net profits, which shall be paid by _____ of the following year."

based on partnership capital

"Management fees shall be paid to each general partner on ___(dates)___ in an amount equal to _____percent of the total partnership capital as of the close of the last fiscal year."

LIQUIDATION

priorities

"In the event of a voluntary dissolution, the partners shall continue to share profits and losses during the period of liquidation in the same proportions as before. Proceeds from the liquidation of partnership assets shall be applied according to the following priority:

(1) Payment of partnership debts to creditors, other than general partners, in the priority provided by law;

(2) Payments to limited partners for their share of profits;

(3) Payments to limited partners for the credit balances of their capital accounts;

(4) Payments to general partners for any amounts the partnership owes them, other than for their share of profits or their capital accounts;

(5) Payments to general partners for their share of profits; and

(6) Payments to general partners for the credit balances in their capital accounts."

SIGNATURE PROVISIONS

these can eliminate burdensome signature requirements

"An amendment to the certificate of limited partnership may be signed, personally or by an attorney-in-fact, by:

(1) A general partner and the new partner if the amendment is caused by the addition of a new partner;

(2) A general partner, the substituted limited partner, and the assigning limited partner if the amendment is caused by the substitution of a limited partner; or

(3) A general partner if the amendment is caused by the retirement, death, or insanity of a general partner and the partnership business is continued."

C. Resources for Further Research

Here is a list of some of the materials we found useful in writing this book. It isn't an exhaustive index of all legal materials on partnerships or small businesses, but it does contain the books which we believe are the most useful to the reader who wishes to do further research. Where appropriate, we've added brief comments. Many of these books are too expensive to be purchased by the average individual and are available in libraries, which are usually open to the public. We supply order information only on books we consider to be reasonably priced.

Partnership Books

Aronsohn, *Partnership Income Taxes* (Practising Law Institute). A general tax review, useful if you have one or two areas you want to check out.

American Law Institute (ALI) Resource Materials; *Partnerships*. Includes several sample partnership agreements, and some good discussion on specialized problem areas beyond the scope of our book.

C.C.H. (Commerce Clearing House), *Standard Federal Tax Reports, Corporation-Partnership-Fiduciary filled-in Tax Return Forms*. A yearly publication that's a great help if you're doing your own tax returns or want to stay one jump ahead of your accountant. Available from C.C.H., 4025 W. Paterson Ave., Chicago, IL 60646.

Desmond & Kelly, *Business Valuation Newsletter*. Contains statistics on valuation price for different types of businesses that can be useful for buy-out valuation clauses. Available from Valuation Press, 661 Washington St., Marina del Rey, CA 90291.

McKee, Nelson & Whitmire, *Federal Taxation of Partnerships and Partners,* two-volume edition, or abridged one-volume student edition (Warren, Gorham & Lamont). The best single treatise on partnership taxation. It's thorough, accurate, and as clear and well-written as tax books are likely to be—i.e., still tough going, at times. Other partnership tax sources include proceedings of the New York Institute on Federal Taxation (Mathew Bender Co.); proceedings of the Tax Institute of the University of Southern California School of Law (Prentice-Hall, Inc.); and portfolios published by Tax Management, the Bureau of National Affairs, Inc., Washington, D.C.

Mulder, *The Drafting of Partnership Agreements* (American Law Institute). A practical book on some of the problems involved in partnership agreements.

West's Uniform Laws, Annotated, Volume 6 (West Publishing Co.). Contains the text of the Uniform Partnership Act, Uniform Limited Partnership Act, and Revised Uniform Limited Partnership Act.

Willis, *Partnership Taxation* (2 volumes, McGraw-Hill Book Co.) is another standard treatise.

McKeever, *Start-up Money: How to Finance Your New Small Business* (Nolo Press). The best book on how to write your own business plan and loan package.

"Tax Information on Partnerships," IRS publication 541.

Partners in Business: How to Choose and Build the Relationship Most Vital to Your Success, by Melvin Wallace, Enterprise Publishing (725 Market St., Wilmington, DE 19801). This book focuses on the interpersonal side of partnerships. It is really a psychology book, but a good one.

The Partnership Book

Small Business Books

Kamoroff, *Small Time Operator: How to Start Your Own Small Business, Keep Your Books, Pay Your Taxes & Stay Out of Trouble* (Bell Springs Publishing). As we said several times in the text, the best book we know on the accounting, bookkeeping and tax aspects of small business management. If you are starting a small business and don't have this book, get it. Available from Nolo Press, 950 Parker St., Berkeley, CA 94710.

Mancuso, *How to Form Your Own California Corporation, How to Form Your Own Texas Corporation, How to Form Your Own New York Corporation, How to Form Your Own Florida Corporation* (Nolo Press, 950 Parker St., Berkeley, CA 94710). If you are interested in incorporating and live in California, Texas, New York, or Florida, these are the books for you.

McKeever, *Start Up Money: How to Finance Your New Small Business* (Nolo Press). An excellent book for anyone about to start or revamp an existing one. It helps you evaluate whether your business plan is a sound one and it shows you how to write a proposal to obtain financing. Sources of financing for small businesses are discussed.

Phillips & Rasberry, *Marketing Without Advertising* (Nolo Press). The best small business marketing book available. If you follow the advice in this book, customers will do your advertising for you by bragging about your business to their friends.

Seigel & Harold, *Successful Small Business Management* (Fairchild Publications, 7 East 12th Street, New York, NY 10003). It is a fact that certain personality types are more likely to succeed in a business than others. This excellent 340-page book identifies and discusses these human traits in a logical and well-organized manner. It covers pre-startup, getting started, different types of businesses, pricing, selling, advertising, and even accounting, from the personal perspective of the business owner.

Feldman, *Home Based Business* (Till Press, P.O. Box 27816, Los Angeles, CA 90027). A good general introduction to running a business out of your home. Another good book in this field is *Mail Order Moonlighting* by Cecil C. Hogue, Ten Speed Press (Box 7123, Berkeley, CA 94707).

Small Business Administration Pamphlets: The SBA publishes a good many useful books and pamphlets covering everything from finance to insurance to exporting and franchising. One of the best is "Starting and Managing a Small Business of Your Own." Most pamphlets are available in the reference section of your library. Or you can get a list from Superintendent of Documents, U.S. Government Printing Office, Washington, D.C. 20402. Ask for order form 115B (for Sale Management Assistance Publication).

Bank of America Pamphlets: The Bank of America offers an unusually well-written series of pamphlets on a number of small business topics, such as "How to Buy or Sell a Business," "Financing Small Businesses," "Understanding Financial Statements," "Steps to Starting a Business," and many more. Single copies are free at Bank of America branches in California. If you are out of state, write Small Business Reporter, Bank of America, Dept. 3401, Box 3700, San Francisco, CA 94137 and ask for order information.

Small Business Legal Problem Solver, by Arnold Goldstein, Inc., CBI (286 Congress St., Boston, MA 02210). This book answers a number of questions about business law, from bank accounts to bankruptcy. The information about contracts, sales agreements, etc. is excellent. A good general reference.

Elias, *Legal Research: How to Find and Understand the Law* (Nolo Press). An excellent book on doing your own legal research, something that small business people should really know how to do.

Warner, *Everybody's Guide to Small Claims Court* (Nolo Press) is your best resource should you ever find yourself holding a handful of bad checks. It is your best guide on how to properly prepare a small claims court case—which is far more than half the battle. It also contains good advice on who, where, and how to sue.

D. Sample Partnership Termination Agreement

___("AT")___ and ___("KC")___ *agree as follows:*

I. RECITALS:

1. Partnership. *AT and KC have been and are now partners doing business under the name of AT & KC ASSOCIATES with its principal place of business in Oakland, California.*

2. Partnership Agreement. *The parties entered into said partnership and have continued in partnership under the provisions of an agreement in writing dated _____, 1977.*

3. Desire to Dissolve. *The parties now desire to adopt a plan for a sale of part of the partnership and for dissolution of their partnership and liquidation of its affairs, in two steps.*

4. Valuation. *The parties agree that each partnership asset disclosed on the partnership balance sheet has a present fair market value equal to its book value to the partnership and that consideration in excess of book value reflected in this agreement is attributable to good will not shown on the balance sheet.*

II. DISSOLUTION:

1. PURCHASE BY AT. *AT hereby purchases forty-nine (49) percent of the partnership interest of KC, and KC hereby sells and irrevocably assigns to AT the said forty-nine percent interest, in consideration of: (A) AT's $5,500 negotiable promissory note in the form of Exhibit A hereto and (B) AT's agreement to hold KC free and harmless from all partnership debts and liabilities.*

2. GUARANTEED PAYMENTS. *KC has received since January 1, 1979 and shall continue to receive through calendar year 1979, guaranteed payments from the partnership, by way of remuneration for services rendered, at the rate of $1,000 per month. Except for such guaranteed payments KC shall receive no other amounts from the partnership.*

3. AMENDMENT OF PARTNERSHIP AGREEMENT. *The Agreement of Partnership is hereby amended to provide that from and after _____, 1979, AT alone shall exercise management and control over partnership decisions, and that from and after that date the profits and losses of the partnership with corresponding items of taxable income or deductible loss will be shared ninety-nine percent (99) for AT and one percent (1) for KC.*

4. COMPETITION PERMITTED. *From and after _____, 1979, each partner shall be free to conduct consulting activities apart from the partnership, even to the extent of competing with the partnership.*

5. INSURANCE. *KC shall continue to receive health and automobile liability insurance coverage under the partnership's policies through December 31, 1979.*

Upon execution of this Agreement, KC shall be entitled to assume the life insurance policy on her life presently carried by the partnership.

6. LEASE. *AT and KC both shall continue to be named as lessees under the existing lease for the partnership's present principal office. However, AT shall pay all rent accruing from and after* _____, *1979.*

7. ACCESS. *KC shall, for the present term of the existing lease on the partnership's principal place of business, have full access to and use of an office in the partnership premises and access to its files.*

8. NAME. *AT shall not use the partnership's name or any name confusingly similar thereto in any new business conducted by him following liquidation of the partnership.*

(a) During the period from _____, *1979 through* _____ *either partner shall be entitled to refer to the partnership name solely for purposes of indicating transition from the partnership to his or her new business.*

(b) After _____, *either partner's use of the partnership name shall be only to the extent necessary to identify prior projects that either has completed.*

9. TERMINATION AND LIQUIDATION. *On December 31, 1979, the partnership shall purchase KC's remaining one percent (1) interest for a price of* _____ *and the partnership shall be dissolved, liquidated, and terminated. Upon such termination and liquidation, AT shall own all of the assets of the partnership and shall satisfy all its debts and liabilities, subject to the restrictions on use of the partnership name as specified in Paragraph 7 of this Agreement. From December 31, 1979 on, except for the purpose of carrying out the liquidation of the partnership, neither of the parties shall do any further business nor incur any further obligations on behalf of the partnership.*

III. LIQUIDATION:

1. ACCOUNTING. *As of December 31, 1979 the parties shall cause an accounting to be made by the then partnership accountants of all of the assets of the partnership and of the respective equities of the creditors and the partners in the assets as of the effective date of the dissolution.*

2. DISCLOSURE. *Except as appears by the books of the partnership each of the parties represents that he or she has not heretofore contracted any liability which can or may charge the partnership or the other party, nor has he or she received or discharged any of the credits, moneys, or effects of the partnership.*

3. SETTLING ACCOUNTS. *Upon completion of the accounting, the parties shall pay all of the liabilities of the partnership including those owing to the partners other than for capital in accordance with [the applicable state law]. Payment of liabilities owing to the partners shall include payment of profits for the current accounting period computed on the basis of actual cash receipts to completion of the accounting. All amounts received after completion of the accounting shall be the sole property of AT.*

IV. EXECUTION AND ENFORCEMENT:

1. SURVIVAL OF REPRESENTATIONS. *The representations and agreement set forth herein shall be continuous and shall survive the taking of any accounting.*

2. SUCCESSORS AND ASSIGNS. *This Agreement shall inure to the benefit of and bind the successors, assigns, heirs, executors and administrators of the parties.*

Executed on _____, 1979 at Oakland, California.

_____

AT

_____

KC

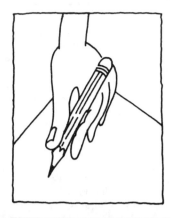

ABOUT THE AUTHORS

Denis Clifford is a partner in the Oakland, California law firm of Clifford, Curry & Cherrin, which has represented many partnerships and small businesses. A graduate of Columbia Law School, where he was an editor of the Law Review, he has been a law clerk for a federal district judge, a law professor, a government legal consultant, and has practiced law in numerous ways, including working with downtown San Francisco law firms specializing in financial affairs of wealthy clients and managing for some years a neighborhood legal services law office in East Oakland. He describes his "career" as being "a soldier of fortune," and loves painting, playing basketball, and sleeping late.

Ralph Warner is a leader of the self-help law movement and a co-founder of Nolo Press. Warner has a license to practice law, but doesn't use it. Instead, through books, lectures, and workshops, he teaches non-lawyers to handle everyday legal problems. Warner has been involved in two partnerships, has successfully started several small businesses, and has talked with a number of small business people about the legal intricacies of getting their enterprises started.

NOLO PRESS SELF-HELP LAW BOOKS

■ BUSINESS AND FINANCE

How To Form Your Own Corporation
By attorney Mancuso. Provides all the forms, Bylaws, Articles, minutes of meeting, stock certificates and instructions necessary to form your small profit corporation. Includes a thorough discussion of the practical and legal aspects of incorporation, including the tax consequences.

California Edition	$24.95
Texas Edition	$21.95
New York Edition	$19.95
Florida Edition	$19.95

The Non-Profit Corporation Handbook
By attorney Mancuso. Includes all the forms, Bylaws, Articles, minutes, and instructions you need to form a non-profit corporation. Step-by-step instructions on how to choose a name, draft Articles and Bylaws, attain favorable tax status. Thorough information on federal tax exemptions, which groups outside of California will find particularly useful.
California only $24.95

The California Professional Corporation Handbook
By attorneys Mancuso and Honigsberg. In California a number of professions must fulfill special requirements when forming a corporation. Among them are lawyers, dentists, doctors and other health professionals, accountants and certain social workers. This book contains detailed information on the special requirements of every profession and all the forms and instructions necessary to form a professional corporation.
California only $29.95

Marketing Without Advertising
By Phillips and Rasberry. A creative and practical guide that shows small business people how to avoid wasting money on advertising. The authors, experienced business consultants, show how to implement an ongoing marketing plan to tell potential and current customers that yours is a quality business worth trusting, recommending and coming back to.
National Edition $14.00

Billpayers' Rights
By attorney Warner. Complete information on bankruptcy, student loans, wage attachments, dealing with bill collectors and collection agencies, credit cards, car repossessions, homesteads, child support and much more.
California only $12.95

Bankruptcy: Do-It-Yourself
By attorney Kosel. Tells you exactly what bankruptcy is all about and how it affects your credit rating, property and debts, with complete details on property you can keep under the state and federal exempt property rules. Shows you step-by-step how to do it yourself; comes with all necessary forms and instructions.
National Edition $15.95

The Partnership Book
By attorneys Clifford and Warner. When two or more people join to start a small business, one of the most basic needs is to establish a solid, legal partnership agreement. This book supplies a number of sample agreements which you can use as is. Buy-out clauses, unequal sharing of assets, and limited partnerships are all discussed in detail.
National Edition $18.95

Chapter 13: The Federal Plan to Repay Your Debts
By attorney Kosel. This book allows an individual to develop and carry out a feasible plan to pay most of his/her debts over a three-year period. Chapter 13 is an alternative to straight bankruptcy and yet it still means the end of creditor harassment, wage attachments and other collection efforts. Comes complete with all necessary forms and worksheets.
National Edition $14.95

Start-Up Money: How to Finance Your Small Business
By Business Consultant McKeever. For anyone about to start a business or revamp an existing one, this book shows how to write a business plan, draft a loan package and find sources of small business finance.
National Edition $12.95

Small Time Operator
By Kamoroff, C.P.A.. Shows you how to start and operate your small business, keep your books, pay your taxes and stay out of trouble. Comes complete with a year's supply of ledgers and worksheets designed especially for small businesses, and contains invaluable information on permits, licenses, financing, loans, insurance, bank accounts, etc. Published by Bell Springs.
National Edition $10.95

Getting Started as an Independent Paralegal (two audio cassette tapes)
By attorney Warner. In these two audiotapes, about three hours in all, Ralph Warner explains how to set up and run an independent paralegal business and how to market your services. He also discusses in detail how to avoid charges of unauthorized practice of law.
National 1st Edition $24.95

The Independent Paralegal's Handbook: How to Provide Legal Services Without Going to Jail

By attorney Warner. More and more nonlawyers are opening legal typing services to help people prepare their own papers for divorce, bankruptcy, incorporation, eviction, etc. Called independent paralegals, these legal pioneers pose much the same challenge to the legal establishment as midwives do to conventional medicine. Written by Nolo Press co-founder Ralph Warner, who established one of the first divorce typing services in 1973, this controversial book is sure to become the bible of the new movement aimed at delivering routine legal services to the public at a reasonable price.

National Edition $12.95

■ ESTATE PLANNING, WILLS & PROBATE

Plan Your Estate: Wills, Probate Avoidance, Trusts and Taxes

By attorney Clifford. Comprehensive information on making a will, alternatives to probate, planning to limit inheritance and estate taxes, living trusts, and providing for family and friends.

California Edition $15.95

Nolo's Simple Will Book

By attorney Clifford. This book will show you how to draft a will without a lawyer in any state except Louisiana. Covers all the basics, including what to do about children, whom you can designate to carry out your wishes, and how to comply with the technical legal requirements of each state. Includes examples and many alternative clauses from which to choose.

National Edition $14.95

WillWriter—a software/book package

By Legisoft. Use your computer to prepare and update your own valid will. A manual provides help in areas such as tax planning and probate avoidance. Runs on the Apple II family, IBM PC and compatibles, Commodore, Macintosh .

National Edition $49.95
Commodore Edition $39.95

How to Probate an Estate

By Nissley. Forms and instructions necessary to settle a California resident's estate after death. This book deals with joint tenancy and community property transfers as well as showing you how to actually probate an estate, step-by-step. The book is aimed at the executor, administrator or family member who will have the actual responsibility to settle the estate.

California Edition $24.95

■ FAMILY & FRIENDS

How to Do Your Own Divorce

By attorney Sherman. This is the original "do-your-own-law" book. It contains tear-out copies of all the court forms required for an uncontested dissolution, as well as instructions for certain special forms.

California Edition $14.95
Texas Edition $12.95

A Legal Guide for Lesbian/Gay Couples

By attorneys Curry and Clifford. Here is a book that deals specifically with legal matters of lesbian and gay couples: raising children (custody, support, living with a lover), buying property together, wills, etc. and comes complete with sample contracts and agreements.

National Edition $17.95

The Living Together Kit

By attorneys Ihara and Warner. A legal guide for unmarried couples with information about buying or sharing property, the Marvin decision, paternity statements, medical emergencies and tax consequences. Contains a sample will and Living Together Contract.

National Edition $14.95

California Marriage and Divorce Law

By attorneys Ihara and Warner. This book contains invaluable information for married couples and those considering marriage or remarriage on community and separate property, names, debts, children, buying a house, etc. Includes prenuptial contracts, a simple will, probate avoidance information and an explanation of gift and inheritance taxes. Discusses "secret marriage" and "common law" marriage.

California only $15.95

Social Security, Medicare & Pensions: A Sourcebook for Older Americans

By attorney Matthews & Berman. The most comprehensive resource tool on the income, rights and benefits of Americans over 55.Includes detailed information on social security, retirement rights, Medicare, Medicaid, supplemental security income, private pensions, age discrimination, as well as a thorough explanation of social security legislation.

National Edition $14.95

How to Modify & Collect Child Support in California

By attorneys Matthews, Segal and Willis. California court awards for child support have radically increased in the last two years. This book contains the forms and instructions to obtain the benefits of this change without a lawyer and collect support directly from a person's wages or benefits, if necessary.

California only $17.95

How to Adopt Your Stepchild

By Zagone. Shows you how to prepare all the legal forms; includes information on how to get the consent of the natural parent and how to conduct an "abandonment" proceeding. Discusses appearing in court and making changes in birth certificates.

California only $19.95

The Power of Attorney Book

By attorney Clifford. Covers the process which allows you to arrange for someone else to protect your rights and property should you become incapable of doing so. Discusses the advantages and drawbacks and gives complete instructions for establishing a power of attorney yourself.

National Edition $15.95

How to Change Your Name
By attorneys Loeb and Brown. Changing one's name is a very simple procedure. Using this book, you can file the necessary papers yourself, saving $200 to $300 in attorney's fees. Comes complete with all forms and instructions for the court petition method or this simpler usage method.
California only $14.95

Your Family Records: How to Preserve Personal, Financial and Legal History
By Pladsen and attorney Clifford. Helps you organize and record all sorts of items that will affect you and your family when death or disability occur, e.g., where to find your will and deed to the house. Includes information about probate avoidance, joint ownership of property and genealogical research. Space is provided for financial and legal records.
National Edition $14.95

■ *LANDLORD/TENANT*

Tenants' Rights
By attorneys Moskovitz, Warner and Sherman. Discusses everything tenants need to know in order to protect themselves: getting deposits returned, breaking a lease, getting repairs made, using Small Claims Court, dealing with an unscrupulous landlord, forming a tenants' organization, etc. Sample Fair-to-Tenants lease, rental agreements, and unlawful detainer answer forms.
California Edition $14.95

The Landlord's Law Book: Rights and Responsibilities
By attorneys Brown and Warner. Now, for the first time, there is an accessible, easy to understand law book written specifically for landlords. Covers the areas of discrimination, insurance, tenants' privacy, leases, security deposits, rent control, liability, and rent withholding.
California only $24.95

The Landlord's Law Book: Evictions
By attorney Brown. This is the most comprehensive manual available on how to do each step of an eviction, and the only one to deal with rent control cities and contested evictions including how to represent yourself in court if necessary. All the required forms, with directions on how to complete and file them, are included. Vol. 1 covers Rights and Responsibilities.
California only $24.95

Landlording
By Robinson (Express Press). Written for the conscientious landlord or landlady, this comprehensive guide discusses maintenance and repairs, getting good tenants, how to avoid evictions, record keeping and taxes.
National Edition $17.95

■ *REAL ESTATE*

All About Escrow
(Express Press) By Gadow. This book gives you a good understanding of what your escrow officer should be doing for you. Includes advice about inspections, financing, condominiums and cooperatives.
National Edition $12.95

The Deeds Book
By attorney Randolph. Adding or removing a name from a deed, giving up interest in community property at divorce, putting a house in joint tenancy to avoid probate, all these transactions require a change in the way title to real estate is held. This book shows you how to choose the right deed, fill it out and record it.
California Edition $15.95

Homebuyers: Lambs to the Slaughter
By attorney Bashinsky (Menasha Ridge Press). Written by a lawyer/broker, this book describes how sellers, agents, lenders and lawyers are out to fleece you, the buyer, and advises how to protect your interests.
National Edition $12.95

For Sale By Owner
By Devine. The average California home sold for $130,000 in 1986. That meant the average seller paid $7800 in broker's commissions. This book will show you how to sell your own home and save the money. All the background information and legal technicalities are included to help you do the job yourself and with confidence.

California Edition $24.95

Homestead Your House
By attorney Warner. Under the California Homestead Act, you can file a Declaration of Homestead and thus protect your home from being sold to satisfy most debts. This book explains this simple and inexpensive procedure and includes all the forms and instructions. Contains information on exemptions for mobile homes and houseboats.
California only $8.95

■ *COPYRIGHTS & PATENTS*

Legal Care for Your Software
By attorney Remer. Shows the software programmer how to protect his/her work through the use of trade secret, trademark, copyright, patent and, most especially, contractual laws and agreements. This book is full of forms and instructions that give programmers the hands-on information they need.
International Edition $24.95

Intellectual Property Law Dictionary
By attorney Elias. "Intellectual Property" includes ideas, creations and inventions. The Dictionary is designed for inventors, authors, programmers, journalists, scientists and business people who must understand how the law affects the ownership and control of new ideas and technologies. Divided into sections on: Trade Secrets, Copyrights, Trademarks, Patents and Contracts. More than a dictionary, it places terms in context as well as defines them.
National Edition $17.95

How to Copyright Software
By attorney Salone. Shows the serious programmer or software developer how to protect his or her programs through the legal device of copyright.
International Edition $24.95

Patent It Yourself

By attorney Pressman. Complete instructions on how to do a patent search and file for a patent in the U.S. Also covers how to choose the appropriate form of protection (copyright, trademark, trade secret, etc.), how to evaluate salability of inventions, patent prosecution, marketing, use of the patent, foreign filing, licensing, etc. Tear-out forms are included

National Edition $24.95

Inventor's Notebook

By Fred Grissom and attorney David Pressman. The best protection for your patent is adequate records. The Inventor's Notebook provides forms, instructions, references to relevant areas of patent law, a bibliography of legal and non-legal aids, and more. It helps you document the activities that are normally part of successful independent inventing.

National 1st Edition   Special Price $17.95

■ RESEARCHING THE LAW

California Civil Code

(West Publishing) Statutes covering a wide variety of topics, rights and duties in the landlord/tenant relationship, marriage and divorce, contracts, transfers of real estate, consumer credit, power of attorney, and trusts.

California only $17.00

California Code of Civil Procedure

(West Publishing) Statutes governing most judicial and administrative procedures: unlawful detainer (eviction) proceedings, small claims actions, homestead procedures, wage garnishments, recording of liens, statutes of limitation, court procedures, arbitration, and appeals.

California only $17.00

Legal Research:
How to Find and Understand the Law

By attorney Elias. A hands-on guide to unraveling the mysteries of the law library. For paralegals, law students, consumer activists, legal secretaries, business and media people. Shows exactly how to find laws relating to specific cases or legal questions, interpret statutes and regulations, find and research cases, understand case citations and Shepardize them.

National Edition $14.95

■ RULES AND TOOLS

Collecting Court Judgments

By Ginny Scott. Winning a court judgment is only half the battle. This book covers skip tracing (how to find someone who owes you money), how to get paid while keeping good will, how to use collection agencies, and how to find out what property is available to satisfy your debt.

California 1st Edition $19.95

Fight Your Ticket

By attorney Brown. A comprehensive manual on how to fight your traffic ticket. Radar, drunk driving, preparing for court, arguing your case to a judge, cross-examining witnesses are all covered.

California only $16.95

Make Your Own Contract

By attorney Elias. Provides tear-out contracts, with instructions, for non-commercial use. Covers lending money, selling or leasing personal property (e.g., cars, boats), leasing and storing items (with friends, neighbors), doing home repairs, and making deposits to hold personal property pending final payment. Includes an appendix listing all the contracts found in Nolo books.

National Edition $12.95

The Criminal Records Book

By attorney Siegel. Takes you step-by-step through the procedures available to get your records sealed, destroyed or changed. Detailed discussion on your criminal record what it is, how it can harm you, how to correct inaccuracies, marijuana possession records and juvenile court records.

California only $14.95

The People's Law Review

Edited by Warner. This is the first compendium of people's law resources ever published. Contains articles on mediation and the new "non-adversary" mediation centers, information on self-help law programs and centers (for tenants, artists, battered women, the disabled, etc.); and articles dealing with many common legal problems which show people how to do-it-themselves.

National Edition $8.95

Everybody's Guide to Small Claims Court

By attorney Warner. Guides you step-by-step through the Small Claims procedure, providing practical information on how to evaluate your case, file and serve papers, prepare and present your case, and, most important, how to collect when you win. Separate chapters focus on common situations (landlord-tenant, automobile sales and repair, etc.).

National Edition $10.95
California Edition $14.95

How to Become a United States Citizen

By Sally Abel. Detailed explanation of the naturalization process. Includes step-by-step instructions from filing for naturalization to the final oath of allegiance. Includes a study guide on U.S. history and government. Text is written in both English and Spanish.

National Edition $9.95

Draft, Registration and The Law

By attorney Johnson. How it works, what to do, advice and strategies.

California only $9.95

Murder on the Air

By Ralph Warner and Toni Ihara. An unconventional murder mystery set in Berkeley, California. When a noted environmentalist and anti-nuclear activist is killed at a local radio station, the Berkeley violent crime squad swings into action. James Rivers, an unplugged lawyer, and Sara Tamura, Berkeley's first female murder squad detective, lead the chase. The action is fast, furious and fun. $5.95

29 Reasons Not to Go to Law School

By attorneys Ihara and Warner, with contributions by fellow lawyers and illustrations by Mari Stein. A humorous and irreverent look at the dubious pleasures of going to law school. 3rd Ed. $7.95

NOLO PRESS SELF-HELP LAW BOOKS

ORDER FORM

Quantity	Title	Unit Price	Total

Prices subject to change

Subtotal _____

Tax (CA only): San Mateo, LA, & Bart Counties 6 1/2%
Santa Clara & Alameda 7%
All others 6%

Tax _____

Postage & Handling

No. of Books	Charge
1	$1.50
2-3	$2.00
4-5	$2.50

Over 5 add 5% of total before tax

Postage & Handling _____

Total _____

Please allow 3-5 weeks for delivery.
For faster service, add $1 for UPS delivery (no P.O. boxes, please).

Name _____

Address _____

_____

☐ VISA   ☐ Mastercard

_____ Exp. _____

Signature _____

Phone ( )_____

☐ Please send me a catalogue

ORDERS: Credit card information or a check may be sent to NOLO Press, 950 Parker St., Berkeley CA 94710

Use your credit card and our **800 lines** for faster service:

ORDERS ONLY (M-F 9-5 Pacific Time):

US: **800-992-NOLO**
Outside (415) area **CA: 800-445-NOLO**
Inside (415) area **CA: (415) 549-1976**

For general information call: **(415) 549-1976**

Libraries contact: NOLO PRESS DISTRIBUTION, Box 544 , Occidental CA 95465
(800) 822-8382 in California
(800) 433-6656 outside California

UPDATE SERVICE
· Introductory Offer ·

Our books are as current as we can make them, but sometimes the laws do change between editions. You can read about law changes which may affect this book in the NOLO NEWS, a 16-page newspaper which we publish quarterly.

In addition to the Update Service, each issue contains comprehensive articles about the growing self-help law movement as well as areas of law that are sure to affect you. (regular subscription rate is $7.00)

To receive the next 4 issues of the NOLO NEWS, please send us $2.00:

Name —————————————————————————

Address ————————————————————————

————————————————————————————

Send to: NOLO PRESS, 950 Parker St., Berkeley CA 94710

part 3/87

Recycle Your Out-of-Date Books & Get 25% off your next purchase!

Using an old edition can be dangerous if information in it is wrong. Unfortunately, laws and legal procedures change often. To help you keep up to date we extend this offer. If you cut out and deliver to us the title portion of the cover of any old Nolo book we'll give you a 25% discount off the retail price of any new Nolo book. For example, if you have a copy of TENANT'S RIGHTS, 4th edition and want to trade it for the latest CALIFORNIA MARRIAGE AND DIVORCE LAW, send us the TENANT'S RIGHTS cover and a check for the current price of MARRIAGE & DIVORCE, less a 25% discount. Information on current prices and editions is listed in the NOLO NEWS (see above box). Generally speaking, any book more than two years old is of questionable value. Books more than four or five years old are a menace.

OUT OF DATE = DANGEROUS

This offer is to individuals only.